RACISM, ETHNICITY AND THE MEDIA

Other titles in the series

Australian Television
Programs, pleasure and politics
Edited by John Tulloch and Graeme Turner

Dark Side of the Dream
Australian literature and the postcolonial mind
Bob Hodge and Vijay Mishra

Fashioning the Feminine
Girls, popular culture and schooling
Pam Gilbert and Sandra Taylor

Featuring Australia
The cinema of Charles Chauvel
Stuart Cunningham

Framing Culture
Critism and policy in Australia
Stuart Cunningham

From Pop to Punk to Postmodernism
Popular music and Australian culture from the 1960s to the 1990s
Edited by Philip Haywood

Myths of Oz
Reading Australian popular culture
John Fiske, Bob Hodge, Graeme Turner

Making it national
Uses of nationalism in Australian popular culture
Graeme Turner

National Fictions
Literature, film and the construction of Australian narrative
Graeme Turner

Out West
Perceptions of Sydney's western suburbs
Diane Powell

Resorting to Tourism
Cultural policies for tourist development in Australia
Jennifer Craik

Stay Tuned
The Australian Broadcasting Reader
Edited by Albert Moran

Temptations
Sex, selling and the department store
Gail Reekie

Australian Cultural Studies
Editor: John Tulloch

RACISM, ETHNICITY AND THE MEDIA

Edited by Andrew Jakubowicz

Written by Heather Goodall, Andrew Jakubowicz, Jeannie Martin, Tony Mitchell, Lois Randall and Kalinga Seneviratne

ALLEN & UNWIN

First published 1994
Allen & Unwin Pty Ltd
9 Atchison Street, St Leonards, NSW 2065 Australia

National Library of Australia
Cataloguing-in-Publication entry:

Racism, ethnicity and the media.

Bibliography.
Includes index.
ISBN 1 86373 364 7

1. Plurism (Social sciences)—Australia. 2. Racism—Australia. 3. Mass media and minorities—Australia. 4. Mass media and race relations—Australia. [5.] Aborigines, Australian—Mass media. I. Goodall, Heather. II. Jakubowicz, Andrew. (Series: Australian cultural studies).

305.80994

Set in 10/11 Garamond by DOCUPRO, Sydney
Printed by Chong Moh Offset Printing, Singapore

10 9 8 7 6 5 4 3 2 1

GENERAL EDITOR'S FOREWORD

Nowadays the social and anthropological definition of 'culture' is probably gaining as much public currency as the aesthetic one. Particularly in Australia, politicians are liable to speak of the vital need for a domestic film industry in 'promoting our cultural identity'—and they mean by 'cultural identity' some sense of Australianness, of our nationalism as a distinct form of social organisation. Notably, though, the emphasis tends to be on Australian *film* (not popular television); and not just *any* film, but those of 'quality'. So the aesthetic definition tends to be smuggled back in—on top of the kind of cultural nationalism which assumes that 'Australia' is a unified entity with certain essential features that distinguish it from 'Britain', the 'USA' or any other national entities which threaten us with 'cultural dependency'.

This series is titled 'Australian Cultural Studies', and I should say at the outset that my understanding of 'Australian' is not as an essentially unified category; and further, that my understanding of cultural is anthropological rather than aesthetic. By 'culture' I mean the social production of meaning and understanding, whether in the inter-personal and practical organisation of daily routines or in broader institutional and ideological structures. I am *not* thinking of 'culture' as some form of universal 'excellence', based on aesthetic 'discrimination' and embodied in a pantheon of 'great works'. Rather, I take this aesthetic definition of culture itself to be part of the *social mobilisation of discourse* to differentiate a cultural 'élite' from the 'mass' of society.

Unlike the cultural nationalism of our opinion leaders, 'Cultural Studies' focuses not on the essential unity of national cultures, but on the meanings attached to social difference (as in the distinction between 'élite' and 'mass' taste). It analyses the construction and mobilisation of these distinctions to maintain or challenge existing power differentials, such as those of gender, class, age, race and ethnicity. In this analysis, terms designed to socially differentiate people (like 'élite' and 'mass') become categories of discourse, communication and power. Hence our concern in this series is for an analytical understanding of the meanings attached to social difference within the *history* and *politics* of discourse.

It follows that the analysis of 'texts' needs to be united from a single-minded association with 'high' culture (marked by 'authorship'), but must include the 'popular' too—since these distinctions of 'high' and 'popular' culture themselves need to be analysed, not assumed.

The field of cultural studies embraces the practices, patterns of meaning and symbolic systems of everyday life; and in particular it focuses on the way in which social divisions are made meaningful—or, alternatively, effaced. Jakubowicz, Goodall, Martin, Mitchell, Randall and Seneviratne note in *Racism, Ethnicity and the Media* that issues of social power (and the media's role in sustaining that power) can all too easily be constructed by the media in a way that 'dissolves our sense of conflict and struggle and offers instead an endless plane of opportunities and choices'. In contrast, their book shows 'how differences between cultural groups are constituted by the media, which differences are valued and how, and which are denied or debased. For within the multidimensional hierarchy of social statuses, of class, of gender, of race and ethnicity (and we might add age and disability and sexuality), the media is hard at work letting some things in and keeping others out. It is one of the strengths of this book that ethnicity and race are continuously considered in the context of their real and representational relations with these other categories of social difference. As the authors say, 'In carrying out our analysis, we do not wish to privilege "ethnicity" or "race" as a dimension of social difference and inequality: we have chosen it as a problem to be investigated, arguing throughout that race and ethnic relations cannot be separated from gender and class analysis' or indeed, as they say elsewhere, from the representation of age. Thus, they argue in their discussion of media products in Part 3 of the book, often a secondary code about age accompanies 'the elaboration of the contrasts elaborating social difference, so that the "equals lesser" term (female, black, working class etc.) was associated with "child" and "immature" '.

Culture, as Fiske, Hodge and Turner say in *Myths of Oz*, grows out of the divisions of society, not its unity. 'It has to work to construct any unity that it has, rather than simply celebrate an achieved or natural harmony.' Australian culture is then no more than the temporary, embattled construction of 'unity' at any particular historical moment. The 'readings' in this series of 'Australian Cultural Studies' inevitably (and polemically) form part of the struggle to make and break the boundaries of meaning which, in conflict and collusion, dynamically define our culture.

JOHN TULLOCH

FOREWORD

Ever since I can remember, the one question I have been constantly asked is how do I define my identity. The fact that my mother was Aboriginal and my father was Anglo-Irish troubles those with whom I have had contact over half a century of living. There is implicit in the question a sense of uneasiness, if not fear, about my difference.

For many such as I, our lifetime experience has been one of racism at the individual level, reinforced by the powerful institutions of the law, government (of which the education system is part), and without a doubt, the media. There have been many challenges to the institutional racism practised and promoted by law and government. By way of contrast however, there has been very little challenge to the media about the way in which that institution practises, promotes and perpetuates racism, dissension and disharmony in the community.

One reason for this is that the law and government are seen as being of the people, and (in theory at least) representing the interests of the people, including minorities. However well or poorly the theory converts into practice, the community perceives that it has the right to call these institutions to account to some extent.

Notwithstanding attempts from time to time to implement certain controls on the media (and the effectiveness or otherwise of those attempts are discussed in this book), the media is generally viewed as the private institution it is, run by exceedingly powerful independent proprietors who are not answerable to the populace. It is a view that is promoted by the media, of course, which has fostered a consensus about the undesirability of placing controls on its actions. It is usually promoted in terms of freedom of the press, more often articulated nowadays in terms of freedom of speech. Neither term is really appropriate to the situation, as the discussions set out in this book clearly show, since so much of the manner in which messages (concepts, ideologies, etc.) are transmitted are electronic and non-verbal. Thus it is that powerful media interests and popular broadcasters have been able to get away with their expressions of overt racism, and in the process inflame the racist passions of others.

For almost twenty years now, Australian governments have mounted community education programs aimed at counteracting racism. These programs rely on the government having access to the media in order to disseminate the government's informations and policies on the issues involved. At the same time the media, as the authors point out herein, have been engaged in the constant promotion of a particular ethnocentric and racist image of the society that we live in, which is, on the surface, in direct conflict with the government's policies and programs.

As a society we rarely challenge the media in its practices. Experience has taught us of course that it is difficult to succeed in any such challenges we might mount. We rarely think about the extent to which the media influences reach into the very souls of our being; but those who own and control the media—those who have access to the media for the purposes of transmitting their particular socio-political ethos—know only too well that this is the case.

If we are to be a mature, intelligent society however, then we must be prepared to confront the views of the media that that particular institution is beyond our control, challenge its authority to set the pace (as it were), and analyse the ways in which media operates to transform our notions of ourselves.

This book expands that process.

P. J. O'SHANE, AM
Sydney, February 1994

CONTENTS

Part III Dimensions of difference

Part IV Media practices and audience perceptions

Part V The way forward

ACKNOWLEDGEMENTS

We would like to thank the many individuals and organisations who helped us with this research. Our conclusions and comments are of course our own responsibility. We are especially grateful for the many indigenous people and people from non-English-speaking backgrounds who gave of their time and energy as subjects to be interviewed, as participants in seminars, and as colleagues in various campaigns.

We acknowledge the financial support of the University of Technology, Sydney through the Internal Research Grants Scheme which provided equipment and salary support for the research assistants; the Australian Research Grants Scheme for a large grant in 1991 which supported a significant part of the fieldwork; the Office of Multicultural Affairs in the Department of Prime Minister and Cabinet, which provided a research grant and invited us to participate in a consultancy project on ethnic audiences; and the Human Rights and Equal Opportunity Commission which invited Andrew Jakubowicz to undertake a study for the Inquiry into Racist Violence. The School of Humanities at UTS provided support through its technical staff under the leadership of Reg Collins, who organised the taping sessions in 1990 and 1991.

We also wish to acknowledge the owners of the copyright in illustrations we have used and thank them for their permission: John Fairfax Pty Ltd for the use of the print of Mary Coustas and Tracey Callender from the *Sun Herald*, News Ltd for the advertisement for the *Daily Telegraph Mirror*; SBS television for the news clip of the official Navy video; Young and Rubicam for the stills from the *Pajero* television advertisements and ABC television for stills from the National Television News.

A special thanks to our editors—John Tulloch, Elizabeth Weiss and Lynne Frolich, for their mixture of stimulus and discipline. They helped dramatically in moving us from a huge collection of material to a more focussed and accessible book. The final document is our responsibility alone.

Finally, our partners have been well aware of the gestation of this project—we appreciate their support and tolerance, and their contribution to the intellectual and domestic labour which allowed the writing of this book.

■ CONTRIBUTORS

Heather Goodall has worked as a researcher and historian for a number of Aboriginal organisations, including Tranby Aboriginal Co-operative College, the Western Aboriginal Legal Service in NSW and the Pitjantjatjara Council. Her research work has included Aboriginal community histories in central Australia and NSW, the history of British nuclear testing on Aboriginal lands, the deaths of Aborigines in police or prison custody and the representations of Aborigines and Aboriginal women in the media. She is currently lecturing in Applied History at the University of Technology, Sydney.

Andrew Jakubowicz has a PhD in Sociology and has worked at universities in Australia and the UK. He first became involved in work around ethnic issues in the early 1970s when he served on the Migrant Task Force, and in the early 1980s he was a board member of SBS. Since 1987 he has lectured at the University of Technology, Sydney, where he was head of the Humanities School from 1991 to 1994. He is currently researching on disability and representation.

Jeannie Martin is a lecturer in the School of Humanities, University of Technology, Sydney. She has published material on immigrant women and multiculturalism, and co-edited *Intersexions: Gender/Class/Culture/Ethnicity* (with Gill Bottomley and Marie de Lepervanche).

Tony Mitchell received an MA in English from Auckland University and a PhD in Drama from Bristol, and is currently a senior lecturer in Performance and Cultural Studies at the University of Technology, Sydney. He has published widely in Australian and international journals on performance studies, popular music studies, multiculturalism and the mass media, and his published books include *Dario Fo: People's Court Jester* and *North Meets South: Popular Music in Aotearoa/New Zealand* (with Philip Hayward and Roy Shuker).

Lois Randall is a media researcher/policy advisor and an independent film and video maker with a broad background in production and technical operations. She has lectured in all aspects of video production at AFTRS, UWS and Metro TV, and has more recently worked as a researcher for the Communications Law Centre, and as Executive Officer of the Australian Screen Directors Association. She was the co-author of *Let's do a Video: A Practical Guide to Community Video Making.*

Kalinga Seneviratne was born and educated in Sri Lanka. He has been broadcasting with Radio 2SER-FM for over 13 years, receiving a United National Media Peace Prize in 1987 and the Public Broadcasting Association of Australia's inaugural Singapore Airlines Education Award in 1992 for his radio work. He has been a part-time researcher, lecturer and tutor at the University of Tecnology, Sydney for the last four years, and is currently the Australian and South Pacific correspondent for the Inter Press Service news-agency.

PART 1

FRAMED AS/NAMED AS DIFFERENT

CONTEXT

A boat chugs across a tropical sea. It is packed with people. The camera zooms in on their density, their wretchedness. Soon the boat is at rest, its Asian passengers twisting and turning in a stream of water hosed on them from above. The camera withdraws; the boat and its burden framed on one side by a naval gun barrel and on the other by the Australian flag. The commentary tells of Cambodian boat people arriving under guard in Broome, Western Australia.

A few seconds of television introduce the themes of this book. Australia, a colonial settler society, its history corroded with the suppression of the Aboriginal and Torres Strait Islander people, its present being formed out of the lives of people from every part of the world, is moving into a new period of cultural and social challenges. These are not merely set by the new world order arising in the wake of the demise of the Soviet bloc. They are generated internally by a society in deepening economic crisis, and externally by a region with dynamic economies and burgeoning population, and by a world in which the movement of people now seems synonymous with conflict and violence. This conflict and violence has been characteristic of Australia's past and for many is scarcely masked by the present.

Australia is both colony and coloniser—both dominant and subordinate. Many old certainties—or myths—are dissolving under pressure and new myths are being forged to make sense of the changing future. The manufacture of myths and images and truths is growing in the major media of social communication—newspapers and magazines, television and radio. Our understanding of the relations between different segments of society, even our sense of what the groups are and how we should conceptualise social difference, is formed partly by the labels and divisions repeated and reinforced by the mass media. These social groups are linked in a web of explanation that maintains the existing social order in the face of apparent threats to cultural and moral hierarchy.

There seems to be a problem in the myth-making—the new myths appear ever more distant from Australia's multicultural and multiracial society, as though the bards are not merely unaware of the diversity around them, but urging the suppression of that diversity in favour of a safer and perhaps more monochromatic vision.

We want to ask four questions of the Australian media, and to see how many answers we can wrest from them:

- How do the media represent Australia in its cultural diversity and social difference?
- Are these representations the result of conscious manipulation and active decision-making by individuals or media groups?
- Are they the consequence, intentional or otherwise, of the way power is organised in Australian society, a power structure which in terms of class, gender, ethnicity, race and political priorities is merely replicated in the media as it is elsewhere?
- What are the characteristics, if any, of communication industries in a post-colonial society such as Australia?

As you will see, our answers to these questions (and yours may well be different) are not firm statements but rather an acknowledgment that they take us only some of the way towards understanding ethnicity, race and media. These questions go to the heart of the debates about the role of media in Australian society and whether any changes are possible in the ways the media represent our society. As the book progresses we will use these questions as levers to open up five spheres of concern—the range of meanings of 'Australia' and the points at which other meanings or experiences are quietened; the ideological work being done (by whom?) to make the nation and call up the people (Pettman 1992:5); the creation of what cultural studies call the 'Other'; defining boundaries, imposing categories, manipulating identities (Pettman 1992:4); and the possibilities of change.

The questions lead us to the political economy of the media, where the crucial dimensions are those of ownership and control. The media, even in a liberal democratic society, are said to construct social discourse to suit the interests of those who are powerful—individuals, corporations, social elites, social classes.

The questions also open other doors—into the analysis of popular culture as an arena of contest and conflict. Many of the social values communicated in the media are ideologically biased distortions of the world to suit the interests, for instance, of advertisers—the main goal of commercial media managers has been described as the creation of audiences for sale to advertisers as consumers. However, popular culture also emerges from the 'masses' who constantly subvert attempts to direct and control them. They demand an opportunity to create meanings that are relevant to their experiences. In the manufacture of popular culture the most creative and dynamic minds of the age explore, criticise and reinterpret contemporary tensions and troubles. We want to present a view that acknowledges the value of the active participation of audiences in the creation of meanings, but one that also recognises that there are 'economic, technological and political determinations' (McGuigan 1992:6) of culture.

The celebration of popular culture generates its own criticism. The sophistication of the creative act is not sufficient to disguise the processes of power. In a post-colonial society the unresolved antagonisms of race are confounded by class and gender until the popular culture becomess a circus for the exploration and reinforcement of and occasional resistance to the more dominant, homogenising tendencies identified by media critics. For instance, *The Sun* newspaper in Britain has a huge readership, and survives on a never-ending cycle of sexism and racism: does this mean that these values are merely reflected in *The Sun* from its readership? Surely it has become imperative to place the popular desire for exploitative and oppressive cultural products in a broad structure of social hierarchies, threatened minorities, and rapid and severe social dislocation (McGuigan 1992: 181ff; Searle 1989; Gordon and Rosenberg 1989).

Considerable attention has been paid by American empiricist social scientists to the mass media treatment of minorities. As Greenberg and Brand (1993a,1993b) demonstrate, there has been a long history of analysis of the representation of minorities, and an exploration of the social implications of these patterns. They note that the electronic media have mostly been characterised by a ghetto treatment of minority characters, either by stereotyping them into subordinate roles or constricting them in minority content programs. They conclude that. . .

. . .in both child and adult programming, the races [in their case Blacks, Hispanics and Whites] are separated more than they are brought together. Half the programs contain no minorities. . .Hispanics remain rarely visible in any programming from the networks. . .the overall numbers [of Blacks] are confounded by concentration on few shows, very little cross-race interaction, and so forth. . .Youngsters turn to TV to learn about life, to learn about people and to learn more about themselves. There is ample evidence that most characterisations of minorities stand out for them, because they are infrequent. (Greenberg and Brand 1993a:44–6)

American research remains unclear, though, about the effects of these characterisations and practices—whether minorities resent the representations they see, whether they use the narratives in fictional and factual accounts to structure their expectations and behaviour, whether they are concerned with the quality rather than the quantity of the appearances and interactions portrayed. Greenberg and Brand argue for programmatic research which is experimentally based and concentrates on social behaviour.

These programmatic approaches do not exhaust the range of academic and popular debate about the media and the construction of race and ethnicity, which is the focus of this book. As we will see, there are many different avenues along which one can pursue knowledge and understanding about two of the most contentious and difficult social issues of this era—the role of the media in social relations, and the bases of racial and ethnic identity and conflict.

2
THE RACISM AND MEDIA PROJECT

This book has been written because we share a belief that the work that the media do on cultural products has profound effects on the nature of Australian society. The media are not separate from society, but closely implicated in its core relationships—of women with men, of classes, of ages, of race and ethnic groups. We conceive of the media as a process of producing meanings. This process consists of several conceptually distinct elements. We begin with the creators of the messages and their industrial environments: the producers. We are interested in how the creation of media products is affected by the mechanisms of production, the recruitment and socialisation of the producers, and the dynamics of moving ideas and messages into the public realm. Then we examine the messages themselves, with their often ambiguous or multiple meanings, and present both aesthetic and sociological critiques of their content. Then we examine the many audiences, consumers of media products, who are also involved in creating meanings, interacting in often unexpected ways with the media, yet indispensable in their responses to the producers. We need some sense of how audiences interpret and use what they consume.

When we began work on this project in the late 1980s, the media were involved in the 'celebration of the nation' that marked the bicentennial of European invasion and settlement. Various government agencies began to deal with the racism and violence manifest in the society that prided itself on being the most successful 'multicultural community' in the world. It was becoming apparent that the Aboriginal–coloniser relationship had not been resolved and that the deep struggle by Aboriginal people to defend and enhance their heritage was continuing against the apparent indifference if not hostility of the invaders' descendants. Aboriginal deaths in custody focused attention on the role of the culture industries—education and media—in maintaining values and attitudes that systematically undermined Aboriginal self-respect and reinforced non-Aboriginals' stereotypes and ignorance of them.

The long debate about Australia as a multicultural society was being reinvigorated by a new wave of boat people, refugees apparently using well-organised 'escape' routes to reach the north Australian coastline. Media personalities were taking a higher profile, and some were 'charged' before the Australian Broadcasting Tribunal for indulging in racial vilification. The national broadcasters (the Australian Broadcasting Corporation—ABC—and the Special Broadcasting Service—SBS) were put under increasing pressure by community organisations to take their multicultural charters more seriously—regular meetings were held between the senior management of these bodies and groups such as the Federation of Ethnic Community Councils of Australia (FECCA). The commercial television sector was presenting racialist outbursts by public figures as 'good television' (Jakubowicz 1990: 65ff), and the print media (local, metropolitan and national) also took part in the debates on the makeup of Australian society 200 years after the invasion (itself a highly controversial term for the colonisation of Australia, at that time assumed by the dominant society to have been Terra Nullius—no-one's land).

We developed the racism and media project on which this book is based as a co-operative exercise to achieve several different but related objectives. We recognised the huge gap in our knowledge about race and media in Australia, and the major problem that this lack of information would create for people wanting to teach about the media. So we were concerned to develop a well-informed analysis of the Australian media, one that integrated structural analyses of the industry with wider cultural analyses of Australian social relations.

We were also concerned that the media industry's awareness of race and ethnicity issues was fairly limited, and that despite the public debate about race and culture the industry was not taking any responsibility for the production practices it encouraged, nor for the media products it created. Thus we sought to influence industry thinking and behaviour.

There was evidence that the regulatory mechanisms put in place over the past decade were ineffectual in influencing media practices—they neither encouraged good practice, nor really prevented poor practice. The most they did was to provide an outlet for public outrage over overt racism. In the print media this was the most that seemed possible (to the voluntary industry self-regulating Press Council). In the broadcast media the regulatory procedures were cumbersome, bureaucratic, and ultimately self-defeating (a situation not improved by the abolition of the ABT in 1992 and its replacement by a Broadcasting Authority that had no standards of its own yet depended on industry self-regulation).

We also found evidence that Aborigines and ethnic minorities were facing large-scale exclusion as media workers—they found it difficult to gain employment, and once employed, to have their experience deemed as legitimate as that of 'Anglo-Australians'. We were interested in playing some part in enhancing the capacity of minority media workers to make a more significant impact on the media. The capacity of Aboriginal and ethnic communities to influence media industry decisions about programs and content apart from their isolated behaviour as consumers also seemed an important issue to focus on. The racism and media project consisted of several elements—

- A research program which monitored broadcast and print media intensively in 1990 and 1991 and analysed a short period of radio, television and print material.
- A close analysis of issues and how they were treated in the media over a particular period (e.g. the boat people; Aboriginal/non-Aboriginal relations; the 'making' of Redfern, an inner area of Sydney with a strong Aboriginal population; the representation of the Third World; the Gulf War; sexuality and race).
- An analysis of particular broadcast programs that raised some of the issues involved (e.g. comedy; children's television; music television and Aboriginal music; drama series).
- A series of interviews with Aboriginal and ethnic minority media workers concerning their experience with the media.
- A series of interviews with 'mainstream' media workers including managers and production staff, and with staff of the Federation of Australian Commercial Telecasters (FACTS) and the Australian Association of National Advertisers (AANA).
- Participation in various media industry training projects, including those for screenwriters with the Australian Film Television and Radio School, and for the ABC.
- Submissions to government and statutory body inquiries.
- Consultancies with major government inquiries (Aboriginal Deaths in Custody, Racial Violence).
- Specific research exercises for government bodies (media content, audience perceptions, especially for the Office of Multicultural Affairs).
- A series of academic and public seminars, and participation in conferences etc.
- Student media projects on race and ethnicity, based on specific programs, stories or advertising campaigns, and examining their makers' intentions and effects.
- Participation in an international comparative research project on ethnic conflict and the media.

This book brings together much of this material, and in particular, empirical research on media content and how it reveals media practices as well as their wider social context.

The empirical material was collected from several sources to provide depth and breadth of data. In April 1990 we recorded two weeks of midday and prime-time television on five Sydney channels—2, 7, 9, 10, SBS (not midday) plus the music video programs *Rage*, *MTV* and *The Noise*, and several hours daily of five radio stations (2FC, 2BL, 2GB, 2KY and 2MMM) with Aboriginal radio from Radio Redfern and SBS's 2EA. All the major newspapers, news magazines, women's and youth magazines were collected. In May

1991 another week of Channel 9 (the channel with the highest ratings) was recorded, and newspapers for the period were also collected. The material was then coded to identify all specific references to ethnic minorities, Aborigines and Torres Strait Islanders, and all instances of general claims to be speaking for or about Australia. For the work on children and television (September 1991 to March 1992) we used *The Afternoon Show* and *Couch Potato* (ABC), Agro's *Cartoon Connection* and *Saturday Disney* (Channel 7), and *Kids' Stuff* (Channel 10).

For during the racism and media project we also collected other material—regularly clipping issues in the print media or following up broadcasts of news, current affairs, drama, music and comedy material. In 1992 a research project on ethnic audiences and the media was undertaken for the Office of Multicultural Affairs. At the request of the Office we prepared a discussion group schedule and media diary which OMA used to collect material from over 60 discussion groups and 700 individual participants in all states and the Northern Territory. We then analysed the material and reported the findings to the OMA (Coupe and Jakubowicz 1993). Some of this material has also been included in a description of ethnic audience responses to and opinions about the mass media. The audience perspectives provide a valuable corrective to our own 'deconstruction' of the media texts we have used, at times demonstrating the very different interpretations that arise from people's experiences and cultural values.

These varying perspectives can be thought of as ideologies, systems of values and ideas by which experience can be interpreted and action determined. 'Ideology' has various genealogies in the social sciences. It ranges from a perspective which contrasts ideology (a self-serving, distorting framework of interpretation) to science (usually described as 'Marxist historical materialism'), through to a more flexible approach in which all perspectives are seen as ideological or partial views of reality. In each case, though, there is a sense that a deeper truth or reality lies beyond the ideology and that it is accessible through analysis.

3

AUSTRALIAN MEDIA STUDIES AND ISSUES OF RACE AND ETHNICITY

While there has been vigorous community debate in the media about issues of race and ethnicity—Aboriginal and Torres Strait Islander Land Rights, the 'Boat people', refugees, etc.—most academic investigation of the media has neglected the issues. Two of the more widely referenced texts that set out to provide an overview of the Australian media—Bill Bonney and Helen Wilson's *Australia's Commercial Media* (1983) and Keith Windschuttle's *Australian Media* (1988)—make little reference to the issues, even though they both explore gender and class (from different perspectives) in some detail.

Even more recent attempts to address these issues have not managed to move much further. Albert Moran's edited collection on broadcast media (Moran 1992) includes a short excerpt from an anonymous government consultant for the Special Broadcasting Authority, and makes no reference to Aborigines. John Henningham's *Issues in Australian Journalism* (1990) includes Michael Meadow's analysis of the media portrayal of Aborigines, but no discussion of ethnicity or cultural pluralism. The Tulloch and Turner collection on Australian television (1989), which is subtitled 'Programs, Pleasures and Politics', makes passing reference to cultural chauvinism by including Stuart Cunningham's discussions of the late 1980s mini-series *Cowra Breakout* and *Vietnam*, which he describes as 'major documents contributing to setting the emergent discourse of multi-culturalism on the national agenda' (Cunningham 1989:44). However, the work that television maintains on ethnicity, race and their links with nation does not feature. Moran and O'Regan's *The Australian Screen* (1989) allows a wider perspective on the constitution of the nation. Here we find dimensions of cultural difference generated by race and ethnicity in Moran's discussion of the migrant as subject in institutional documentaries, and a recognition of immigrant experiences in a discussion of Sophie Turkiewicz's work as a film director by Annette Blonski and Freda Freiberg (p. 205). In the same collection Sean Maynard offers a chapter that discusses the representation of Aboriginality and the relationship between blacks and whites in Australian cinema. He acknowledges that, as a white writer, he does not offer a full exposure of the issues, and admits to a certain romanticism (p. 235). The Cunningham and Turner (1993) collection on the media in Australia addresses cultural pluralism and racism in a limited way—through a compressed summary of Jakubowicz's analysis of SBS radio (Jakubowicz 1989) and occasional references—examples in terms of mini-series, films, television. However, there is no sustained analysis of the ethnic press (not a single mention) nor any discussion of ethnic or Aboriginal audiences, except of some 'migrant girls' in an excerpt from Tulloch and Moran's study of *A Country Practice* (1986:266–71).

Government-sponsored research into media and race has been generated by the Office of Multicultural Affairs, mainly by the authors of this book and by Phillip Bell (Bell 1993), as well as by the Human Rights and Equal Opportunity Commission (HREOC 1991, Jakubowicz 1990), and most recently by the Australian Broadcasting Authority. The former Tribunal conducted neither research nor inquiry into the issues. The 1993 project undertaken jointly by the ABA and the British Broadcasting Standards Council (Nugent et al. 1993; Bostock 1993), dealt with three issues—the frequency of representation of Aborigines and NESBs, the nature of the portrayal, and what might be done about the findings. Using a series of qualitative research clinics, a national telephone survey and an analysis of selected programs, the report concluded that audiences felt that 'television was considered to be an influential medium which should actively promote harmonious community relations between different cultural groups. . .an educative role which in turn should promote better understanding' (Nugent et al. 1993:36). The point was made that for minority groups the issue of representation (extent and type) was a significant concern—for Anglo-Australians it had a low priority and required 'numerous prompts' (p. 38). The main concern was on the exclusion of Aborigines and ethnic Australians, rather than how they were portrayed on screen—except in the case of Aborigines where there was 'some evidence of a perceived lack of positive images' (p. 39).

The response to issues of race and ethnicity in many of the more academic studies seems to have been constructed from a self-confident central point looking out towards the margins. Thus we are enveloped by resurgent cultural nationalists with their feet firmly set in Anglo-Australian tradition, seeking to understand the meaning of 'these others'—the others into whose realm they have strayed (Aborigines and Torres Strait Islanders), and the non-Anglo immigrants who have wandered into the paddock after they have built the fences.

This problem of perspective emerges very clearly in a more recent study of Australian television culture which springs from the same celebratory approach to the renewed Australia (O'Regan 1993). For the first time, a serious study of television has made a significant attempt to examine the nature of the 'television service' by assessing what is described as the 'different cultural and spatial levels' and its 'minoritarian, ethnic, indigenous and 'established' Australian manifestations' (p. iv). Rather than setting up polarities, as in monocultural against multicultural, O'Regan argues for television as a mosaic of sites, levels, and so on. Viewers move through these easily, he suggests, adopting different identities as they travel, dipping in and out of minoritarian and 'established' forcefields. Overall Australian television has become the 'site for competition, synergy and antagonism' (p. 105) between levels and interests and projects. In a two-chapter foray into the Special Broadcasting Service, the first of which surveys the symbolic politics of multiculturalism, and the second of which encompasses the service itself, O'Regan argues that SBS has taken on an ever-expanding role as presenter of a world view predicated on a unitary Australian interest, into which the culturally pluralist communities that make up the audience can be enrolled. Australia's fundamental tensions within ethnic fragments and between them and the wider society have been dealt with by importing images and narratives from the homeland and by the presentation of the multicultural image by ethnic Australians. The great majority of local ethnicities appear only in informational programming, leaving the fictional programming to imported material. Concluding about the politics of the scene, O'Regan claims that 'multiculturalism and SBS have always been in the business of managing ethnicity and social marginality in ways consonant with government policy. . .[although] SBS actively enlists and allows ethnic and marginal aspiration to significantly shape them' (p. 177).

Such an approach to understanding the processes of multicultural television begins from an assumption of marginality, and tries to explain how that marginality is managed in the interests of overall social harmony. In doing so it provides useful insights into the changing struggles over content and ideology. It does not, however, come to grips with the exclusion and control of cultural differences which continue to characterise the 'established 'Australian' media.

Such an approach reaches this impasse because it fails to comprehend two dimensions of struggle and conflict. One dimension is the daily negotiation by ethnic minorities for cultural and personal integrity and survival against elements of a culture which defines itself as 'mainstream' and 'established'; the other dimension involves the structural processes that reinforce hegemonic control within media and other social organisations against the perceived threat of the Others and their challenge to the competence and capacity of the dominant social order. Simply put, the question remains: why have the established television services remained more or less incapable of changing to allow a more multicultural service? The multicultural project at SBS television has been not so much about managing minorities (though a certain element of that explains the low level of funding and the constant problems with service delivery) but rather about internationalising the Australian middle class, in the face of a globalising communication and production environment against which that class remained resistant.

The rhetoric of cultural pluralism for ethnic communities at SBS has allowed the television industry in general to remain largely unaffected by the cultural changes wrought by migration. The 'infotainment' programming of the channel during prime time allows a stronger engagement with Australia's ethnocentrism, but why has it had such little impact on the other services targeting this same audience? Our argument is that the current media structures exist to maintain particular cultural hierarchies, and that change occurs only when these practices are challenged whenever they are produced, however stimulating and enjoyable they may be.

Australian media studies have begun to examine the issues of racism and the media, though seldom with any direct attack. They do not place social power and the role of the media in sustaining that power in a context of conflict and struggle but offer instead an endless plain of opportunities and choices. Since we need to clarify the central importance of the media in those processes of social power, we shall now examine the relationship between ideology and the media.

4

IDEOLOGY AND THE MEDIA

The construction of media content is inevitably a conflictual process, yet such conflict need not be hostile: it is often creative and expansive. New ideas challenge the old, new attempts to communicate the social mosaic to audiences find spaces already occupied. The material to which audiences have access offers milieus through which social difference and diversity can be explored, represented, contested, reproduced and modified. The mass media thrive on a variety of genres and sites, yet always try to set these in terms of the known and comfortable. Audiences are shown 'real life' in forms such as news or current affairs—these world views are also tied into conflicts scripted as sport, or drama, or comedy; as quiz shows, dance contests and cartoons, in soaps and serials. In magazines they read news reports and evaluative pieces, editorial comment and explanatory articles, comic and cartoon representations. They read recipes and advertisements, 'how to' do everything from baby care to car repair. They can pursue fantasies of body, dress, lifestyle, or analyses of major social, economic and scientific issues.

Such a melange of opportunity suggests that any simple line of argument will flounder in complex alternative. This must be partly true as the ideologies pervading the media are problematic sets of values and aspirations, strongly affected by the diversity of responses from audiences no matter what interpretations are proffered by producers, writers and editors. Ideology can serve as a shorthand term for that 'complex set of meanings and a structuralisation of the processes of production and consumption of meaning on the part of audiences' (Hodge and Tripp 1986: 23).

However, these ideologies are not 'unattached', suspended in some space in which ideas alone struggle for dominance. Ideologies have real material roots—in the economic and social structures of society. We are not, however, taking the simplistic line that all ideologies can be identified by their social contexts, but proposing that they are patterns of ideas that link individual identity and consciousness to wider social practices and forces. These wider social forces and values interact with individual rationales and perceptions in a reciprocal process of reinforcement. Ideologies can disguise material interests and can be used to confuse the general with the specific (for instance, where one group presents its interests as though these are the nation's interests).

We have at time found ourselves overwhelmed by evidence of a sharper sense of ideology—ideology as a set of ideas deliberately constructed to advance a particular group's interests. Group interests are an important dimension in comprehending ideology at work. When we ask media workers, such as television current affairs producers, why a particular pattern of representation recurs in the media, we have to deal with two levels of analysis. For example, when the low level of Aboriginal representation in the media is explained to us by producers and editors either in terms of unavailability of 'talent' or expected hostility from audiences, we must first analyse the media's explanations of what we see; then we have to draw our own conclusions about their explanations—are they merely self-serving rationalisations? Are deep beliefs about the 'real world' being put forward? Or evidence chosen to support a predetermined position? We had one discussion with a prize-winning senior television producer, himself an immigrant from Britain, who proudly proclaimed to us that he knew nothing about Australia before he arrived. He then announced that 'ethnic people are not as good as Australian journalists, and we appoint on the basis of merit—if you want us to have more ethnics you'll need an instruction from management that we have quotas, and that we have to take them'. Clearly there is more than ignorance going on here—there are deeply entrenched hostilities and perhaps a sense of material threat engendered by the new arguments for a multicultural and non-racist media.

Since the media are organisations for the production, dissemination and consumption of meaning, how are meanings produced, disseminated and consumed? Ien Ang (1991) has spoken of meaning being increasingly produced globally but consumed locally—of large systems and corporations commodifying meaning and distributing it across the world to be interpreted, negotiated, modified, twisted, reconstructed before re-emerging intertwined with local history and culture, never the same nuance or pattern twice, always different. The local then becomes analogous to difference. Difference is produced by localising human experience, in the face of globalising processes that tend to homogenise. But how is difference possible if the production of meaning is becoming more concentrated in fewer hands, each with public and conservative political agendas?

5

POWER AND THE MEDIA: CONCENTRATION

The political economy of the media—that symbiotic interaction between the ownership and organisation of media production, the action by government (as the state in capitalist society), and the broader society—has been one of the major paradigms used to interpret media–society relations. The political economy approach assumes that the material aspects of production in the media industries affect the content (conceived of as ideology) to such an extent that everything that occurs in the media is shaped by these material aspects, to fit in with the interests of media's owners and controllers. Content, especially, is 'commodified', and the ideas and values communicated through the media are transformed by the processes of production into commodities to be exchanged in the marketplace. The two related components proposed by this political economy paradigm are (1) the ideological function designed to reinforce the values favoured by the economic and politically dominant groups; and (2) the material function of commodification with its power to reconstruct popular culture into a culture of consumption of commodities. As McQuail (1987:64) has noted in his summary of the mainly British debate from this perspective (Murdoch and Golding 1977; Curran et al. 1986), the political economy approach does allow a focus on the integration of media industries into the global economic environment. It also offers an explanation in structural terms of the systematic exclusion of lesser voices, presenting the media as an arena in which only those who are powerful enough to participate can exert any influence. All others gain access (Andy Warhol's fifteen minutes of fame in a lifetime) only when their experiences are either interesting or bizarre enough to be of material value to the more powerful, especially advertisers.

Herman and Chomsky (1988) have argued that media content, particularly news and current affairs, is heavily influenced by which corporations own and control the media and what other interests they might have. They write of the media as 'manufacturing consent', developing and communicating propaganda to sabotage revolutionary struggles against imperialism, and to validate social forces that act in the US government and multinational corporation interests in the Third World. Such a view directly challenges any claims to democratic independence and impartiality in the presentation of international and national news. According to them, the key filters on news are the size and scope of media ownership, the power of advertisers, and the sourcing and choice of news.

Ownership and control of the media in Australia has promoted fierce debate and widespread concern over recent years. The broad structures may have changed but the net effect has been the concentration of the commercial media, particularly the press, in fewer hands, and the precarious survival of other mass media outlets (television and radio). The effects of economic boom and bust, changing legislative constraints, changing federal communications ministers in the Commonwealth government under the Australian Labor Party, and free market trends have produced a situation where two longer-term trends—concentration and globalisation—have come to dominate media practice.

The national newspaper market has effectively moved into the hands of two players. Rupert Murdoch's News Ltd in reality controls (i.e. has no competition in) all the metropolitan markets, save for Sydney and Melbourne; in early 1992 a consortium put together by Canadian publisher Conrad Black won control of the failing Fairfax newspaper group—the *Sydney Morning Herald*, the Melbourne *Age* and the national *Financial Review*. Black has rebuilt an earlier alliance with television and magazine publisher Kerry Packer. This alliance was dissolved to avoid political interference by forces who viewed Packer's involvement in the Fairfax papers as a very dangerous increase in the concentration of ownership and influence (and a potential breach of the restrictions on cross-media ownership), but Packer soon returned to the game, purchasing a significant holding in Fairfax in 1993.

The battle lines were drawn, with Murdoch trying to position his national morning paper, *The Australian*, as the voice of the conservative and technocratic elite of Australia. The *SMH* and *The Age* had been rather more liberal in their perspectives, though there was growing apprehension that they too would be driven to a more politically conservative position by Black; his purchase of the *Jerusalem Post* allegedly moved it in that direction.

In the electronic media, and television in particular, major changes in ownership have occurred as technological change has accelerated, shadowed by the possibility of cable TV, and these changes have resulted in a much more polarised broadcasting marketplace. Three commercial networks, each controlling a string of regional stations throughout the country, have had varying financial fortunes. Packer's Nine Network came through the recession of the late 1980s in strong shape: in 1987 Alan Bond bought the stations from Packer for over $800 million, but was forced to sell back to Packer in 1990 for $200 million. Only in the Northern Territory, where he was the single largest private landowner, was Packer less than successful—there the Australian Broadcasting Tribunal awarded the central Australia licence to Imparja TV, a commercial station with strong Aboriginal involvement through the Central Australian Aboriginal Media Association.

Both the other commercial networks were put into receivership, put up for sale or placed under tight financial management. Their capacity for innovation was limited, or so they argued, and their capacity to sponsor Australian material was consequentially reduced. The key role of the banks in the networks' survival strategies meant that enlarging their audiences became a fairly crucial goal—not one to be easily offset against the apparently riskier business of stressing multicultural social goals.

Until recently, television programming directors have relied on safe, familiar formats and with material that rarely challenged audiences. Claims to certitude, dependency on regular presenters (some with over 30 years in television) and a concentration on the activities of the powerful had various consequences. The 'reality' that was the concern of news and current affairs, or which formed the background narrative of script ideas for serials and soaps, remained almost uncompromisingly Anglo-Australian; or if it was 'internationalised' it catered for North American domestic audiences.

The magazine market also became increasingly competitive—indeed, as the 'broadcast' media became less satisfactory for dollar-strapped advertisers, the capacity of magazines to deliver a message to a smaller but clearly defined audience became a more attractive proposition. The integration of *The Bulletin* (a magazine in Packer's Australian Consolidated Press group) with *Newsweek*, an American magazine published by the *Washington Post* paralleled the introduction of an Australian edition of *Time* magazine. These magazines reflected a much more clinical segmentation of their audience—a move also affecting women's and teenagers' magazines such as *New Idea*, *Woman's Day*, *The Australian Women's Weekly*, *Cleo*, *Cosmopolitan*, *Dolly* and *Boyfriend*.

The national media sector—ABC, SBS—was also affected by changing economic and political pressures. With the ABC's real resources reduced, and with its argument for being the only 'national' network eroded by the government's policy of 'equalisation' and the creation of the three commercial networks, the ABC continued to move towards more cost-efficient practices. As the pressure mounted to extend its equal employment opportunity policies to a greater intake of minority groups, the ABC was forced to cut staff, and so initiatives have tended to rely on additional funds from outside organisations—the employment of Aborigines sponsored by the Department of Employment, Education and Training, or the engagement of 'ethnic' trainees sponsored and paid for by the Office of Multicultural Affairs. There is increasing evidence of the ABC's resistance to targeting the employment of ethnic minorities, or in making multicultural programs. The rationale for this resistance is the declining real resource base and the reluctance to give preferential treatment to groups previously excluded.

The Special Broadcasting Service also began a major transformation. Under new legislation it has replaced commercial sponsorship announcements on television with advertisements. The effect of this has been to put prime-time broadcasting under some pressure to gain a significant audience, to rely heavily on English language programs between 7.30 p.m. and 9.30 p.m., and to move broadcasting in other languages to more marginal timeslots.

In radio, SBS sought to reprogram the service given to larger and well-established communities to accommodate new immigrant groups. In 1991 this created a major conflict in Sydney, with large public meetings of these communities condemning the move, and demanding that SBS not disenfranchise them—many had significant numbers of monolingual elderly. The outcome of this was a commitment by the Labor Party in its 1993 federal election manifesto to provide SBS with another radio network, thus allowing it to meet the demands of a wider number of ethnic communities.

6

POWER AND THE MEDIA: GLOBALISATION

Ownership and control obviously affect media production practices. The globalisation of production (e.g. Jacka 1992) has also put significant pressure on local media production futures. Industries are becoming organised on an international, if not global scale; the audiovisual industries in particular are taking on a form in which technology and product are becoming more closely integrated. Sony, the Japan-based hardware manufacturer now owns CBS music (the software) in the USA, thus reinforcing its control over sound technology. News Ltd, which now owns Fox cinema and television, has thus gained a global interpenetration of film, television, magazines and newspapers.

Sklair notes in his discussion of globalisation that the transnationalisation of the media is really a transnationalisation of the economic structures of society, eroding the nation state and creating a culture-ideology of consumerism (Sklair 1991: 139; Roncagliolo 1986). This culture-ideology is central to the process of 'assimilation' of immigrants into Australian society, for it is their transformation into consumers of media-advertised commodities that represents one of the key transformations of culture they often experience (Jakubowicz 1987; Coupe and Jakubowicz 1993). Immigrants often try to understand Australian society by consuming commodities presented to them as appropriate by the media. Globalisation does not necessarily lead to a homogenisation of content, but it will spread consumerism as a cultural form. This spread of consumerism is also identified by Aboriginal leaders as one of the greatest dangers facing traditional Aboriginal peoples with the coming of television to remote parts of Australia.

If economic pressures prompt a conservative surge by the media towards the uncontroversial and safe, to make audiences feel more secure and certain about their prejudices, then the opportunities for diversity diminish. For instance, the declining numbers of newspaper owners means that the international network of information sources is reduced. Similarly, the former Fairfax papers may be facing a future of declining autonomy of sources and an increased use of other Conrad Black news sources due to an economic rationalist logic that looks for the elimination of duplication of resources. The domination of the metropolitan newspaper market by News Ltd restricts the range of opinion and input available. *The Australian* and Sydney's *Telegraph Mirror* already have a track record of hostility to cultural diversity in Australian society, let alone intellectual diversity within their own pages, so the future in that regard is less than hopeful.

Similar problems exist in other elements of the national and international news systems. Most international news for television comes from two sources—ITN and Visnews. The ABC maintains reporters in several countries, and Channel 9 has links with the USA and UK. However, the remainder of news inputs are tied to the priorities of the international agencies and their interests in the North American marketplace.

Since the Commonwealth parliament's print inquiry in 1992 failed to recommend any action to maintain if not increase diversity in the press (Bowman 1992), and since the government has replaced the Australian Broadcasting Tribunal by an even less interventionist body (The Australian Broadcasting Authority) that is far more likely to respond to commercial media interests, it appears likely that the 'free market' will be allowed to intrude further into the politics of information in Australia.

The Australian government is also coming under pressure from the international trade community, and in particular from the United States, to abandon its restrictions on overseas-produced television material, including both advertisements and television programming. Under the General Agreement on Tariffs and Trade negotiations, the Australian content rules of the old ABT have been identified as potential obstacles to trade. Abandoning these rules under American pressure could well have devastating consequences for the local production industry and for its small steps towards a more open and diverse representation of Australian society.

4

CULTURAL CRITIQUES AND AUSTRALIAN (DIS)CONTENT

The political economy approach is important for understanding not only the media but also the processes through which ideas about society are formed and communicated. Post-modern critiques of political economy and the rise of cultural studies that concentrate on the text and argue that the structures which produce the texts are of marginal relevance, have come to prominence in recent work on the media.

Strongly influenced by French deconstructionist analyses and semiotic studies of the content of media discourses, these approaches have emphasised the ambiguity of meanings in texts, focusing on the tension between the intention of the author (or even the author as a concept) and the power of audiences or readers to discover their own meanings in the texts, drawing on their experiences and references. The texts are removed from the process of their industrial production and set in a landscape of ideas and values, without a relationship to any material interests. The subjectivity of the reader is given paramount place, with great attention paid to the discontinuities between author and audience. Subcultures are celebrated as the milieus of resistance, or as strategies for psychic survival in the face of the 'end of ideology' and the 'death of history'. Style, imbued with semiotic density, becomes the focus for exploration and analysis, a venue for the articulation of cultural identity and social difference.

The reaffirmation of subjective sensibility offers a necessary corrective to both the structural mechanism of Althusserian theories of ideology and more conspiratorial views of the capitalist/imperialist project, which removed the opportunities for subversion and adaptation by those at the receiving end of the communication blitz. However, this reaffirmation can also lead to the mass media's uncritical celebration of the popular, especially of youth sub-cultures which can find themselves celebrated merely as oppositional and selfconsciously subversive (McGuigan 1992).

One example of this problem in Australian media studies occurs in the debate over Australian content in Australian broadcasting (and in cinema), and thereby over the relationship between the state, media and national culture. At present the arguments seem to have reached an impasse—over whether there should be government intervention to define and defend national culture, or more exploration of what a national culture might be in a period of increasing globalisation of communication and media production.

The first step then is to assess the arguments over whether there should be Australian content regulations for Australian cultural development. Under pressure from the United States during the Uruguay round of the GATT talks, Australian government negotiators have had to dwell with some intensity on the economic and social rationale for rules that constrain the entry into the Australian television and film marketplace of foreign-produced television material.

The Australian Broadcasting Tribunal raised this question in its Inquiry into Australian Content in 1987–8 (a sort of Bicentennial project all on its own). The Tribunal issued a background paper which canvassed some of the key dimensions of the policy guidelines; it reflected on Canadian film development policies, on funding criteria adopted by the Australian Film Commission, and on the Commonwealth Government's Department of the Arts during the period when Section 10 b(a) of the Taxation Act supported films seeking certification as 'Australian' for taxation write-off purposes. These structural supports to local production had a great deal to do with employment in the film industry and offered a spin-off in local movies, but did not specifically address the cultural content of the product—only its key personnel, and sources of funds.

The ABT was also interested in the idea of an 'Australian look', a content approach that would allow the allocation of a higher points score to fulfil local production quotas, imposed by the Tribunal on commercial broadcasters. The points system had been introduced in 1973 by the Broadcasting Control Board (precursor to the ABT) to induce greater quality and diversity in programming. However, the Board tended to become captive of the industry it was designed to regulate, and thus had to be 'freed' to operate in the wider public interest (which it was also called upon to define). John Docker, in a strong argument against Australian content regulation, has attacked the whole question of state discipline in relation to popular culture (Docker 1991). Docker is highly critical of the division between high and popular culture implicit in the ABT policy of Australian content. He argues that conservative visions of the State's role in protecting audiences from the supposedly corrosive effects of mass culture (particularly imported material) and in stimulating audiences by ensuring access to 'high quality' programs, particularly drama, have emerged from a long tradition of bourgeois distaste for the potentially oppositional tendencies in popular entertainment—the subversion of authority implicit, say, in the carnival tradition.

Public interest groups, Docker says, confront the community with a constrictive perspective on the choices they might want—the public in fact have a great deal of power to signify their interest or lack of it to commercial broadcasters. Arguments for regulation, he continues, are arguments for elitism, which are fundamentally contemptuous of the authenticity of popular opinion and the capacity of the population at large to make choices in terms of their own needs and pleasures. It is a struggle by popular culture against repression, suppression, censorship, moralising, surveillance, and impositions (Docker 1991: 24).

Yet what are we to make of this argument when the effect of existing regulation, minimalist as it is in relation to Aborigines and ethnic minorities, and even where it is written into the charter of the ABC, has had so little effect (according to David Hill, ABC chief executive, quoted by the *Sydney Morning Herald* on 17 February 1993 as saying that 'reporting of Aboriginal affairs in the Australian media ranges from responsible to appalling and even racist')? This is particularly problematic for Docker as he ties his attack on the high culture bias of regulation to the advocacy of internationalising program flows. He suggests that there is no danger in the Americanisation of Australian television, as here again the cultural marketplace will assign value and in time resolve the conflicts through the active participation of audiences.

One is reminded of the old Marxist adage, that people make their own history, but not on terrain of their own choosing. It seems as if Docker has sought to rescue the role of the audience as subject from what he saw as the torment of structuralist imposition, only to lose a handle on that process and its context. Stuart Cunningham offers a similar critique of Docker when he suggests that Docker is being disingenuous in his presentation of commercial broadcasters as 'acutely sensitive' to popular interests, aiming to serve the carnivalesque desires of the working class, and being constantly hampered by regulatory bodies and interest groups (Cunningham 1991:29).

From another perspective, there is some strength in Terry Flew's argument that existing structures of control (despite ABT Television Program Standards (14[1]b) which attempt to recognise the Australian community's diversity of backgrounds) have not done very much to overcome the marginalisation of ethnic communities and Aborigines in television discourses (Flew 1991). Indeed, there are far more Blacks and non-Anglos in American material on Australian television than in any Australian series, a point we make below in relation to advertising on children's television, which is often made for the American market. The popularity of *The Cosby Show* and the findings of the ABA report on cultural diversity (1993) suggest that it is not necessarily Australian audiences that have a problem with these issues—rather, Australian program-makers appear to have been as reluctant as the regulatory system to offer diversity.

The strongest arguments against Australian content rules have come from the advertising sector, particularly from the Australian Association of National Advertisers (many members of which are either transnational companies or local distributors of transnational products) and from the Advertising Federation of Australia, representing agencies. The ABT listed 61 submissions in its summary of submissions (ABT 1988c), of which 24 came from the advertising industry. Their overall claim was that current practices increased the cost of production and requirements should be removed. Against their position submissions from Actors Equity, several independent production houses, and some professional associations (e.g. Writers Guild, Teachers of Media) stressed the importance of maintaining controls to protect and enhance the industry.

The Australian content debate has significant implications for the position of ethnic minorities and Aborigines in the Australian media, although the nature and extent of these implications are not obvious. The cultural marketplace does not necessarily produce cultural diversity or complexity—if a mass audience drives the provision of media product, and that audience is significantly racist, even substantial minorities may have little influence on the outcome. Furthermore, in the face of the media's assimilationist messages non-Anglo immigrants and Aborigines may be less than anxious to join a debate in which the majority values have such a residual and minor place for them. The argument that they can influence the marketplace if they so choose begs the question—if there is precious little evidence of images, issues, voices and faces with which they can identify, what is the likelihood they will demand such things? Or indeed, for the Anglophonic mass, what chance do they have of seeing or enjoying diversity if it is denied them?

The Australian content debate provides a useful avenue for exploring the value of different theoretical approaches to understanding the media, for it demonstrates that material interests are closely tied to ideologies about the national interest and how it should be advanced. However, we need the insights from cultural studies to understand media treatment of race and ethnicity, and in particular, what it means to talk of the Australian media as racist.

8

RACES AND RACISMS

Racism can be understood as the set of values and behaviours associated with groups of people in conflict over physical appearances, genealogy, or cultural differences. It contains an intellectual/ideological framework of explanation, a negative orientation towards 'the Other', and a commitment to a set of actions that put these values into practice.

While we are specifically interested in how the media represent racial conflict, it is important to understand its broader social context. Explanations for such conflict vary from the materialist to the idealist, if not metaphysical. Some researchers (e.g. Miles 1982; Wetherell and Potter 1992) have placed contemporary racism in the framework of imperialism and colonialism, as an ideology specifically generated to justify the conquest and expropriation of colonised (native) people by European metropolitan powers. They explore the processes that legitimise racism, and find in people's discourses about racial difference their evidence for the apparently unfathomable disjunctions between public tolerance and the maintenance of racist structures and behaviour (Wetherell and Potter 1992: 206ff). Since the ideology has a material basis it is unlikely to change so long as the material relations between and within societies are those of inequality and exploitation. Furthermore, if the colonised are brought into the metropolitan society as immigrant workers, their colonised, subordinate position will accompany them and will be reinforced by low status jobs, poor housing and schooling, and negative cultural stereotypes and representations.

Earlier versions of this materialist account have been criticised as being too reductionist, and insensitive to the complexity of racial and cultural attitudes and practices. One such materialist approach that sprang from the work of Stuart Hall and his colleagues at the Birmingham Centre for Contemporary Cultural Studies in the decade after 1975 argues that 'Race is the modality in which class relations are experienced' (Hall 1978 quoted in Gilroy 1982). Race had its roots in an experience that preceded capitalism, and is now inextricably intertwined with inequality and oppression. Consciousness of race and class cannot be pulled apart for black people (nor for white), while gender relations permeate consciousness of difference for women and men. Black women's experience of white societies is structured by patriarchal relations of power—race and class are experienced in gendered forms (hooks 1992).

Issues of race cannot be singled out from those of gender and class. The intersection of these dimensions of social cleavage is fundamental to our study, for the media provide the structure on which many of these intersections are worked through in symbolic form. The stage comedy *Wogs Out of Work* grew out of an ethnic (mainly Greek) working-class experience in Australia. It was created by the children of immigrants, showing the world through the perspective of the second generation. They stood some distance from the Anglo-Australian 'mainstream' culture yet their new class position (as tertiary-educated children of 'uneducated' immigrant parents) created many of the tensions over gender roles and relations from which the comedy springs.

Since we are concerned with the representations of cultural minorities and their relationships with the wider society, we have chosen 'race' and 'racism' as shorthand terms for extremely complex and ambiguous processes. We have already noted that talking about cultural difference has a legitimate place in any social discourse. Yet given the difficulties with the idea of race, can we maintain the usages we have sought to establish?

'Race' has no scientific basis as a term for the relationship between skin colour, physical features and gene pool on the one hand, and social and cultural behaviour on the other. The range of genetic diversity within physiologically distinctive communities is often as great as differences between communities (Rose et al. 1985:119ff). While crude demagogic claims persist with this simplistic 'biological' connection, it is not part of contemporary social science. On the debate over sociobiology we agreee with Steven Rose and his colleagues when they note that 'any use of racial categories must take its justifications from other sources than biology' (Rose et al. 1985:127). So 'race' has primarily social meaning—the next step is to explore the range of social meanings and their implications in attempting to understand how the media interprets, represents and communicates race and races.

There are several fairly innocuous uses of the term—the most obvious being the human 'race', where broad ideas of common descent (in evolutionary models) or of creation (in more religious contexts) allow us to explore shared cultural and historical experience. It may also be used to describe apparent physical differences, but such use already verges on evaluation, ranking and hierarchical ordering against some external value set. Fuzziness also intrudes—people may speak of the white race, or the Black race, or the European race, or the Chinese race. Immediately there are problems of interpretation—does race stand for skin colour, or geographical place of birth, or nationality, or culture, or something else—some essential psychic or moral quality that can be differentiated? Here we are moving into a tougher linguistic territory fraught with potential tensions, where different appearance, behaviour, or even geographical origin suggest impossible barriers of hostility between peoples.

In popular and policy discourses the idea of 'race' as a metaphor for culturally distinct communities is often simply used to distinguish, not to discriminate. So under what conditions does the use of 'race' move towards *racism*—where cultural or physical distinctiveness is used to explain social behaviour, and sometimes to justify discrimination, oppression or even extermination? Racism concerns the use of power by one group against another on the basis of an idea of racial differentiation. It is at issue, we believe, not simply where difference is noted but where difference is mobilised to justify the domination of one section of society by another. Thus the media are deeply implicated, through their constitution of meanings, in public discourses about social inequality. One apparently trivial example—a leading current affairs television journalist allegedly described as untrustworthy the character of the then NSW Premier Nicholas Greiner (a Hungarian-born immigrant) in relation to a 'political deal' with a former colleague—his coda for the criticism being 'never trust the Hungarian' (*Sydney Morning Herald* 15 May 1992:7). This broadcaster, three months previously, had been an active participant in a training session on multiculturalism for news and current affairs journalists where he had reiterated his hostility to racism and his support for the multicultural project. Yet he slipped easily into behaviour which, on reflection, he agreed was offensive.

We use 'race' to refer to the social processes of differentiation based on physical features and geographical origin. We use 'ethnicity' to distinguish groups in terms of cultural and community practices. Race and ethnicity are and can be used interchangeably in common parlance, with race more likely to refer to people 'of colour', and ethnicity to 'white' communities and individuals of European descent. Racism and ethnocentrism are both embedded in relations of power; racism is now more likely to be justified by a sociobiology argument about the 'natural' territoriality of races. This argument claims that ethnic groups or races 'naturally' resent each other, naturally compete and conflict, and thus 'naturally' should remain in their own spaces and not intrude into communities where their presence must naturally trigger hostility and perhaps violence (Blainey 1984; Ruxton quoted in Jakubowicz 1990). Such claims are racist because they maintain that the privileges of one group should prevail over those of another purely on the basis that cultural differences are incompatible. They also uphold the idea that cultural difference necessitates competition and therefore hostility.

We can talk of structural racism occurring where regular patterns of unequal access to power seem to recur, and to be solely associated with race or ethnic factors. For example, a mass media organisation may vigorously oppose public racism, including racist language, yet in a more covert way sustain the environment in which such behaviour survives. An organisation may do this simply by applying professional and institutional values, such as its policy of employment on merit, or news values. These values may thereby create an employment milieu from which cultural minorities are either excluded, or in which they feel intimidated, and a news and current affairs output that speaks nearly always with the voice and from the perspective of what *The Australian* newspaper has so unselfconsciously and proudly referred to as the 'dominant race' (Editorial, *The Australian*, 28 August 1989).

'Who speaks for the subaltern?' asks Indian intellectual Gayatri Spivak, 'who can voice the worlds of the voiceless?' Spivak (1988) notes 'Clearly if you are poor, black and female you get it in three ways. . .[but in] seeking to learn to speak to (rather than listen to or speak for) the historically muted subject of the subaltern woman, the post-colonial intellectual *systematically* "unlearns" female privilege'. Spivak concludes that she cannot separate herself from her class, but she can use her analytical skills to deconstruct 'mainstream' accounts of the experience of the voiceless.

Homi Bhabha too finds in the post-colonial contemporary world—the world of migrant workers and transients, the internationalised world of 'ethnoscapes' (Appadurai 1990: 297)—the potential of cultural difference to establish new forms of meaning and strategies of identification. For Bhabha, the migrant experience is to be found where 'the 'loss' of meaning enters as a cutting edge into the representation of the fullness of the demands of the culture. . .Furthermore, migration makes the challenge of reading, into the present of a specific cultural performance, the traces of all those diverse disciplinary discourses and institutions of knowledge that constitute the conditions and contexts of culture' (Bhabha 1990:313). The contemporary world of the new settler has embedded in it the residues of all those worlds from which all migrants have come.

Our analysis focuses on these issues of power—as they appear in the texts themselves, as they position audiences, in the use of language and imagery, in the structure of arguments and narratives. We also examine them as they appear in the political economy of the media in Australia, through government regulation and controls, ownership, internationalisation and globalisation, the rights of minorities to challenge structures of communication; and in the organisational environments in which meaning is produced and disseminated. We will show that the continuous articulation of difference is one of the media's main exercises. As this process continues it has the effect of assuming and reinforcing boundaries, of justifying views of the world and understanding it in terms of race, and thereby, almost because it is so unselfconscious, in accelerating the slide from differentiation to discrimination. This process of cultural development is hedged by what JanMohamed and Lloyd have referred to as 'the pathos of hegemony [which] is frequently matched by its interested celebration of differences, but of differences in the aestheticized form of recreations' (JanMohamed and Lloyd 1987:8).

Those of us determined to combat racism and the deepening social hostilities it disguises and exposes have to deal with the media system as a whole. Cashmore has argued that racism is neither an inborn psychological constant nor simply a problem for minority groups (1987:258). Nor, as Kushnick has shown, is racism merely a matter of individual prejudice; it is more a structural feature of societies where power and social opportunity are distributed unequally to socially differentiated populations (Kushnick 1981). In developing our understanding of race, ethnicity, racism and the media, that broader social context and its forces mark out the arena with which we are concerned.

Yet while we must acknowledge that race is socially constructed and racism is also a social process interpenetrating other relations of power—class, gender, age, sexuality, disability—we also realise that ethnic identification and racial communalism are resurgent, that inequality is becoming more commonly perceived in terms of race and ethnicity, while economic pressures are interpreted as ethnic, racial or national ones. Anthony Smith suggested over ten years ago, before the urban riots in London's Brixton, while Eastern Europe and Northern Asia had only just begun to rumble once more against the Soviet Empire, midway between the Watts of 1965 and the Los Angeles of 1992, that this 'ethnic renaissance has the power to heal the rift in the alienated consciousness of marginalised men and women. . .[ministering] to the special identity needs of those groups which had become estranged from their communities' (Smith 1981: xiii).

Sixty years ago, when racism did not carry the social opprobrium that it does today, two Queensland sociobiologists of that earlier era opened a paean to 'race safety' with the following comments:

> Race safety. . .must be grounded on the experience of history and the immutable laws of evolution. Evolution pursues its relentless course amid the disorganised forces of opposition, impervious to humanitarian experiments, blind to our sufferings and contemptuous of our divided efforts to resist. The weak will be supplanted by the strong. . .(Bostock and Nye 1934: 1)

THE NEW RACISM, COMMUNAL IDENTITIES AND THE NATION

The mass media have now become the main avenue for testing out the new racism with its sociobiological roots, a racism that encompasses both the 'fear and desire' of which Annette Hamilton wrote in her discussion of Australia's filmic representations of Aborigines and perceptions of Asia (Hamilton 1990). Such fear is exemplified by the desire for Asia as an economic solution to Australia's economic crisis in terms of trade, finance and growth, and by fear of Japanese investors, Indo-Chinese boat people, and Chinese refugees.

The constitution of an 'Australian people', an Australian nation in some way defined against the Others, offers what Etienne Balibar has referred to as a 'fictive ethnicity', a community instituted by the nation-state, claiming or inventing for itself an identity of origins, culture and interests 'which transcends individuals and social conditions' (Balibar 1991:96). Here we have 'the symbolic kernel of the idea of race. . .[as] the schema of genealogy, that is, quite simply the idea that the filiation of individuals transmits from generation to generation a substance both biological and spiritual' (Balibar 1991:100). So the media encompass too the transmission of this fictive genealogy, reiterating the constitution of the national community, reinforcing in their silences and in their positioning of 'the Other' the practices necessary to remain part of the 'family of the nation'. The position of women accorded by this fictive genealogy plays a central part in the family that is presented, for the image of the good mother whose role is to nurture her husband and children, and care for those in need, is a dominant theme in media presentations of the nation (see Chapter 2 in the discussion of advertising and women's magazines).

The media have also become the pathway for the development of a consciousness of community and identity among fragmented minorities, so much so that 'the physical survival of minority groups depends on the recognition of its culture as viable' (JanMohamed and Lloyd 1987:9). The media offer sites of particular tensions, dominant discourses, minority resistances, and articulations of minority communalisms. The broad political and economic structures within which the media operate are subject to many of the same pressures and struggles, so that the interests in control often find themselves caught between the pursuit of wealth (by activating audiences and purchasing media) and their own class/race position which might be better served by the suppression of diversity.

The debate over the media as sites for conflict and struggle between majorities and minorities has significantly polarised between demands for equality and demands for differentiation. In the most simplistic terms the tension lies between those who seek to integrate minorities with the 'mainstream', and those who seek to isolate the minority experience so that it can be explored and exposed.

Stuart Hall talks of identity as being 'formed at the unstable point where the "unspeakable" stories of subjectivity meet the narratives of history, of a culture' (Hall 1987:44). He characterises the current era as a time of marginalised, fragmented, unenfranchised, disadvantaged and dispersed identities—particularly so for migrants. More especially, he suggests that the rapidity of change and the globalisation of human interaction are giving us all an increasing sense of 'migranthood', a sense of moving from a certain, predictable world into one of unpredictability and change—what some have referred to as the 'post-modern' condition. Hall notes the immense unease such a recognition of oneself as immigrant brings, and how it prompts you to make a sense of your identity wherever you are. This meant becoming 'black' for Hall, a process of self-constitution in Britain which allowed for history—his Jamaican childhood and desire for escape (from mother and family)—and politics, the experience of racism in Britain and the emergence of the Black British. For Hall this process of 'imagining' communities in which one belongs has to work symbolically, until identity emerges from difference and from understanding both one's own history and the history of those with whom one interacts. Identities are constituted in a most complex way, and are constantly in development.

The imagining of self and community is subjective and private as well as communal and public. To understand both these aspects means that the media and its 'effects' cannot be treated simply, nor dogmatically, nor universally. Yet it is clear that one of the central processes concerns the constitution of community on the one hand (defining of 'us' at the centre of the moving sea) and the naming of difference on the other, who sits outside bobbing along, to be allowed to 'land' when suitably exhausted and penitent. Individual subjectivity is involved in this defining through participation as audience—the subjective and communal effects will vary but will be neither totally unpredictable nor without social consequence.

This is a jungle, as Kobena Mercer (1990) has called it, of shifting perceptions of the immediate problems. Yet some problems persist, or are resurrected, especially those of legitimacy—not only about whom is to be permitted to speak/or acknowledged as speaking on behalf of the 'Australian' people, but what the content of their speech might be. For Aborigines and non-English speaking background immigrants the difficulty in finding a way to retain and develop an at least partly voluntarily chosen identity, and the opportunity to participate more actively in the social, economic and political processes of Australian society, have been such persistent problems.

One of the major constraints they/we face is the perception by those who make key decisions in the media that the world view of minorities is less important than their own perceptions. As we will see, this systematic subversion of minority perspectives recurs in what the Australia media offer about inter-group relations. Hodge and Mishra have written of this Australian '*mentalité*' as they relate the Australian way of life to its literature as follows: 'Our particular concern is with the roles that Australian literature has played in this unceasing and doomed quest for symbolic forms of legitimacy. . .we see the culture and its literature as still determined massively by its complicity with an imperialist enterprise, coexisting in a necessary but compromised symbiosis with moments and forces of subversion from within the society' (1992: x). They conclude their study by arguing that Australian society has developed a legend that is the after-image of a nightmare—white racism carries the cost of superficiality and literality by wilfully refusing to acknowledge injustices to Aboriginal people and to other minorities (pp. 218–19). The media play a crucial role in presenting this superficial response as the popular response.

Since the first settlement of Australia by Europeans the maintenance of social order has been a primary concern of the state. Two broad and related strategies emerged under English direction—a punitive and coercive one, based on the state's monopoly on violence, and a less well articulated but at times equally savage focus on cultural tools.

For Aboriginal Australians this has meant a deadly dialogue between extermination and assimilation, both often indistinguishable in the hands of settlers and police. Learning about private property rights through police actions and formal education replaced traditional communal priorities for clan and family co-operation. The incorporation of chemical warfare—the introduction of alcohol—and the use of police powers to control its effects—has contributed to the majority society's ideology about Aborigines and has steadily destroyed Aboriginal identity (and lives). Anglo-Australian responses to Aboriginal resistance have long recognised how crucial the destruction of traditional Aboriginal identities and their replacement with a subordinated, acquiescent subjectivity has been in legitimating the invasion and its consequences.

Much of the history of Aboriginal and Torres Strait Islander survival in Australia over the past 200 years has been the story of cultural resistance—struggles to sustain a sense of specific (localised) Aboriginal identity. The struggle and its consequences have been documented—*Lousy Little Sixpence*, for instance, is a documentary film of the experience of Aboriginal people who were taken from their parents in welfare raids, to be brought up in state institutions or as state wards. The resurgence of the Land Rights movement in the 1960s and 1970s was closely connected with the establishment of Aboriginal community services—especially health and legal. Closely linked to those movements came the rapid spread of Aboriginal media. These included newspapers such as those produced by the Central and Northern Lands Councils (*Land Rights News*), local community radio stations (e.g. 8KIN, run by the Central Australian Aboriginal Media Association in Alice Springs), local video and television projects (such as those at Ernabella and Yuendemu), and now a regional television station in Central Australia (Imparja) (Dowmunt 1992).

The assertion of Aboriginal identities in contemporary Australia is greatly strengthened by Aboriginal and Torres Strait Islander control of their own media, and the inclusion of Aboriginal programming in various other community outlets. Both the national broadcasters—the Australian Broadcasting Corporation (ABC) and the Special Broadcasting Service (SBS)—have developed specific programming for Aboriginal productions. The ABC has established an Aboriginal and Torres Strait Islander Production Unit in television, and SBS commissions Aboriginal current affairs programs and has a code of conduct for media workers who want to make programs with or about Aboriginal and Torres Strait Islander people.

During the Bicentennial year of 1988, commemorating 200 years of European settlement, the media greatly increased its coverage of Aboriginal issues. One key struggle by Aborigines, to force a full investigation of the deaths of hundreds of Aborigines in prison while under police detention, resulted in a Royal Commission. The Inquiry, reporting in late 1991, drew particular attention to the media and its crucial role. The Commission report recommended that Aboriginal media should receive strong government support 'in recognition of the importance of their function', and that the wider media organisations which reported on Aborigines should have codes of practice, training and employment programs, and much better contact with Aboriginal communities (Aboriginal Deaths in Custody 1991). For Aborigines, identity, community and survival are indeed closely linked to the way the media operates. There are similar dynamics affecting immigrants, and in recent years in particular, Asian immigrants.

For two centuries Aboriginal Australians have had to resist or adjust to the settler society. Their problematic status has moved through extermination, assimilation, separate development for some, integration, cultural pluralism, and ethnic nationalism—all these as descriptions or outcomes of government policy. Non-Anglo immigrants, recruited as workers in the development of Australian capitalism, have also experienced changing values and labels. At the heart of the values issue lies an unresolved engagement with 'difference'. The first 150 years of European settlement was well marked by ethnic clashes and tensions, initially between Europeans and the indigenous people, but soon between the English and the Irish, followed by tensions between Europeans more generally and the Chinese, and then Italians: but not until 1946 did the emergent, fairly insular Anglo-Australian society face a sustained challenge to the values adopted and adapted from Britain. The commitment of the post-war Labor government to a massive immigration program, which drew millions of workers from across the (at first white, European) world, carried with it an implicit and explicit set of values about the sort of society the government and the people wanted. Linking a specific policy of exclusion (White Australia) with an equally specific one of inclusion (assimilationism), government spoke of New Australians being formed under the Southern sky.

The press expressed concern about the threat these immigrants represented to Australian workers—some of the earliest challenges were attributed to Jewish refugees, some of whom had managed to arrive in the late 1930s despite the attempts of the Australian government of that time to avoid accepting them. By 1947 when the displaced persons scheme was in place and the first cohorts from the camps of Europe were to arrive, the government through its joint Ministry of Information and Immigration (a significant combination presided over by Minister Arthur Calwell) sought to ensure that the first press stories would be positive. The first boatload of refugees on the ship *SS General Heitzelman* were selected on the basis of their physical qualities—to appear as much as possible like the ideal image Australians had of themselves—tall, lithe, blond(e) (not unlike the Nazi image of the ideal Herrenvolk), the men handsome and the women beautiful.

The emphasis after that time was on assimilation. The Australian media reproduced the assumptions of a homogeneous society, with only the rising immigrant media enabling the newcomers to move from 'immigrant' to something else—an identity hung between refugee, exile, and emigre, as worker or peasant, as paterfamilias and untermenschen, as mother and wife, as cleaner and process worker. There were many significant openings in the past half-century in which values and attitudes could take hold and crystallise as prejudice and myth: Italian workers protesting against life in the camps in the 1950s and 1960s, gangland murders and standover rackets, illegal body hire rackets, mad Croatian bombers, crazy Yugoslavs, conspiratorial Greeks, fat/ugly/hairy women wrapped in black, eternal earth mothers—a host of simplistic images in which media headlines fed the whirling river of half-formed stereotypes and loosely connected impressions that people drew on to make sense of the rapidly changing social scene.

Immigrant identities have to assimilate pasts, presents and futures that are inevitably disjointed. Alternatives are constantly standing by, unbidden reminders of different pathways, different 'homes'. And in the wider pathways of society these lives have no purchase, no recognition. The boundary of difference, of being named Other, is there in the silences and the absences, as much as in the crueller and cruder statements and narratives.

10

RACE, CULTURAL PLURALISM AND THE MEDIA IN AUSTRALIA: ABORIGINES AND TORRES STRAIT ISLANDERS

Aborigines and immigrants from non-English-speaking backgrounds have been objects of consideration by the mass media in Australia since the establishment of the first press in the 1790s. During the past 200 years the media have produced millions of words, and in recent years images, through which Australians have sought to relate to each other and to the forces of change.

One of the underlying and unresolved (unresolvable?) problems for Australia as a colonial settler society has been the justification of the conquest, the appropriation of Aboriginal lands, brought to sharp focus by the High Court decision in 1992 (the Mabo case) that there was after all a legitimate native title to land. The practices of internal colonialism have involved on the one hand the appropriation and on the other the attempted extirpation of Aboriginal cultures and languages: at times government policy and social practice have been characterised as much by indecision and ambivalence as by any clear sense of purpose.

The media have a long history as the conduit for ideologies which justify the white invasion and the subsequent decimation of the Black nations. In recent years the media or parts of it have become more self-conscious about their representation of Aboriginal and Torres Strait Islander issues, adopting a generally more liberal perspective—that is, an abandonment of the historic perspective of 'primitivism'. In its place we have seen the resurrection of other traditions, of the Aboriginal as victim, as romantic savage, as the authentic expression of a real Australia.

An early version of the argument for the assimilation of Aborigines and their abandonment of their traditional culture appears in the *Sydney Gazette* during the first twenty years of the 19th century. The journal celebrated the life of a young Aborigine, cared for by whites after the death of his parents in the War of Resistance. 'His origin he remembered with abhorrence. . .a rooted and unconquerable aversion to all of his own colour. . .with his early alienation from his sooty kindred he seemed to have undergone a total change of disposition. . .docile, grateful, and even affable' (Yarwood and Knowling 1982:59–60). On the other hand, Bennelong, the first Aborigine to be sent to England, died in 1813, having succumbed to alcoholism and communal ostracism. The *Gazette* noted censoriously of his passing that 'little favourable can be said. . .His propensity to drunkenness was inordinate; and when in that state he was insolent, menacing and overbearing. In fact, he was a thorough savage, not to be warped from the form and character that nature gave him by all the efforts that mankind could use'. (loc. cit.) The sense of Aborigines as menace and threat to Europeans persists today in presentations of Aborigines in relation to crime, inter-communal and intra-communal violence, and health (for instance, in relation to AIDS or hepatitis).

These themes, of 'mankind' seeking to refashion the primitive to civilisation, to celebrate the Aborigine who becomes docile and subordinate to the white, persist in media accounts. Meadows has reported what he refers to as 'institutional racism' in two stories published in the late 1980s: *People* magazine's account of a Cairns police sergeant speaking of Aborigines as 'dingoes' and 'black bastards' to be excluded from white society; and the Brisbane *Sunday Mail*'s series of stories on alleged cannibalism amongst Queensland Aborigines in the late 19th century. Meadows, a journalism lecturer at Queensland University, pursued both these stories with the Press Council. In each case he was unsuccessful. In the former case, the Council accepted that the article would have caused great offence to Aborigines but it was in the public interest to have it known that the police officer in question held such views. In the latter case the Council accepted the defence of satire offered by the editor of the paper, despite the lack of evidence to substantiate any of the claims about Aborigines in the piece (Meadows 1990:89ff).

There are numerous other examples of this oppressive relationship between Aborigines and the press. The Report of the National Inquiry into Racist Violence in Australia (1991) argued that the media play 'a significant role both in communicating and soliciting the ideas, fears and resentments of racism and in informing and educating Australians about each other. . .Many people complained to the Inquiry about what they believed was racism in media reporting. . .[t]his was particularly true of Aboriginal people, who complained of long-standing racism and insensitivity on the part of the media' (Human Rights and Equal Opportunity Commission 1991:355).

In a detailed account of media reporting of Aborigines, in the press and on radio and television, the Inquiry documented evidence from Aboriginal communities in Redfern regarding a *Sixty Minutes* report, 'The County', which reinforced the most popular prejudices about Aborigines. This was achieved 'structurally', not by attacking Aborigines directly, but by placing the TV journalist and thus the audience with the police (with the journalist Mike Munro, congratulating and endorsing the police), and by accepting the police view of events as the only interpretation. The Inquiry also noted the unsatisfactory outcome of community complaints to the Australian Broadcasting Tribunal (Human Rights and Equal Opportunity Commission 1991:116), where the Tribunal found that while the program might have been offensive to Aborigines, it did not breach standards—the Aborigines were recommended to complain to the Australian Journalists' Association. The Inquiry also argued that the media in areas with high Aboriginal populations were particularly problematic—the Perth *Daily News*, the *Sunday Territorian* (Darwin), the *Dubbo Daily Liberal*, and Radio 2WEB in Bourke, New South Wales, were specifically mentioned (pp. 117–18).

Alternative views to these do find a place in the media—yet they occur so occasionally as to be remarkable. There have been some appearances of Aborigines in 'mainstream' entertainment programs, though usually of limited duration—*A Country Practice, Prisoner, E Street* are 'soaps' which have had quite positive and creative images of Aborigines. While 1988, the Bicentennial year of the British settlement in Sydney, allowed for a more extensive examination of Aboriginal concerns, with feature stories and documentaries celebrating Aboriginal activities and creativity, since that time the reports and stories appear to have reverted to the stereotypical and limited accounts—concerned with issues of conflict and locating Aborigines as objects, 'outside' society. In particular, whites' paranoia about Aborigines (described by Hodge and Mishra 1992) came to the fore after the Australian High Court found in the 1992 Mabo case that the doctrine of *terra nullius* was void and that native title to land could be proven. In the same year Boney, a fictional part-Aboriginal detective with primitive and supernatural skills in sensing the spirits of the country, reappeared on Australian television. In his first incarnation he was played by a 'blacked up' New Zealand actor; this time he was an unmade-up Anglo-Australian former soap star. Aboriginal protests went unheard as the character he was to play was 'only one-sixteenth Aboriginal'.

Several themes recur in the range of representations of Aborigines by white media, and on which Aboriginal and Torres Strait Islander audiences have found ways to comment (e.g. in Bostock 1993, and Edmunds and James 1991):

1   an emphasis on tribalism, negative primitivism, entrapment in a backward culture;
2   a concern with the threat posed by Aborigines, through crime, violence, and outbreaks into white society;
3   Aborigines as failures—unable to cope with the contemporary world, as undisciplined and incapable;
4   the victims of whites—the treatment can be sympathetic or unsympathetic;
5   affirmative action, with the celebration of positive Aboriginal images;
6   cultural appropriation—Aborigines and Aboriginality used as a stand-in for Australia, with their primitivism as 'spiritual' (particularly in advertising);
7   the first environmentalists, the spiritual link to the land.

Aboriginality provides the sharpest sense of 'race' and social difference. Aborigines and Torres Strait Islanders hold a specific place in Australian cultural relations, as the prior owners of the space occupied by everyone else, whatever their ethnicity, who came after them. Indeed, one of the elements in the immigration debates of recent years has been the response by some Aboriginal groups and spokespeople to the anxiety expressed over immigration, specifically from Asia, that has permeated media discussions of what has come to be known as 'multicultural' Australia.

RACE, CULTURAL PLURALISM AND THE MEDIA IN AUSTRALIA: IMMIGRANTS

The media response to immigration and the settlement of non-English-speaking immigrants has been rather more diverse than the limited number of plays that have characterised their involvement with Aborigines—immigration has been a staple topic of social and press debate, linked closely to concerns over security and the economy.

Interpretations of the media role in debates about immigration and the relations between cultural groups expose the sorts of controversial theoretical questions with which we wish to engage in this book. The example of news, current affairs and features—'reality' and the media so to speak—offers strongly divergent perspectives from analysts of the Australian media of what effects the media have on society. Rod Tiffen summarises this polarisation as tension between two views. One is a simple 'hypodermic' view, with passive, malleable media audiences having their views modified directly by an injection; the other view has the audience strong and independent, selecting its input at best, at worst simply allowing their experience of the media to wash over them as their attention is really elsewhere (Tiffen 1989:2). A final dimension to this apparently insoluble dilemma has the media as the victims of manipulation, merely 'reflecting' reality in some way and at the mercy of more powerful social forces in which they are enmeshed.

Some consequences of these perceptions emerge in discussions of the immigration debate in Australia. One argument developed initially by Tanya and Robert Birrell (Birrell and Birrell 1987) proposed that the 'agenda' on immigration in Australia was captured by a population and economic growth lobby, for whom immigration was a crucial component in national development. This interest group forged alliances with the bureaucracy of government—in particular the Commonwealth Department of Immigration—and ethnic community leaders, with the aim of sustaining immigration despite demographic and economic evidence which, researchers claimed, did not warrant such a high level. The media, in this perspective, become a crucial weapon in advancing this view, offering through leader pages, editorials and feature stories, a stand-in for the more amorphous notion of public opinion.

Following on from the Birrells, Katharine Betts has suggested that the ideology of immigration has become a metaphor for the broad package of values legitimated by intellectuals, who effectively control the media. Multiculturalism, as a set of values, has been so closely linked to support for immigration that the media identify hesitation on the former as rejection of the latter. Thus Betts argues that the media have become overcome by an uncritical support for cultural pluralism, immigration and legitimation of the values and interests of ethnic community leaders. The values of anti-discrimination have been used to sweep up acceptance of immigration (Betts 1988). Here we see the media treated as though it is a homogenous collectivity, amenable to domination by particular interests or a coalition of interests.

On the other hand, the media are presented as a somewhat anti-immigration element in the analysis developed by the Human Rights Commission. In its review of racist violence on the basis of ethnic identity, the Commission made specific mention of the immigration debate as an important element in stimulating violence against immigrants (Human Rights and Equal Opportunity Commission 1991:172–5). 'There has been a tendency on the part of many media outlets to focus on conflict and extreme views in relation to these issues. The viewpoints of the communities themselves are too often ignored' (HREOC 1991:372).

Can we usefully talk of the media being either captured by social groups, or systematically biased in some way? One way into the problem of this question in relation to news lies in understanding the processes of 'newsmaking', in which industrial and ideological factors both play a role; here complexity rather than simplicity typifies the working environment, and multiple audiences relate to and use the media in their own patterns of social interaction (Tiffen 1989).

Indeed, the media coverage of ethnicity and race issues reveals many facets and value sets. Such evidence as we have about the Australian media suggests a pattern in which generic forms—genres specific to particular forms of media production—play an important role in structuring the content and format of what is communicated. For instance, newsmaking depends for its survival on two elements—the deadline and the newshole—the limitations of time and space. In addition, news production reflects prevailing news values, themselves affected by journalists' and editors' perceptions of audience expectations, desires and responses (Tiffen 1989).

Little research has been published about how newsmaking on immigration, ethnicity and race actually occurs in Australia (see Cunningham and Turner 1993, but also Meadows 1992 on Aboriginal issues), though some overseas studies throw light on the issues. The recent work by Teun van Dijk, a Dutch scholar who has carried out research in Europe and the United States, elucidates particularly well the dimensions of the problems in relation to newspapers. Van Dijk takes the position of a discourse analyst, concerned with language and its interaction with values and beliefs. He notes that the press (he is concerned primarily with print media) plays a significant role in the way people think about the world. He argues that 'the ideological and structural dimensions of racism presupposes complex processes of reproduction. . .discourse, language use and communication play a prominent part in this reproduction of the ethnic consensus of white groups. . .particularly. . .for all forms of elite discourse, including that of the mass media in general and that of the daily press, in particular' (Van Dijk 1989: i).

Another study of the Dutch press also found that ethnic references can cause collective damage and that the frequency of headlines with ethnic references is overestimated. It has been suggested that the newspaper reader tends to interpret the stories in a way that serves to either increase the reader's racism or leave it unchanged, and that ethnic identification does nothing to counterstereotype minority groups. It has also been argued that journalists' reservation about making ethnic references in crime news is necessary, and that they have a responsibility to weigh the importance of fully reporting crime against the possible damage to individuals and groups (Winkel 1990).

The interpenetration of the media with everyday talk and the shared social cognitions of group members led Van Dijk to conclude that 'the various elites have both special interests and play a central role in the reproduction of their own power and that of their own group. . .the pervasive racism [that research has shown exists in all media]. . .is part and parcel of the symbolic power exercised by the white elite' (Van Dijk 1988: 223). He summarises the main findings on research about the news media and the representation of minority groups drawn from studies in Britain, Europe and the USA as follows:

- Minority employment and control in the media seriously underrepresents even their minority status in society, in parts so low as to be negligible.
- Reports of minorities in the press are minimal in size and frequency, and almost always negative, linking them with crime, violence, riots, and problems.
- Reports are stereotypical and tend to blame the victims.
- 'Positive' contributions are ignored, censored or underplayed.
- Whites are presented as kindly and supportive, or as facing difficult problems created by the minorities.
- Discrimination against minorities is reported as deviant and occasional, while elite or structural racism is barely reported (Van Dijk 1988: 224–6).

Van Dijk's methodology is also valuable, and we have drawn on it for some of our empirical work, extending his scope (news accounts and newspapers) to the media and a greater range of material for analysis. Van Dijk focuses on the structure of text and its relationship with context. His approach 'specifically aims to show how the cognitive, social, historical, cultural or political contexts of language use and communication impinge on the contents, meanings, structures or strategies of text or dialogue, and vice versa;

how discourse itself is an integral part of and contributes to the structures of these contexts (Van Dijk 1991a: 38). There is an interaction between the structure of the language used to express ideas and the political and social processes involved—language cannot be apolitical, and language used in media practices is especially open to political involvement with wider ideology.

Structural analysis offers an account of both the surface and underlying levels of meanings. Syntactical and stylistic conventions carry the underlying meanings and fashion them in particular ways for specific ends. Each genre has its own schematic structure, though how these structures are used reveals the social role of the producer, audience expectations and a sense of the context. It is assumed that speakers/producers try to 'optimally realise their communicative or social goals, and go through different functional moves to realize those goals' (Van Dijk 1991a: 40). The contextual analysis requires an understanding of the political and social relationships, as part of an exploration of how specific readers/consumers may interpret, decode, and remember the communication.

The major Australian study of ethnic groups and the media (White and White 1983) focused on media reports of a few cases in one city—Melbourne. Their findings suggested that media reports deliberately incorporate stereotypes of groups, especially Italians. They also suggested that the media (these studies focused on the print media) tended to report the perspectives of the powerful: Anglo-Australian, bureaucratically dominant, with long-established relations with the press and a capacity to withdraw co-operation if the press got too far out of line. Typically Italians came to take on the profile of Mafia standover merchants and thugs; there was no opening provided for other Italian spokespeople to place the criminal groups in the context of a much larger social grouping who were appalled by the violence and extortion at the Melbourne markets.

The issue of how the media responds to the 'reality' of Australia as a multicultural society is closely linked to the broader question of multicultural policy and government involvement in fashioning social responses. The government (the state) has a long history of engagement with the media and attempts to direct their activities.

12

THE STATE AND THE MEDIA IN A CULTURALLY PLURALIST AUSTRALIA

The history of government involvement in race and media issues in Australia reveals a spasmodic process, galvanised at times by social movements demanding action. Not surprisingly, the policy advances in relation to media and cultural difference, and racism, have been generated primarily by activities in the broader realms of race and ethnic relations.

It is possible therefore to see the period of the Labor government in the early to mid 1970s as a national policy turning-point: from a commitment to assimilationsim—and thereby a denial of the legitimacy of difference—to 'integration' and then ultimately to multiculturalism in its diverse and transmuting forms (Jakubowicz 1987, 1989). Under the assimilationist perspectives which had marked the first quarter-century of post-war immigration, and the best part of a half-century of policy in relation to Aborigines, the discourses legitimated by the state and carried in the media sought to expunge difference for the sake of 'the new Australian' and to save a dying race.

Thus while Australian radio carried the occasional program in the 1960s in Italian (Al Grassby, the Labor Immigration Minister of the 1972–4 period, broadcast in Italian in the Riverina area of New South Wales in the 1960s), there were no widespread ethnic language programs, there were legislative controls on broadcasting in languages other than English, and the national broadcaster's *Teaching English* constituted its main response to the immigrant presence. The Aboriginal presence, seldom recognised in any specific programming, emerged most often as appropriated and iconic representations of the 'old Australia', with the struggles of the Aboriginal people rendered invisible.

The election of the Labor Party to national government in 1972 carried with it a series of consequences—the first serious moves to recognise Aboriginal Land Rights, the commitment of resources to support Aboriginal community organisations, and Aboriginal survival placed firmly on the national agenda.

Concerns of immigrants also became identified more specifically, with Grassby establishing a series of migrant task forces to advise him on the areas requiring most urgent action (Jakubowicz et al. 1984). The government moved to shorten the waiting period for citizenship, and with the development of Medibank, a health insurance program, sought strategies for communicating more effectively with the newly enfranchised, predominantly non-English-speaking working class. By late 1974, with Grassby losing his Federal Parliamentary seat in a racist campaign against him, the government appointed Grassby as Commissioner for Community Relations. He was charged with establishing the first ethnic radio programs funded by the Commonwealth through the Department of Attorney-General. These programs, run initially by volunteers in five languages in Sydney and Melbourne, were broadcast under a licence to Grassby as Commissioner. Although they were an immediate success, attracting significant audiences, they did not save Labor from defeat in the coup and election of 1975.

The return of the Liberal Country Party coalition to Federal power reinforced the importance of ethnic communities and the role of the ethnic media, including radio stations. The new Prime Minister, Malcolm Fraser, worked through one of his advisers, Petro Georgiou, to establish a review of ethnic radio and of general services to immigrants. Under the chairmanship of Melbourne lawyer Frank Galbally (defence lawyer in the Melbourne Markets murders of the early 1960s which led to widespread media publicity of Mafia and Mano Nero control in the Italian community; see White and White 1983), the Committee of Review recommended the establishment of the Special Broadcasting Service to maintain and extend ethnic radio, and signalled the need for a multicultural television service.

After apparently futile negotiations with the Australian Broadcasting Commission over the cost of and responsibility for the service, the Fraser government committed itself to an independent TV service, which it later decided to integrate with SBS, creating an 'ethnic' radio service and a television service that was to be 'multicultural'. The rationale for government involvement was twofold—radio programs were to provide information on settlement issues for immigrants, and allow for cultural maintenance. The television programs were designed to open to the whole Australian 'community' the culture of all nations that had contributed to the Australian population, and furthermore, to give monolingual Anglophones information and perspectives about the world which were denied to them in the mainstream media.

At the same time the ABC charter was being reviewed, in prospect for its translation into a 'corporation'—one key element of its charter was the requirement that it take into account the multicultural nature of Australian society. When Labor returned to government in 1983 its reform agenda was far more subdued than the one that had existed a decade before. The goals were now rather more influenced by concerns for deregulation, reduced government intervention, and equality in the marketplace. From the outset Labor flagged a reduced commitment to national broadcasting, and a concern to moderate government interference in the activities of the media marketplace. The revamped Australian Broadcasting Tribunal developed its standards on racism and cultural pluralism only marginally, focusing on the prohibition of racial vilification and allowing the marketplace to determine cultural content—except for the Australian content rules, which did not place any particular emphasis on either Aboriginal or ethnic issues or concerns.

The Federal government's strategy in 1983 in relation to the national broadcasters was circumspect but clear, if only in retrospect. The ABC, now a corporation, was to have a Board representative of Australian society, but without any members with an 'ethnic' or multicultural constituency. The Aboriginal people were to be represented by an Aboriginal former Liberal senator. The new Board of SBS was to have only 'ethnics', no Aborigines, with the sole Anglo-Australian member representing the broadcasting industry's interests.

The structural tension between the two national broadcasters—the ABC a major production house in its own right, SBS a meagrely funded body contracting out most of its limited local production in television—that was established in the early 1980s continued into the 1990s in a worsening economic climate. By 1993 SBS was selling advertising on TV, after several years of sponsorship, and was moving closer to a cut-down version of the UK's Channel 4 in programming philosophy and audience profile. The ABC had been offered a charter which initially dropped any reference to Australia as a multicultural society, but by 1993 had reasserted its commitment to the policy issues. This reassertion could be found in areas of radio and television, particularly current affairs, in the establishment of a multicultural unit (and its suspension late in 1992), the role of which was to prompt the rest of the organisation to think multiculturally, the engagement of ethnic trainees (funded by the Office of Multicultural Affairs), and a series of training courses for producers and managers. The on-air programming had changed very little, despite a series of meetings that began in 1989 between senior administrators and members of ethnic communities.

Although we will look more closely at recent issues in both SBS and the ABC concerning multiculturalism and the media later on in the book, it is important to note here that the national broadcasters have tried to deal with rather than avoid these issues. The commercial broadcasting sector, and the press, have mostly maintained a range of behaviour that reflects hierarchies of power in Australian society—priority representation given to male, middle-class and powerful actors, in nearly all genres except those targeted at women. Their gender perspectives may be altered marginally but race and ethnicity remain problematic.

13

THE DIRECTION OF THE BOOK

When we draw together these threads we are presented with a perspective on the media in Australia which contains the following elements:

1   The media operate under two imperatives—an economic imperative, which seeks to secure significant audiences to sell them to advertisers (at least for all but one of the television networks); and a cultural imperative, in which the media offer sites for ritual confirmations of the legitimacy of the social order.

2   Media audiences are neither as 'free' nor as 'programmed' as protagonists of the 'merely reflect society' or the 'hypodermic propaganda' analyses of media effects suggest. The relationship between the media and its audiences is symbiotic: the audiences seek security in media rituals, the media seek audiences that they can secure, a symbiosis in which social values are offered confirmation and reinforcement.

3   In societies in which racial differentiation and ethnic hierarchies are significant components of social conflict and inequality, normal media practices will reinforce the existing relations of power between and within groups; it is possible to challenge these practices and induce changes that will reduce the megaliths of cultural uniformity; these challenges will themselves meet resistance, and if the challenge is diminished then former inequalities will increase.

Four broad 'problems' in social relations have been implicated in media representations of ethnic minorities and Aborigines. We refer to them here as 'national identity' (the framing of the content and the definitions of who's in and who's out); dimensions of difference (what strategies are discernible in the media's differentiation between groups, the delineation of group boundaries, and the characterisation of groups in relation to each other); the exotic (a specific category of differences, emphasising cultural practices from the erotic to the bizarre and supernatural); and 'media practices' (an account of how the media works, with emphasis on the experience of media workers from minority and Aboriginal backgrounds).

This book works through these problematic relationships in a series of analyses and essays, in which some of the material we have collected is presented in thematic assessments, in others as a careful reading of the texts collected during the intensive period of research on the Sydney media (1989–92), and in others through the interviews with media workers from Aboriginal or ethnic backgrounds. The first of these explorations deals with Australian national identity and media roles.

PART II

REPRESENTING AUSTRALIA: NATION AND NATIONAL IDENTITY

14

DREAMING UP THE NATION

The absence of Aborigines and Torres Strait Islanders and ethnic minorities from the centre of discourses about the nation suggest that our first task concerning national identity and representation should be to examine what is said about the nation. Homi Bhabha (1991) has described this problem as one of 'narrating the nation', whereby the idealised community is constituted through waves of stories to help place the audience/reader within that imagined history. To explore how minorities are represented we must therefore first ask how does the 'dominant race' (Editorial, *The Australian*, 28 August 1989) tell its own stories?

This approach enables us to avoid preoccupation with the racialised subject and to focus on the generalised idea of Australia which at first sight does not have any bearing on race. Australia makes periodic self-conscious attempts to assert a national cultural identity that makes of 'Australia' something more than a geographic mass or a legal–political unit. Historically defining 'national identities' for Australia, finding a cultural identity, spelling out a *symbolic space*, a *sacred* and *redemptive* space, that defines the nation, has been the task of historians, the literary and artistic world, and most important, the mass media (Willis 1993).

This concern for establishing a cultural identity distinct from, say, Great Britain, or like one-time imperial powers, has re-emerged as a concern of government, and the 'cultural' producers have again been mobilised to the cause. The concern of the Prime Minister Paul Keating to define Australia as a nation independent from Britain during the 1993 Federal Election and in the lead-up to the centenary of Federation is an example of this movement.

A concern with national identity has always dogged multicultural policies and immigration policies in Australia. The demise of the White Australia Policy notwithstanding, and partly in response to right-wing racist agitation, the concern with national identity has been explicitly privileged in multicultural policies in Australia since 1982. Consequently our research led us to look at how an abstract entity 'Australia' was put to work in media products and events. Unsurprisingly then, the concern with defining 'Australia', and asserting a distinctive 'Australian' cultural identity was very marked in the years we recorded and collected data (the five years following the Bicentenary celebrations). A preoccupation with 'Australianness' was unmistakably a reassertion of an Anglo (and occasionally an Anglo-Celtic) Australianness, and was carried in a range of locally produced media and genres; for example, ads, feature items, series, soaps, stories, news items, romances, historical events, style and fashion, decor and so on. The only exception to the relentless Anglo-ness of imagery and narratives about 'Australia' lay in the deployment of symbols of Aboriginality—but more of this later.

For most media consumers the single most powerful form of information comes to them through advertising. Advertising relies on the myths and symbols that can draw from the consumer the appropriate response—purchase of the commodity advertised. In the waves of nation-imaging in the past decade, media techniques have entailed the articulation and reiteration of sentimental concepts of cultural homogeneity—or rather, the symbols, icons and sentiments associated with mythological formations. These focus on an abstract communality via techniques such as:

- The use of historical sketches, particularly for the early 1950s, the period defined in popular mythology as existing before feminism, multiculturalism and Land Rights struggles (for example, television advertisements for pork).
- The use of images of the landscape, particularly the beaches and empty bush peopled only by an Anglo presence.
- The extensive use of family imagery, or images of domesticity.
- The use of personality and heroic imagery (laconic, pragmatic, Aussie battlers, diggers, bushmen, sports persons etc.).
- The evocation of nostalgia: for a history, the land, the hearth etc.

As we viewed the hours of television, and read our collection of newspapers and magazines, we realised that the most significant use of non-Anglo Australians was to mark boundaries. Non-Anglo Australians were included as contrast with the 'normal'—the audience addressed by the advertisements but also the audience that was expected to be watching the news or reading the press. These others, these 'non-normals', were included either as exotic accessories to the physical backdrop for example in food advertisements, as tourist attractions or as threats to boundaries—boat people, for example.

Aboriginal populations have an even more curious role. They were not portrayed as true-blue Aussies but as non-Aussies. They were present as artefacts, as landscape features, or as abstract Aboriginality—the redemptive, metaphysical element at the centre of the 'land'. Aboriginality, the abstract attribute of the subjects of colonisation, seems to get inserted as a mystical allusion to long-past roots: roots into the land and into whatever is sacred about Australia. We find them mysteriously appearing in night-time corroborees, stamping in body paint, faded in and out over images of Japanese four-wheel drives racing through the Kimberley hills. And here too, there is a discomfort about the physical boundary of 'Australia': Anglos appear in the margins of an indistinct and shifting physical boundary, as intruders. It is almost as though fear about the transience of white settlement has been commmodified for the four-wheel drive to relieve.

Some initial comments about national identities:

1   National identities are not fixed: even within an Anglo position they are competing and these are played out across media products.

2   Although discourses of national identity aim to hold disorder at bay (especially in times of economic crisis) they are nonetheless internally *plural*. A single discourse of national identity aims at cultural coherence by deploying a range of stories, histories, images, icons and so on, a range necessitated partly by the abstractness of the phenomenon but also by the diversity of the population involved. The discourse itself is not necessarily coherent or logical; that is not its function. Discourses of national identity function very much like myths.

3   A national imagination functions as a point of reference, not a model for behaviour or for 'the real Australia'. Hence discourses of national identity are immune to arguments from 'reality' (the reality of Australia; no-one is like this in Australia; not all Australians are blondes, etc.).

4   Discourses of national identity partake of the poetic and aesthetic, more so than the 'scientific' or the 'rational'. They have more to do with the imagination, emotions and sentiments than with the practical or the objective. While they deal with everyday aspects they sublimate the mundane (Aussie families: a beach, a ritual, a backyard cricket match, tea, Arnott's biscuits, boys/fathers playing, girls/mothers serving).

5   National identities nonetheless have an economic and social value especially in times of economic crisis. But they also have an export value: concretely, in the export of mass cultural media products (TV soaps, docos etc.), but more abstractly in selling Australia and Australian products to an overseas market (finance, goods, tourism etc.). 'Selling Australia' also blurs Australia's boundary.

Australia is also sold to Australians. In a sense Australians are tourists and purchasers of Australia and Australian products, in much the same way as the rest of the world, and the same images of Australia are used; to be a national citizen is to be a world consumer, a process in global acculturalisation that dominates the narratives of the media.

Discourses of racial differentiation may simultaneously be discourses of sexual differentiation; one may be used to reinforce the power relationships embedded in the other. In such cases we have racialised genders, and sexualised races. Any investigation of racial distinctions and inequalities must also examine how systems of sexual differentiation are implicated. Non-Anglo and Aboriginal women were therefore an extremely important focus of our research for they stand in a crossfire of racism and sexism.

Nowhere is this confusion of boundaries and struggle to define national identity more evident than in the multiple discourses about Aboriginality.

15

DEFINING/CONFINING THE ORIGINAL NATIONS: ABORIGINES AND TORRES STRAIT ISLANDERS—IN AND OUT OF THE NATION OR PUTTING PEOPLE IN THEIR PLACE?

An ambivalence in Australian constructions of national identity has in the past led ironically to the portrayal of Aborigines as symbols of a white Australia. This ambivalence recurs in contemporary Australian media practices.

Aborigines cluster in two media genres: advertising and news/current affairs programs. In soaps and serials Aborigines have made occasional, but no long-term or permanent appearances (Bostock 1993). In advertising (and consumer-oriented programming on television such as *Burke's Backyard* or *The Great Outdoors*) and news, however, Aborigines are depicted in divergent and contradictory ways.

Where Aboriginal people are represented in advertising, it is invariably in positive and sympathetic images, but they are extremely limited ones. The American-produced United Airlines ad, for example, opens with an image of David Gulpilil, posing cross-legged in traditional dress on a red inland desert rock, gazing at the horizon. An American voice-over says 'From the heart of Australia you can see to Paris'. The ad continues with images of soaring planes and some other juxtapositions of countries, although not with the same 'primitive/cultured' contrast. In its final frame it takes a mildly satirical position, showing Gulpilil on the Eiffel Tower, in European dress, with a faint, ironic smile.

Although selfconsciously playing with the established representations, this nevertheless reiterates them: the lone, Aboriginal male in the most remote, threatening region of the continent, is depicted as 'traditional' in dress and pose, and so is distant in time and culture as well as geography from most contemporary Australians. Yet this location is the one that most frequently identified as iconic, the 'heart' and 'centre' of Australia, whether adversely characterised as the 'dead heart' or positively romanticised as the 'red centre'. The Gulpilil figure symbolises here the 'heart' of Australianness, an irony in itself as David Gulpilil is a coastal Arnhemlander.

A completely non-ironic version of this identification of traditional Aboriginal men with iconic 'Australian' landscape occurs in a recent Japanese-produced Mitsubishi Pajero ad, in which images of the car speeding through the Bungle Bungles in the Kimberleys are intercut with images of a

Mitsubishi Pajero in the Bungle
Bungles: Aboriginal dancers and
Pajero dissolve into the
sunset/Aboriginal flag.

group of Aboriginal men dancing in traditional ceremonial dress, amidst dust and sunlight. A Japanese-accented male voice-over says: 'To make the world's most advanced four-wheel drive, we tested it in the most rugged country on earth'. The filtered light and the Aboriginal men's face-paint distances the viewer from the individuality of the men, and they seem more like icons, like the land itself, there to naturalise/nationalise the imported car. Such abstraction of Aboriginal people is suggested by another version of this ad, identical except that the Aboriginal men have been replaced by an eagle soaring over the Bungle Bungles, suggesting perhaps that either men or bird can provide the appropriate 'Australian' symbolic content.

Some advertisements do not include images of Aboriginal people, but use works of Aboriginal culture, usually didgeridoo music or Aboriginal art, to suggest either 'Australianness', or central desert locations, or both. For example, in the recent Northern Territory tourist agency ads to encourage internal tourism, music and commissioned Aboriginal art work were presented as *essentially* Australian, and, therefore, *owned* by *all* Australians, 'Your *own* Territory'.

A more lighthearted play on the association of Aboriginality, traditionalism and central Australian landscape is made in the Telecom ad featuring Aboriginal Tom Lewis as a Telecom technician who can predict the weather. His white companion is awestruck, and asks whether Lewis knows this from 'the spirits', prompting Lewis to laughingly declare that he heard it over his mobile phone. Here Lewis is the knowledgeable master of the most modern technology, and his companion's expectations about traditionalism are mocked.

These ads present a range of standpoints and goals, and there are differences in the ways Aborigines are portrayed as admirable. Most show Aboriginal people in the most 'traditionalist' roles, dress, poses, and activities. While often shown as 'exotic' in that they are unusual and different from the 'normal', they are nevertheless presented as 'primitive', and 'rugged', associated with beautiful but harsh landscape—that is, with the old concept of the 'hard savages' of the 18th century, as opposed to the 'soft savages' of Tahiti and Polynesia in general. The Telecom ad, however, shows an Aboriginal man in a contemporary setting, and not only in contemporary day clothes but as employed and in control of sophisticated technology.

Yet although there are such differences among these representations, they all share a common element: they place those admirable Aborigines in harsh desert surroundings in contrast with the video clips from Yothu Yindi (*Treaty*) and Warumpi (*My Island Home*) over which there was at least some Aboriginal production control. These clips make frequent references to the *contemporary* existence of the Aboriginals portrayed, even when juxtaposed with images of very traditional activity (*Treaty*), and both concentrate on Arnhem Land *coastal* scenes. The shock-effect of these coastal scenes reminds us that all the other images shown on television, even those of coastal people like David Gulpilil, are in harsh, iconic central desert.

This can be contrasted with the representations of Aborigines in the news and current affairs programs in which these advertisements are often embedded. In the news genre, Aborigines are consistently shown as sources or victims of crime, causes of general disorder, involved in protest, complaint and conflict, fighting among themselves (political 'factionalism'; 'tribal' 'payback'); 'primitive' and violent: 'payback'; victims of 'oppression' but violent, drunk and hopeless as a result (see Greenberg and Brand 1993a for a comparison with the US situation). They are usually shown in these roles in urban settings (Redfern, Mt Isa or the remote but still urban Alice Springs) or occasionally in big, rural settlements (Wilcannia, Arukun, Palm Island).

Perhaps the whole text of news and advertisements aims to convey Aborigines as admirable only in 'natural' environments (for instance, presenting Ernie Dingo in the 'au naturel' sequences of *The Great Outdoors* as if he has a special, privileged relationship with primordial spaces and places), where they are 'close to nature', whereas they are depicted as 'most trouble' in the 'unnatural' but 'real' and *close* city. There may be some parallels with the ads that depict African Americans and Carribeans as erotic and enticing, and with the treatment of 'other' cultural and racial groups in children's animations. In all of these, the identifiable and most positive images are traditionalist, not contemporary, urban images and/or these positive characters may be remote geographically. In either event, they are separated from the 'normal' (white) viewer whether by time or by physical distance. Their television appearances (increasing but still nowhere near their proportion of the population) were so rare that in our 1990 survey of television advertising, Aborigines appeared for three seconds out of the 100 000 seconds captured, and the only images were still photographs of Aboriginal children in face-paint, used to sell a Japanese camera.

The thrust, therefore, of even the more positive images is to trap Aborigines in the most remote, 'ancient', 'rugged' *place* as well as the most remote cultural *time*, and as *objects* of the white gaze. The symbolic use of landscape in advertising imagery fixes Aborigines as distant and iconic, rather than people here and now and real!

The nation is perhaps most succinctly defined through its relations with other nations, other peoples. We will use two sustained media discourses to explore the processes through which ideas of the nation are intertwined with definitions of the foreigner, especially as threat and enemy. We refer here to the media treatment of the Gulf War of late 1990 and early 1991, and a continuing element in Australian political life since 1976—the boat people of Indo-China and southern Asia.

16

BOUNDARIES OF THE NATION: THE GULF WAR

The ample evidence of the Gulf War of January–February 1991 as a media-managed event suggests that the capacity of governments to manipulate the media to achieve a general level of societal acquiescence has increased dramatically in recent years (Andersen, 1991; LaMay et al. 1991). The Gulf War is pertinent here because the role the media played in seeking to gain support for the UN intervention against Iraq used images of the Orient well entrenched in Australian society—the Orientalism that Edward Said described as an ideological interpretation of complex and historic societies, drawing on racist stereotypes dating back to the Crusades. Some Australian media outlets seemed aware of the dangers of applying indiscriminate and simplistic stereotypes to all Arabs, Moslems and people from the Middle East (see Shboul 1988).

Edward Said (1978) has written of the western engagement with the Arab and Islamic worlds as a voyage into Orientalism, the construction of a vast edifice of interpretative writing and imaginings which serves to subordinate this world to the values, interests and priorities of the European/North American/white western project of cultural and economic hegemony. Within this edifice there are practices which re-emerge, evocations of a civilisation at once cruder and more sublime, erotic and savage, passionate and uncaring, a world of vicious retribution and the subordination of women and their relegation to the private sphere of domesticity. Every dimension is comparative—their behaviour as against ours, their totalised being against our individuality. This process of orientalisation accelerated during and after the Gulf War, but the rhythms to which the media warriors of the Gulf War were to march were already clearly discernible in media practices well before the Iraqi invasion of Kuwait.

The 10 April 1990 edition of *The Bulletin* carried a story which had this as the inside cover teaser:

> Thanks to more than 250,000 Moslem immigrants from around the world, Islam is Australia's second-biggest religion. Our perception of Islam, which is more a way of life than a religion, is to a large degree coloured by events in the Middle East and such episodes as the late Ayatollah Khomeini's death sentence on author

Salman Rushdie. Some Moslems claim that the media's tendency to highlight any discord within elements of the Moslem community here doesn't make for understanding or acceptance. Bruce Stannard talks to some believers. [Illustration of mosque and minarets in an Australian suburban street]

The story on Islam is assigned to the 'Issues' section of *The Bulletin*, an area for short pieces and background and is thus defined as 'soft', compared with the 'harder' reality of news. The sequence of short pieces which make up *The Bulletin*'s response to this Islamic challenge to media bias include an introduction on Islam and Australia, opening with a comment on the first Australian Moslems, the Macassan fishermen of Arnhem Land in the 16th century. The introduction asks: 'Moslem Australia—is it getting a fair go?'. The writer concludes that indeed 'the media seem obsessed with the notion that Moslems in Australia are a dangerous tribe or regional minority. . .in a country which is supposed to pride itself on acceptance of diversity, freedom of religion and a fair go'. An interview with Sheikh Taj el-din Hilaly follows, under the headline 'Media are to blame'. Taj is mullah of the Ali bin Abi Taleb mosque in Lakemba, a Sunni congregation of many thousands. The interview is reported directly, and in it Taj is at pains to make two points— that the media pursuit of sensationalism is destructive, and that Moslems in Australia are one flower in the bouquet of the multicultural Australia. The final interviews are with Silma Buckley, an Anglo-Australian convert to Islam who runs a Moslem primary school in Sydney, and Nada Roude, a Lebanese Australian woman who has been involved in the development of a Moslem women's refuge.

The interview with Roude explores two issues—the position of women in Islam and Roude's experience growing up in Australia as a small child from Lebanon. We read of her suffering racist attacks; living in the western suburbs of Sydney is described as 'living in the middle of a racial battlefield'. Roude maintains that women in Islam are more like sacred objects than sex objects, that physical contact between men and women outside the family provides an opportunity for the devil by evoking the possibility of illicit sexuality. Yet 'beyond the veil, she is charming, intelligent, forceful, compassionate and completely committed', writes the journalist, 'far from the dour Moslem ideologue so often portrayed in the media'.

Here then we have a sensitive, intelligent story which, while gripped in places by stereotypes (for instance, a picture of women praying illustrates the Taj interview, with a subtitle 'Women worship separately: it keeps Satan at bay'), nevertheless presents a sequence of Moslem perspectives. The interrogation of Roude is done by advancing stereotypes; she is then invited to criticise these, and offer alternative and more subtle explanations of Islamic practices. For instance, she condemns domestic violence by Moslem men, pointing out that Sheikh Taj el-din Hilaly had strenuously supported the rights of Moslem women to an independent education and need for a refuge from domestic violence.

The edge of orientalist mythology is blunted slightly—we see modern active people, part of Australian society, critical of materialism (as would be many Christians) and anxious to participate in the multicultural society, concerned still with racism and the dangers of intra-communal and inter-communal conflict and violence should the media continue with their crassly racist stereotypes of Islam. The Roude story demonstrates that some media workers can resist bias and distortion.

The story on Islam in Australia ends on page 45. There follow three pages of display advertisements and then the *Newsweek* section—the first page has Saddam Hussein, 'The dark knight of Baghdad', 'Public Enemy No.1', the '800 pound gorilla of the Middle East', in a story about Iraqi attempts to purchase nuclear warhead capacitors as part of the armament strategy. The story, which reports the US government indictment against Iraqi agents, runs for 112 column cm; 2 column cm of this, near the end of the story, quotes an Iraqi spokesperson in Baghdad—the remainder of the story is made up of commentary and quotes from US officials.

It is difficult not to compare these two stories—the former, a feature piece full of sympathetic quotes from 'good Moslems', agrees that the media is problematic in its representation of Islam; the second is a hard news story with all the stereotypical representation of the Arabs as a threat to the social order of the world (or at least the USA, with the lead headline reminiscent of the 1930s and the American government painted as the Untouchables). To make these comments on the story is not to condone the Iraqi attempts to develop nuclear weapons but to demonstrate the tension between a selfconscious attempt by a magazine to avoid stereotype in one context, and its almost uncontrollable use of it in another. As Van Dijk has demonstrated, [the press use headlines as a type of raft to attract attention in a swiftly flowing river of ideas and information. The dominant currents of prejudice or stereotype are launched by headline writers to draw readers into the body of the story. The headlines may be marginal to the story but they reinforce what people have come to understand as the 'reality' of the world, and provide an apparently new instance of this reality; from here, readers can proceed to understand or interpret the story presented to them.]

The Gulf War period, particularly the months after the invasion of Kuwait by Iraq, but before the UN offensive, were marked by rising hostility to Australian Arabs and Moslems. The emotional and physical attacks were exacerbated by the reporting of the events, and the pursuit by the electronic media in particular, of potential interviewees whose loyalty to Australia could be tested on national television. Two television events of that period exemplify the poles at which media sophistication can sit in these circumstances.

Soon after the arrival of the Australian naval flotilla in the Gulf as blockade support, the Australian Navy released a public relations video showing the ships cruising, practising manoeuvres, and so on. Well into the tape the video showed sailors dressed up as 'Arabs' wearing sheets and drawing on black moustaches, to play the 'locals' in an enactment of a search and seize raid by other sailors in uniform. The 'Arabs' performed with histrionics and exaggerated caricature, and parodied the daily prayers of devout Moslems. Most media outlets showed a short clip on the evening TV news of 10 October 1990 of ships sailing around, with a comment on their role to intercept any ships that might try to break the UN blockade against Iraq. SBS, on the other hand, identified the hard news story as the parody by the sailors and the offence it might give to Australian Arabs whose loyalty was already under test by the media.

The material in question was shown by an SBS TV journalist to two representatives of the Australian Arab community, who expressed extreme concern not only at the behaviour of the sailors, but at the fact the Navy seemed unaware that circulating such a video might indeed offend (*SBS World News* 10 October 1990). A public uproar rapidly developed (*SBS World News* 11 October 1990), leading to an apology from the Naval high command to Australian Moslems, which culminated in senior Naval officers going to a meal in inner western Sydney, on 'Moslem turf' with local Moslem leaders.

Dressing up: SBS's Navy video

In this case we saw a journalist identifying the 'hard news' story within an ostensibly much 'softer' item—he saw institutional racism as a structural problem for Australian society, while the other channels saw only a colour piece on boats at sea.

In a rather different approach to that taken by the SBS news, the ABC's *7:30 Report*, an evening current affairs program, ran a story on Australian hostages in Iraq and the role of Radio Australia in sending messages to them from their families. The narrative was nationalist and concerned with the feelings of the families whose relatives were unable to leave Iraq during a time of great danger. At the end of the item there was a wipe into the 'other side', a journalist and camera crew on the streets of Lakemba, an inner western suburb of Sydney, in pursuit of Arabs. A couple of vox pops, Arabs saying in poor English they thought Saddam Hussein was a good man, and then the ethnographic encounter. The journalist finds a nameless Arab to take her into Iraqi land in search of the local Iraqi club. Here she begins to question people about their loyalties—to Australia, to Iraq, which?

The microphone and camera become weapons as she pursues people, demanding they answer, refusing to accept poor English as an excuse. She pursues a man whom she claims had said he supported Hussein—another tries to say to her that most Iraqis are loyal Australians, many of them Christians and refugees from Hussein themselves.

Local Arab and Iraqi reaction to the ABC approach was hostile. Within ten days another *7.30 Report* program had been made, condemning the media for its insensitivity and bias (including in this condemnation its own segment, but extending the complaint to commercial television). The program interviewed several Arabs (Christian and Moslem) and allowed them to express their concerns about growing racism and hostility, eliciting comments on the role of the media. Once more though, the program opened with a shot of a mosque in the evening shadows, allowing the viewers to assume all Arabs were Moslems, and all Moslems Arabs. Only in the body of the story do we find Christian Arabs talking about their feelings.

A commercial current affairs program which focused on whether Arabs/Moslems could be Australians undertook some quite hostile interrogations of Arabs and Moslems in Sydney. Channel 9's *60 Minutes* (26 August 1990) gave itself the title 'Divided Loyalties'. Here we saw interviewees pushed to 'declare' themselves; the following week viewers' responses declared that the Moslems concerned should return to their countries of origin if they were not prepared to unequivocally condemn Iraq and support the Australian government.

During that period of media excitement, when social commentators from Australian nationalist perspectives were urging Arab attestations of loyalty to Australia, several Arab Australians became aware of the importance of monitoring the media and confronting the media newsmakers. The Committee of Arab Australians began to take action, by complaining to the Anti-discrimination Board in New South Wales, and by attempting to negotiate directly with what was then the *Daily Telegraph* (to become the *Telegraph Mirror*), perhaps the worst offender in the print media through its editorials and cartoons. A meeting was organised between the Arab Australians and the *Telegraph Mirror*. One result was a rather more careful consideration of their perspectives in later stories, under direction from the editor David Banks.

At the end of the war, ABC Television broadcast a special issue of its weekly current affairs show, *Four Corners* (4 March 1991), which, as its presenter Andrew Olle put it, 'takes you to the heartland of Arab Australia'. It was entitled 'The Home Front', as though there had been a real war on in Australia between Arabs and other Australians. *Four Corners* departed from its usual format by going out to Sydney's western suburbs, where a forum discussion at the Bankstown City Hall was recorded. The program asked whether the Gulf crisis had, instead of increasing understanding, merely turned ignorance into prejudice. The media reaction to the war was one of the key issues.

The participants were predominantly Arabic Australians with two Anglo Celtic media people and a police officer from Bankstown. The Arabic Australians who spoke from the floor were mostly very fluent English speakers; some had typically Australian accents. The discussion was clearly defined in three stages: the international dimensions of the conflict; how the conflict affected the local Arabic community; and how this harassment was influenced by media reports of the conflict.

The debate about media coverage involved Fahmi Hussain from the NSW Islamic Council, Joe Wakim, Mary Reheby, David Banks, the editor of the *Telegraph Mirror*, Wafa Shafic, Frank Devine, a columnist for the *Australian* and Andrew Olle himself. It is interesting that Olle and Banks were both on the defensive. 'We in the media are perhaps a little ignorant about the issues and I have to say myself that I've learnt a heck of a lot in the last few days researching for this program, which I had no idea about', acknowledged Olle; he then asked Banks if it was fair to say that 'we haven't done our homework in many ways'.

'I think it's a lot longer than 10 years we haven't done our homework. I think that people do live in bubbles, they live in bubbles created by the societies which brought them up. I mean, frankly, most of the journalists in this country would be, I suppose, Anglo and would be Christian, you know—Anglo-Australian and Christian', replied Banks.

The Gulf War marked an important moment in the public awareness of the media role in defining the nation, its members and its enemies, and in demonstrating how the boundaries are constituted and contested. Tension persists over the boat people, the refugees who seem to be a continuing source of 'contamination' to the media's concept of the purity of the nation.

17

BOUNDARIES OF THE NATION: THE BOAT PEOPLE

One of the most important sagas of the nation's recent political life in relation to immigration has been the series of narratives and analyses concerned with the arrival of refugees by sea onto the northern coast of Australia. The history of the boat people was interrupted in the late 1970s, after an intensive period of arrival following the fall of Saigon—in that case the refugees were overwhelmingly Vietnamese. However, in 1990 a new group of people began to appear. The first were refugees from Cambodia, but by the early 1990s there were also arrivals from China in an apparently well organised illegal migration program (*Sydney Morning Herald* 6 June 1992). We take up the story where, almost fortuitously, the second of the 'new wave' boats came into Australian waters in April 1990. There are two issues here—first, how images of the boat people are used to define the boundaries of the nation; and second, how the threat to the nation is articulated (in some cases rather more overtly racist, in others without any apparent racist import).

On Monday 2 April 1990 the story of the arrival of 118 Cambodians the day before in a boat off Broome in Western Australia was picked up by 2BL News at 8.25 a.m. The people were described as 'refugees' and 'Cambodians in a boat'. The words 'boat people' were not used at all. At 8.39 a.m. on radio station 2KY in Sydney, Ron Casey, a talkback radio host (who had been inviting listeners to comment on immigration all morning) received a phone call from 'Helen':

> I've been through the *Sydney Morning Herald* and there's not a word about these freeloaders from Kampuchea they've towed into Broome. Now what are they going to do with this crowd?

Casey responded:

> These are the boat people. . .It's been played down by the newspapers. . .let me make it quite clear—the boat people, because they come from an underdeveloped country, they can bring tuberculosis, they can bring all sorts of diseases—they have just lobbed up on our doorstep. And now we have to face up to the problem of all the do-gooders trying to stop their deportation. . .Now if we don't fly

them back or tow them to Timor. . .and let the Indonesians cop them they'll keep coming. There are so many places where Asian people could go if they wanted to descend on a nation. Why don't the boat people head for Taiwan, why don't the boat people head for Indonesia? There's plenty of vacant space in Borneo, I can tell you that for sure. Where do you think they got that saying 'wild man from Borneo'?

This is followed by a musical promo: 'That's why you're listening. Ron Casey, 2KY'. The placement of the Casey/2KY promo immediately after these statements (during which Casey's manner was very agitated or excited) identifies this highly emotive style of discussion of the immigration issue as the reason 'why you're listening' as Casey's signature theme. He seems to be trying to excite his audience over the issue of Asian immigration, to attract callers to his talk-back program. He also seems to harness fears based on racial difference and ignorance, making false assumptions about the Cambodians to vilify anyone of Asian descent. The equation is established: all 'Asian people' are presented as 'boat people'; all people from developing countries carry disease and therefore all immigrants are threatening. What is also significant about Casey's treatment of the incident is the idea that 'they'll keep coming'. He uses language such as 'descend on a nation', 'Asianisation', and the 'giving away of the northern part of Australia' throughout the period monitored.

The news coverage of the Cambodians' arrival by the commercial media, the *Sydney Morning Herald* and SBS TV, takes a similar perspective. The story was covered on Monday evening by SBS TV, ABC TV and Channel 9 News. Channel 9 News ran a 20-second story: 'A boatload of more than 100 Cambodian refugees has arrived in WA. . .118 people were jam-packed on board; men, women and children. . .They'll be taken to Broome where authorities will decide if they can stay'.

ABC TV News ran an 80-second story, introduced by Richard Morecroft, against a picture of a different, smaller boat full of people (actually file footage of an earlier arrival), with the caption 'Boat People':

A boatload of more than 100 Cambodians has arrived in Broome after being intercepted by the navy off the north coast of West Australia. Claiming to be refugees, the group is one of the largest to come to Australia since the late 70s.

The report by Melanie Ambrose from Broome took a sympathetic angle:

This 20 metre boat has been carrying 118 people with food and water for over three weeks. Those on board say they are Cambodian. . .back on dry land the toll of the journey to freedom became clear. [The vision at this point is of a woman being carried or dragged between two naval or customs officers.] Despite the travellers' exhaustion authorities began their interviews which are expected to last for many months because of a lack of identification. . .although officials haven't got to the bottom of the story yet the group has been classified as one of the biggest to enter Australian waters since the influx of Vietnamese refugees here in the 70s.

SBS World News ran a 93-second story with the following introduction:

Immigration officers are investigating the identity of 118 boat people now in detention at Broome in West Australia. Although those on board claim to be Cambodian, the authorities have yet to be convinced.

The SBS report from Broome:

Crammed aboard this 20 metre boat were 70 men, 30 women and 18 children. They are one of the largest groups of boat people to be intercepted off the coast of West Australia in more than 10 years. Although they claim to be refugees from Cambodia, many are said to have travelled without the documents that could prove their identity. . .If they are to find a refuge in Australia they'll first have to prove their identity and then conform with the UN criteria for gaining

ABC TV News: Journey to freedom, 2 April 1990

refugee status. So far the Immigration Department isn't prepared to call them anything more than unauthorised arrivals.

On Tuesday 3 April the story was dropped by Channel 9. Channel 7 ran a 50-second story on its morning news/current affairs program *Eleven AM*: 'In just under an hour the biggest boatload of Cambodian refugees ever to arrive in Australia will be flown out of Broome'. Again, the language used suggests that a great many 'boatloads' of Cambodian refugees had arrived in the past, even though this was only the second group to arrive. The report goes on to describe the group as 'boat people'. *SBS World News* ran only a small headline: '118 occupants of small boat. . .flown to Melbourne' with a head: 'Boat people to be flown to Melbourne'.

On Thursday 5 April Channel 7's *Eleven AM* ran a short headline: 'The crew of a boat that brought 118 Asians here at the weekend could be fined. . .they claim to be Cambodian. . .' *SBS World News* ran a 125-second story with the introduction: 'Immigration officials may prosecute the five crew members who brought more than 100 Asian boat people to Australia last weekend. . .'. The description has changed from Cambodian to Asian.

ABC News ran : 'Immigration officials said it could take at least 6 months to decide the fate of the Cambodian boat people. . .'; they are still Cambodian but are no longer described as refugees.

By Thursday the descriptive language had shifted to 'Asian boat people' (SBS) and '118 Asians' (Channel 7). At this point all stations except SBS dropped the story. SBS ran a different version on *Asia Report* on Friday 6 April—a 228-second re-edit of the material used in Thursday night's news. Presenter Lee Lin Chin introduced the story as follows:

> The Australian government is convinced that this week's arrival of a large group of South-East Asians doesn't spell the start of a new wave of unauthorised visitors. Immigration officials say the recent tightening of our laws on illegal entry means we won't be seen as an easy mark.

Karen Milliner then reports:

> . . .these are the second arrivals on our shores in recent months. . .This latest arrival has raised concerns of a new wave of unauthorised visitors. . .

Immigration spokesperson Jean Shannon points out that. . .

> . . .we've only had two boats in the last 10 years, so we've virtually had a decade free of boats. It's not the same situation as the 70s. . .I really don't think at this stage that there's any reason to be alarmed. . .

The shift in language from Cambodian refugees to South-East Asians and Asian boat people reflects the increasing control of the agenda by the Immigration Department. The certainty that the people were Cambodian and refugees had deteriorated during the week to the point that their nationality had been replaced by a racial denotation, and their political status transformed from one of people needing our help to people posing a threat. The trajectory of the story seemed to follow the line of exclusionists such as Casey, that all 'Asians' are 'boat people' and they're all the same.

The electronic media stories reflected the government line, even though the treatment of their plight ranged from cool to sympathetic. However, no background was given on Cambodia, nor was there any discussion with local Cambodians nor assessment by refugee bodies of the government position. The print media were more expansive but reinvoked 'Yellow Peril' images of the 1950s and 1960s to carry the story. Thus the Sydney Morning Herald noted (5/4/90:12):

> 118 ASIANS HOPE FOR RESIDENCE
> A group of Asian boat people flown to Melbourne from Broome in Western Australia will be held in custody until Federal Immigration officials finish questioning them. . .They claim to be Cambodian and are being held at the Enterprise migrant centre at Springvale. They are regarded as unauthorised arrivals by the Department of Immigration. According to the assistant secretary of the Immigration Department's policy secretariat, Ms Sue Ingram, they will have to leave Australia if it is found that there is no basis on which they can seek permanent residence.

The news story is placed between a sympathetic profile of an earlier Vietnamese boat person, and a background piece on the context. It is linked to the political story of Hewson, the Federal leader of the Opposition and NSW's state Labor Opposition leader, Carr, debating the overall immigration level and where immigrants and refugees settle. The story 'Premier choice for refugees' offers a map with a star and arrow coming from China: 'Indochinese arrivals 1988/89'. Such maps, used by all TV stations in their introductions to the story, like Casey's use of the words 'descend on a nation', evoke 'yellow peril' propaganda.

Both the *SMH* (5/4/90, p. 12) and ABC TV news (2/4/90) described the voyage as a 'journey to freedom', which is ironic considering that the Cambodians actually landed in detention in Melbourne and many were still there four years later!

Ron Casey's 2KY treatment of the arrival of the Cambodians, his fear of their bringing 'all sorts of diseases', and his use of language such as 'descend on a nation', seem to be drawn from a 'sub-narrative' that runs through the news and current affairs coverage of this story. All the stations ended the first

(Monday night) news story with the image of the hosing down of the arrivals. Despite even the ABC's sympathetic narrative this scene conveyed the impression that they were so filthy they had to be hit with a jet of water from a huge fire hose—almost sterilised—before landing.

The continuing narrative of the boat people was sustained from 1990 into 1992. By April 1992, two years after the seizure of the boats off Broome and the arrest of their occupants, the Australian government had decided to try to send the boat people, now definitely identified as Cambodians, back to Cambodia. The public debate had been heightened by the discovery, at the end of 1991, of a group of Chinese illegal immigrants who had beached their boat on the Kimberley coast of north-west Australia, and walked hundreds of kilometres to a remote outback station, from where they were transferred to Darwin. The rescue of the people had been a story of high drama in January 1992, following air and land searches across inhospitable terrain. The press reports offered two themes throughout the period—the 'vulnerability' of Australia to illegal Asian entry, and the 'strength and resilience' of the boat people in surviving the ordeal in country where 'no white person would go'—it was 'blackfella country', too savage, too dangerous, yet they had wandered through it almost unharmed. This capacity for survival, heralded initially as a 'positive' value, began to be reinterpreted as threat once more—a threat exacerbated by the apparent difficulty the government had in repatriating the new arrivals—or indeed any of the boat people from previous years.

A particularly significant intervention was made by *Four Corners*, the ABC's flagship current affairs program, in March 1992. The program, produced by Marian Wilkinson, concentrated on the plight of the refugees—as the government sought to resolve the tension between the rights of the refugees and the problem of the rapidly increasing internationalisation of populations which characterises contemporary world affairs. The program pointed to the poor conditions under which the refugees were being kept, their desire to remain in Australia, the contradictory standards of the government, and the 'search for freedom' that the voyages and the arrival in Australia signified. Another theme emerged: Australia's vulnerability to 'penetration', suggesting that the state could not adequately protect the nation/ethnic group/family from danger and pollution. This subterranean theme found final expression in the extended close-up of the abandoned Chinese vessel burning in a mangrove creek, set alight we assume by customs officials to destroy any disease it might have harboured. It also gave another message: that for these people there would be no returning to wherever it was they had come from, using the transport that had brought them, no 'going back'—burning boats rather than bridges behind them.

The Other as a threat, to be 'washed' or 'burnt' into purity, before being carried into detention, recurs as a marker of difference—the images allow 'us' to say what 'we' are not: not them; 'we' are not Asian, not refugees, not scared to the edge of insanity, not driven to flee through exhaustion into the totally unknown, lost, without location or place. . .we are clean, uniformed, white, humane, ordered, placed, our territory neatly defined. Yet we are told of our need to be wary, suspicious, our bluff outgoing culture already corroded into hesitancy and violence, not by 'our' choice, but through 'their' doing, their arrival, their desire. Indeed, the more intensely they desire (us?) the more urgently we fear (them?).

On one hand then we have the boundary defended, but we also have the heartland celebrated. If the nation is to be sustained it must be fed, and mum must feed it. The nation and the blonde mum sit together.

18

THE BLONDE AUSSIE MUM, THE AUSSIE FAMILY AND THE AUSSIE NATION: TELEVISION ADS

The absence of non-Anglo Australians is most pernicious in a particular genre of television ads, aimed at prime-time family viewing, that speak 'Australia' and 'the Australian way of life' as a uniformly Anglo country based on a 'typical Aussie family'. These ads are almost totally concerned with food staples (margarine, breakfast cereal, biscuits, meat), and with institutions aimed at family responsibilities, (banks, insurance, family cars). They are given a 'typical Aussie' family setting—the sentimental core of Australian social life. Their message is that in a world of dissipated cultural identifications, domesticity is the irreducible core of Australian national life, and the source of what is consistently Anglo. The association of family and nation, their alliance in language and symbol, is a common phenomenon—the Motherland, the family of the Nation, and so forth. However, in a multicultural country the presentation of the family and the nation as monocultural questions the relationship between 'social reality' and the iconic practices of advertising. As one advertiser put it to us, it is not that Australian women and families are 'like that' (the margarine advertisement) but that 'everyone wants to be like that, knows they cannot, but purchases the product to seek a share of the lifestyle, power and security the images hold out'. At the centre of the 'typical Aussie family' is a typical 'Aussie Mum'. The Aussie Mum is the stable factor, the mainspring of the Aussie family and the total embodiment of what is unchangeably Australian (Anglo-ness, tradition).

In these ads the image of the Aussie Mum as blonde is critical. Her blondeness is symbolic: (no-one believes all Aussie Mums are blonde—the image is not meant to be taken literally. It is a potent symbol that condenses a hotchpotch of sentiments, moods and idealised social relations into a totally mundane image—almost a parody—of the Australian family. We are left with a sense that at the heart of 'being Australian' are timeless, unvarying Anglo traditions and a traditional Anglo way of life. Blondeness signifies the nation's undifferentiated and exclusive ethnicity. Blonde Aussie Mums are the bearers of the national ethnicity (Anglo) and the guardians of Anglo ethnic traditions.

The image of the blonde Aussie Mum does a variety of ideological work. It signifies an appropriate division of labour within the family; it tells us how women should behave and to what they should aspire; for people who are not blonde Australians it implies that consumption can help them move towards the unobtainable goal of true assimilation.

The nation requires a history; the history legitimises a master narrative that presents in emotional form the rationale for the social and cultural order, its hierarchies and exclusions. Here we find a family evolving before our eyes:

Voice-over: 'In the Bega Valley the fundamental things still apply, as time goes by.'
A man sits on a colonial verandah as a horse and cart pass by.

Across the screen flashes a montage of black and white images of Queen Victoria, a horse-drawn tram, a group of beach belles, the Sydney harbour bridge under construction, and Donald Bradman playing cricket.

A man (son of the first man) sits on the same verandah dressed in 1950s style as an old truck passes by. A second montage shows black and white images of victory celebrations, a 1950s Bondi surf life-saving procession, an old Holden car, a man riding the waves on a long-board, and the Queen visiting Australia.

A man (grandson of the first man) sits on the same verandah in more modern clothes as a car goes by. A third montage of black and white images shows an aeroplane, the Beatles landing in Australia, Yvonne Goolagong holding up a medal, the Australia Cup, and Bush shaking hands with Gorbachev

A young man sits on the same verandah in contemporary clothes as a late-model car goes by.

Voice-over: 'Bega Cheese. A taste born in the valley. A taste that you remember.'

National identity is constantly defined and redefined on television. In advertisements it is reconstructed as a marketing strategy. Products are sold as authentically 'Australian' or as the items that real Australians buy: 'the fundamental things'. The reactive *'Get some pork on your fork'* ads presented a nostalgic version of pre-multicultural and pre-feminist Anglo Australia through 1950s newsreel-style voice-overs and black and white images, relying on nationalism to sell meat: 'real' Australians eat pork. The Aussie male is often presented as having a particular relationship with the land/nation, driving across the rugged landscape in a four-wheel drive. Masculinity is represented by ownership and conquering the rugged land.

Representations of 'multicultural Australia' in both ads and soaps could be summarised as the cook, the thief, his wife and her grocer. Non-Anglo Australians are often portrayed as marginal to the fundamental unit of the family. They are usually subservient (e.g. cooks, waiters, grocers); or dangerous—a temptation to stray from respectability or a representation of our desire for something dangerous and unknown. In so far as 'multicultural policy' has intruded on the advertising world, it appears to have done so via an emphasis on the search for a national identity, rather than any genuine search for a multicultural audience. Definitions of Australianness are reinforced by the delineation of difference; of what is 'non-Australian'.

The representation of non-Anglo Australians in ads has usually been limited to 'comic stereotypes' in the mould of 'Con the Fruiterer', and most commonly in ads for or about food. In an I & J Light and Crispy frozen foods ad for example, an Anglo woman impersonates 'Sam' the 'ethnic' grocer who sold her the fish. (Likewise in McCains, Pasta & Pasta sauce ads, Mama Fiorelli's, and Asian food ads.) A Red Rooster Chicken Croissant ad shows a stereotyped 'French' chef (played by an Anglo actor) in striped T-shirt and beret presenting the croissants, his 'Aussie' son contributing 'with chips'. A Sara Lee croissants ad shows a 'French' woman eating the croissants: 'This Sara, she's French, no?' In these ads European and Asian immigrants are stereotyped as not particularly intelligent people who have comic accents and whose only positive contribution to Australian culture is their food. They are used in ads to show the authenticity of the foods marketed, yet there is nothing 'authentic' about their own representation as people.

In a recent trend, more multicultural ads have started to appear on television. Most are for large fast-food companies such as McDonalds, often geared towards families in which both parents work and convenience foods are attractive (the working class is fast becoming the ethnic class). The 'great taste of McDonalds' ad, for example, shows people of a wide variety of ages and ethnic backgrounds eating at McDonalds. Some ads draw on American rap music images, where non-whites are cool, to capture the youth market. One series of Palmolive ads, however, was quite different, portraying a variety of Australian women in different situations, including several women from Asian backgrounds—but none of these ads include Aboriginal people in their representation of Australians.

Advertisers seem to have taken the view that Aboriginal Australia is too hard—a few ads have attempted to capture something 'essential' about Australia or the primeval source of humanity by linking a product to Aborigines. For example, in the late 1980s Pepsi-Cola contrasted an Aborigine with a satellite television broadcast to suggest the universal qualities of the drink; the ad was shot in the USA for international release, by an Australian crew. However, in the first of our viewing periods only one ad carried any Aboriginal content—Canon Camera opened its montage 'smile of Australia' with a one-second still of two Aboriginal children with painted faces and huge smiles; all the following shots were of Anglo-Australians. There is no relationship between these children and the rest of the smiling Australians; they stand apart from the the 'story'. This quick, isolated image of Aboriginal children makes a touristic appropriation of Aboriginality, an increasingly common trend followed by the Northern Territory tourism ads.

Advertising agency Saatchi and Saatchi produced a series of Northern Territory tourism ads for which Aboriginal artist Terry Yumbulul was commissioned to produce work in traditional style depicting NT tourist attractions and the Yullara resort. This artwork was then animated and given a non-Aboriginal voice-over—that masculine 'Aussie battler' style that was launched in Bond Corp beer and sports advertising in the early 1980s—mixed with didgeridoo music:

> Today in the Territory you can take a slow train
> to the loneliest pub in the scrub.
> Join the millions of visitors to Kakadu.
> Snap a prehistoric monster.
> Hear waterfalls roaring.
> Eat bush tucker by a waterhole.
> You see there's no place in the world like your own territory.

The waterfalls are waterslides; the 'bush tucker' is traditional European food served on plates with knives and forks, and the waterhole is a swimming pool—all depicted in Yumbulul's work. Similarly, the Yullara resort ad runs:

> Today in the Territory you see the world's oldest river.
> Get a bite of barramundi.
> Visit the world's oldest art gallery.
> Gorge yourself at Catherine.
> Sleep under 75 billion stars,
> or under five stars.
> You see there's no place in the world like your own territory.

Aboriginal people are not depicted in these ads—only their artwork, music and land. The male Anglo voice and the resolve ('You see there's no place in the world like your own territory') imply Anglo-Australian ownership and control of the land and culture and the right to market them as tourist commodities. The concept of 'bush tucker' signifies Aboriginal/white/land relationships. In the past this pidgin phrase was used disparagingly to refer to uncultivated food collected by Aborigines and Islanders. More recently a former army officer has become popular through the ABC television program, *The Bush Tucker Man*, in which he introduces urban non-Aboriginal audiences to the crafts of living off the land.

Playing on the image of the bush tucker man the Kraft Coon cheese ads show us another white Australian roughing it, but able to survive when bush tucker and Aboriginality are thrown away for some 'traditional Australian tucker'—Peter Russell Clark appears out in the bush with a handful of indigenous bush tucker:

> G'day.
> You know Australian bush tucker isn't easy. [Throws bush tucker away]
> You can spend all day scratching around for half a meal.
> And that's why I travel with a bit of traditional Australian tucker in the fridge.
> And you can't get better than Coon.
> Coon's got that tried-and-true you-beaut flavour that. . .Australian families have loved for over 50 years.
> Coon. Australia's favourite tasty.

Anglo-Australian culture is given precedence over Aboriginal culture here, as the 'real' and 'traditional' culture of this country. Aboriginal history, culture and land ownership are trivialised or denied. How extraordinary that this advertisement is for a product called 'Coon Cheese'. 'Coon', a contemptuous term for 'black', evokes America's history of slavery, racism and oppression and Australia's 200 years of ambivalence and hostility to Aborigines and Torres Strait Islanders.

If advertising is the land of desire and fantasy, of dreams raised and offers of fulfilment met by the simple exigency of spending money on the commodity, then short fictions, particularly in weekly or fortnightly magazines or as television soaps, provide a means to keep the ads apart and offer their own moral homilies. We turn now to an exploration of this genre.

19

ROMANCE FICTION, SOAPS AND SERIALS

Romance fiction holds an important place in the lives of millions of readers and viewers. The exploration of the twists and turns of human relationships, the horrors, heartbreaks and delights of both printed and televisual forms, have become the focus of the study of 'pleasure' in contemporary life. This concern for pleasure has developed out of a challenge to the traditional academic interpretations of these experiences, which tend to regard them as 'low culture', not serious, and with few redeeming features. Tulloch has suggested that current soap operas provide a range of negotiated readings that can challenge the dominant views of reality presented elsewhere in the media. Audiences gain pleasure from these processes of negotiation, and from making an interpretation of their own, one that incorporates the advertising accompanying the serial narrative (Tulloch 1989:120–1).

The central dynamic of romantic fiction is its focus on the pleasure of one gender—women. The main fantasy of the soap opera consists of a fully self-sufficient family regularly facing threats of disintegration (Feuer 1986; Modleski 1984); it presents women with a 'deep truth about the way [they] function in culture: as both moral and spiritual guides and household drudges, moving back and forth between the extremes, but obviously finding them difficult to reconcile (Modleski 1984:101).

For our analysis of gender and ethnicity we found a rich source of material in romance fiction and television serials. In the week we researched, the women's magazines we chose carried the following 'fiction':

- *Daddy*, Part II of a new novel by Danielle Steel (*Woman's Day* 3 April 1990 pp. 62 ff)—'Oliver has survived losing Sarah, only to learn that his son is in serious trouble. . .'
- *The Heart of the Continent* by Nancy Cato (*New Idea*, 14 April 1990)— 'In this extract's heartwarming conclusion, the dream of having a family comes true for Alix and Jim. . .'
- *Stagestruck* by Estelle Taylor (*Australian Women's Weekly* April 1990)— 'At last her chance had come, to realise her dreams and see her name in lights. . .'

The *New Idea* story provides a perfect example of how romance can convert history into an untroubling and apparently realistic account of the development of European society after the invasion. The story it hides is as interesting as the one it tells. Nancy Cato is a leading Australian author, and her work has been adapted for several television mini-series.

Cato's story is set in the outback, in 1915. This final episode takes place at Christmas in the Northern Territory, where the heroine, Alix MacFarlane, has arrived with her husband, Jim Manning, at his parents' station at Cappamerri. They have a baby, whom she knows was conceived when she and Tim made love by the banks of the Diamantina River. The child is a daughter instead of the son Jim wanted to inherit the property. Alix returns to the Centre, where we meet the first Aborigines—two stockmen, 'Micky and Jarry', and where the drought breaks and there is celebration. Later, in Adelaide, they go to the movies to see *The Birth of A Nation* (a racist account of the founding myths of America)—which 'Jim liked best'.

Despite Alix's pleas, Jim joins the Light Horse and is killed in Palestine. At war's end Alix returns to Cappamerri with the baby to live with Jim's parents. The family has been reconciled and restored after tragedy, with the woman as mother and carrier of the heart's burdens as heroic men go off across the world to die gallantly.

This is white middle-class life in central Australia, in a period when cattle stations were being carved out of Aboriginal lands, and massacres continued. This is the story Cato does not tell, as it might diminish the heroic grandeur of the pioneers. The fictitious property is somewhere near Clifton Hills on the Birdsville track to Marree. In the 1880s and 1890s when 'Big Jim', Alix's father-in-law, was setting up his station, native police and trackers massacred hundreds of the Yaluyandi, Garanguru, and Yawarawarga people. A few years later more blacks were killed by white settlers when they speared a bullock for meat (Elder 1988:159). Cato's idealised depiction of the Aborigines as stockmen (with Anglo names) and a land devoted to cattle, secures the white history in fictional discourse. Alix's concern for the Aborigines is roused by Jim's comments about their children. In an earlier chapter (7 April 1990) where Jim asks Alix to marry him and come back to the station, Alix sees herself 'bringing the light of learning to these wild children of nature' who, Jim says, can read only 'cattle brands and the letters on kerosene cases'. The narrative reasserts the white right to appropriate and profit, the only check being the vagaries of the weather.

The stories reinforce Modleski's arguments about the nature of romantic fiction—the unresolvable tension between the cooking, cleaning, shopping, baby-feeding and nappy-changing activities implicit in advertising content that makes up much of the rest of the magazines—and the stories (fictional and features) of glamorous women who do none of these things. Yet the history imparted by stories such as these is also important: for many readers these myths constitute the national history. Other national myths are communicated electronically.

Television soaps—serials with regular casts—derive from the tradition of melodrama in literature. The original serials were published in weekly news magazines—Dickens' stories were first published in this format—and were eventually taken up by North American broadcasters trying to attract listeners to the new phenomenon of radio. They were sponsored by soap companies—thus 'soaps'. With the translation into television they tended to lose the ubiquitous, authoritative narrator of the radio form. However, they spread throughout the world, carrying complex and contradictory messages about American and other societies.

One example of the complexity of this genre has been the response to *Dallas*. To investigate how the meanings of *Dallas* are negotiated and sustained, Liebes and Katz (1988) made a wide survey of audiences in Israel and the United States—Arabs, newly arrived Russians, Moroccan Jews, kibbutzniks and Anglo-Americans in Los Angeles. The Moroccan Jews and Arabs viewed *Dallas* as a real representation of American upper-class life, and related to the program as outsiders—them and us. They criticised the behaviour, in particular of the women, whom they considered have low morals. They rejected its values. The Russians saw it in ideological terms—as manipulation of the masses who are told that the wealthy are really unhappy. They accepted, however, that significant classes of people do behave as they are portrayed in Dallas. The Americans and the kibbutzniks dealt with the program more playfully—for them it was only a fantasy that no-one could take seriously.

Since soaps invite multiple readings, presented as they are in a culturally pluralistic environment, it is worth reflecting on two Australian soaps—*A Country Practice*, and the Australian archetype, *Neighbours*.

A Country Practice was for some time the highest rating drama series on Australian television. It has the reputation of being more serious in that it deals with social issues; *Neighbours* avoids issues. *ACP* has been the subject of a major study by Tulloch and Moran (1986), and Tulloch, in a subsequent study, has argued that it plays out the extremes of the soap by conjoining the large problems of human existence with the daily chores (Tulloch 1989:129). However, despite Tulloch's argument that an episode in the mid 1980s explored the relations of class, gender and ethnicity, and despite four episodes that featured Aboriginal actor Gary Foley to introduce themes of Aboriginal deprivation and poverty, the series is essentially white and Anglo-Australian. All its key roles are middle-class Australian—even the comic roles.

In two episodes called 'A Change of Heart' shown in April 1990, *ACP* dealt with the issues of heart transplants and a young solo father trying to bring up his baby on his own. The heart patient dies but his daughter decides to keep on with his farm to live out his dream. The solo father, after first deciding to give up his daughter, is then convinced by another solo father, Dr Kouros, to stick with it. He does so and the family survives.

In these two episodes there were eleven core cast members, and five other speaking parts. None of these parts were played as anything other than mainstream Australian, although there was nothing about the roles that would have ruled out other ethnicities or races.

James Davern, executive producer of *ACP*, has argued that such a perception of the program is misguided and ill-informed. At a conference on industry self-regulation and cultural diversity sponsored by the Office of Multicultural Affairs and hosted by the Communications Law Centre in Sydney in May 1993, Davern argued that non-Anglos had been cast in many episodes, including stories about citizenship (in which a Vietnamese official in the Immigration Department naturalised an English member of the cast); Asian–Caucasian love affairs; a Thai doctor (played by a Chinese Filipina); an intergenerational clash and a Polish–Australian family. He also said that a regular role (a park ranger) had been created for a young Aboriginal actor. As Davern told the conference: 'We've come to the conclusion that rather than put our Aboriginal and ethnic people in on an issue basis, [it is better to] make them an integral part of the town and so our policy is that at least 15 per cent of our extras, for example, have to be Aboriginals or ethnic people or Asians and so when you shoot some scenes in the Wandan Valley Club, you will see these people as a normal part of the community' (Davern, Office of Multicultural Affairs 1993:38).

ACP is just one example of a growing awareness of the issues. By 1993 the Screen Producers' Association of Australia had adopted a policy on the portrayal of cultural diversity in film and television, covering scripting, casting and extras. The policy, described in more detail in Part V of this book, helps producers focus on better practice. Another series, *Neighbours*, has also increased its multicultural mix over the past three years. *Neighbours* was renowned for its quintessential presentation of the 'real' Australia.

Neighbours is shown five nights per week on Channel 10. There were 26 speaking roles in the episodes shown during the week April 2–6 1990. Two female roles may have been Italo-Australian (the character names were Christina and Caroline Alessi) and a black character (Eddie Buckingham, played by Bob La Castra) was introduced. His character developed from a charming London Black whom Harold and Madge Bishop had met on their travels, into a shady character making furtive long-distance phonecalls and being pursued by some un-named London contact. In the 'normal' context of Ramsay Street and the Anglo-Australianness of the other roles, casting a black man as a dubious character seems to be asking the audience to associate his black skin colour with this role.

The community of *Neighbours* is presented as normal and diverse—a cross-section of personalities and problems—and yet there is a falsehood here.

In a society where middle-class suburbs would have at least a sprinkling of Asian faces, there are none. Perhaps this class excludes the Aborigines and Vietnamese, as *Neighbours* is set in leafy groves far from the Cabramattas or Redferns. Yet the program claims to represent Australian life. It is an Australian life idealised and transmuted into what it might have been like if post-war migration had never occurred. It is more than the celebration of the family that pulls together; it is a celebration of a view of race and ethnicity in which the centre is white and unselfconsciously homogeneous.

By 1993 Davern was able to say on behalf of Grundy's, the producers of *Neighbours*, that this perception of the series was also outdated. In a critique of Phillip Bell's analysis, *Multicultural Australia in the Media* (1993), Davern argued that *Neighbours* had given sustaining or lead roles to 'people like Mario Nicolosi, Kristian Schmid, Ben Guerens, Vince Sorrenti, Paula Scholes, Debruska Clemens. *Home and Away* had Dieter Brummer and Rebekah Elmaloglou. Now I'm sorry but those people don't fit the category of blonde Anglo-Australiannness. They were on the screen, somebody didn't see them' (Davern, OMA 1993: 41).

Two different perceptions are evident here—we propose (and Bell agrees) that these programs are essentially drawn from the heartland of Anglo Australia, whose inhabitants look out at the 'marginal' people who reflect the growing diversity of society. How does the core culture of the series deal with and relate to these social changes? The heartland seems untouched by them.

Davern, on the other hand argued that his viewers are getting an increasingly accurate reflection of Australia and that the lapses in verisimilitude occur through no fault of the producers—a Filipina played a Thai because there were no Thais available for the role; a Chinese played a Japanese because there were no mature Japanese actresses available. Yet perhaps Davern pinned down the problem in his account of an episode in which two Indians joined a barbecue and spoke of cricket: 'You must consider the effect of that on our audience which is out there, between here [Sydney] and the Blue Mountains and who probably may or may not have an Indian neighbour who they've never spoken to, and they are confronted by two Indians who are not going to bite or hurt them, but who might like to talk to them about cricket' (Davern, OMA 1993:44). The audience determines for the producer how issues of race and ethnicity will be handled. It is not a matter of the producers reacting to a particular issue; their social perspectives are negotiated over time with the audiences, and the most accessible and least threatening perspectives are chosen.

Whatever their claims, soaps carry significant information about Australian social relationships. However, the question of accurate representation in television radio and press news, current affairs and features require a more sustained analysis of the processes at work. The portrayal of Aboriginal people and their location in the discourses of the nation have already been outlined.

The sustained efforts of the media to represent the Aboriginal experience, when detached from the 'wild', as one of chaos and violence indicates that Aborigines present problems for those involved in such representation. The national project of cultural cohesion and mythic solidarity is disrupted by the Aboriginal presence. So how is this to be handled by the media—exclusion in general, except when inclusion is unavoidable?

20

FRAMEWORKS FOR MARGINALISING ABORIGINAL VOICES: 'FACTIONS', 'DRUNKS' AND 'REAL' ABORIGINES

There are some recurring patterns in how Aboriginal issues were reported in news and current affairs genres in all media in the recording periods. The exclusion of Aboriginal voices as authoritative is persistent. In most of the print and television items recorded, there were few opportunities for Aborigines to state their case. Where Aborigines were interviewed as spokespeople or authorities, their views were invariably placed in the concluding few paragraphs—as, for example, in the coverage of Black deaths in the *Daily Telegraph* in the 1990 research week.

In 1991 a series of stories was carried on the 25th anniversary of the extraordinary political victory of the Gurindji, in the *Sydney Morning Herald* and on ABC and SBS television. The Gurindji are an Aboriginal tribe who were forced off the Vesteys' cattle station in the Northern Territory in the 1960s, and who fought to regain their land through a strike and occupation of Wattie Creek in 1966. The commercial television stations failed to mention this story, just as in the 1990 research week they had failed to carry any positive stories about Aborigines despite several relevant items carried in other media during that week. The SBS news report managed to interview one Gurindji man, but the ABC did not allow any Aboriginal people to speak, interviewing instead Gough Whitlam (whose Land Rights Act could only offer leasehold over the Gurindji land) and Paul Kelly (a white musician with links to Aboriginal communities)! The *SMH* coverage was significantly better because it carried a feature story (28 Aug. 1991) by freelance writer Chips Macinolty, who has worked closely with Northern Territory Aboriginal communities for many years and who is a significant contributor to *Land Rights News* published by the Northern and Central Land Councils. In Macinolty's story Aboriginal interviewees tell the story of the community's past and present, the news coverage of the item (30 Aug. 1991) by *SMH* regular reporter Mike Secombe did not give space to any Aboriginal voice. The absence of Aboriginal voices interpreting 'news' about Aboriginal issues does not leave a vacuum of interpretive guidelines for audiences. Several powerful and persistent 'frames' of expectation about what news relating to Aborigines will be about are evident in how stories about Aboriginal politics are constructed, and how they are interpreted varies from audience to audience. For example, during the 1990 recording period, Channel 9's news story about three youths killed in a crash in an allegedly stolen car after a high-speed police chase identified them as Aboriginal, but did not identify the race or ethnicity of the police or the driver of the third car involved in the accident. A white audience unsympathetic to Aboriginal people might infer from this story that Aborigines are more likely to commit crimes than other people, whereas an Aboriginal audience may draw from it the impression that police never give Aboriginal people time to account for themselves before pursuing them to their deaths. This story may even enhance a sense of Aboriginal political solidarity as Aboriginal audiences across the country see young Aboriginal men unquestioningly accused of criminality by the media and subjected to the same intense police harrassment as they are themselves. So the interpretation of 'news' rests strongly in the individual and shared responses of its many audiences. Nevertheless, such 'frames' of expectation—Aborigines as likely perpetrators of crime in this case—severely limit the interpretative range of this story.

During the recording periods in 1990 and 1991 several other frames of expectation were evident—for example, news about Aboriginal politics which associates Aborigines with disunity and an inability to present a unified voice. This, indeed, may be a ready excuse for failing to interview Aboriginal spokespeople. The most frequent term used in this context is *factionalism*.

'FACTIONS' AND MARGINALISING OPPOSITION

A series of *SMH* articles in April 1990 on the debates about changes to the Land Rights Act in NSW demonstrated clearly the 'frame of expectation' assumed by the journalists and editors involved in the texts of these pieces, but more particularly their graphics and headlines. The work of Stuart Hall and Teun van Dijk is relevant to the *Sydney Morning Herald* handling of this debate. Their studies in the UK and the Netherlands suggest that the press tends to present stories within established frameworks of interpretation (Hall 1988; Van Dijk 1991a). These frameworks are quickly recognised in short pieces, and reflect besides the sources used for stories the journalists' assumptions and expectations about the issues involved.

On 5 April 1990 the *Sydney Morning Herald* featured an article by Matthew Moore about the Aboriginal response to NSW Government proposals to alter the Land Rights Act. Earlier the Greiner Government amendments had met unanimous opposition from Aboriginal people, after which Charles Perkins had been employed as a consultant to the Government to produce a report about ways to effect changes. Perkins' report had just been released, and it too met unified opposition from Aboriginal people. There is, however, no Aboriginal voice in the article. Moore's text and the headline strongly endorse Perkins' report, but the overall arrangement of the article goes far beyond this. The strongest element is the picture, which dominates the page layout, of two Aboriginal faces glaring at each other and arguing. The implication is that Aboriginal people are arguing among themselves, as if Perkins (who is from Alice Springs and has lived since the early 1970s in Canberra) represented a sector of the NSW Aboriginal population rather than his employer, the Greiner Government. This powerful image sets the context for the article and directs readers to view the debate as one between Aborigines rather than between NSW Aborigines and the Greiner Government.

The article is set in a framework so that debates among Aboriginal people become interpreted as 'factionalism' rather than legitimate dissent. There is a strong expectation that Aborigines *should* present a unity of opinion; this expectation seems to derive from a romanticised view of pre-industrial community relations. Aborigines are criticised for 'disunity' if they do not all appear to hold identical opinions. Whereas differing views and argument among Anglo-Celtic Australians are celebrated as the vital basis for parliamentary democracy and liberal free speech, when Aboriginal and other non-Anglo-Celtic people exhibit differences of opinion this is characterised as 'factionalism' which, it is implied, reflects an inability to work within western liberal democratic structures.

This was confirmed by an editorial on the land rights amendments in the *Sydney Morning Herald* of 14 April 1990. It was headed 'Problem of black factionalism' and the first sentence hammered home the point: 'The Aboriginal community is notoriously fragmented. That has to be borne in mind when considering its response to proposed changes to the NSW Land Rights Act'. The editorial produced no evidence of internal conflict within the NSW Aboriginal community, but asserted that this was the case, and reinforced the effect achieved by the graphics in the earlier article, which trivialised Aboriginal opposition to the State Government to the level of internal bickering. As Van Dijk has demonstrated, headlines and leading paragraphs are the most frequently remembered parts of news articles, and so a framework of interpretation established in these elements shapes the entire story and subsequent items.

On Saturday 7 April 1990 SBS television news reported on a conference held by Aborigines in Bathurst to discuss the State Government's proposed amendments to the Land Rights Act. This report was the only significant one made during this recording period, in any media, that showed Aboriginal people organised and debating complex political issues. But the commentary was all voice-over by non-Aborigines and no Aboriginal voices were heard, although at least this time Aborigines were seen speaking. Yet the images of people debating at a heated and angry meeting may not convey the sophistication and organisation of the Aboriginal politics involved; it is more likely to give the impression of disunity and division, which may then be placed neatly into the 'factionalism' paradigm well established in the public discourse about Aborigines. While it may have been difficult for the reporter to locate spokespeople, the report would have been better balanced had it shown some Aboriginal people commenting on the major issues being debated, with a fuller representation of the issues themselves—not just the fact that disagreements occurred.

TURNING CRITIQUE INTO DEBATES OVER ABORIGINAL SPOKESPEOPLE'S AUTHENTICITY

A variation of the expectation frame of disunity is drawn from a long-established distinction made by white Australians between Aboriginal people of different ancestry and culture. Old welfare administrations tried to classify and divide people according to 'caste' or skin colour and the concept persists that some people are 'more' Aboriginal than others, either because of their appearance or their lifestyle. This amorphous concept is used by politicians and bureaucrats regularly to impugn the authenticity of their Aboriginal critics. Media reports, however, continue and perpetuate this framework of interpretation, ignoring more substantive elements of disputes to focus on questions of the Aboriginal spokespeople's 'authenticity' and authority to speak.

During the 1991 recording period, there was an example of this in a story about a debate between Aborigines and government. The *SMH* carried two versions of a Tony Hewitt report (24 August 1991 and 26 August 1991) about the Parliamentary Whip, ALP member Bill Prest, calling an Opposition MP, Bob Katter, a 'gin jockey', and the Queensland Premier Wayne Goss refusing to sack him. In a week in which the Soviet Coup and the Strathfield Massacre were competing for press space with John Kerin's first Budget, the story was given surprising prominence. The Premier was under pressure from his own party and from the resignation of Aboriginal anthropologist and activist Marcia Langton from a senior position in the Queensland Aboriginal Affairs bureaucracy. Her substantial criticisms of the Goss Government focused on its Land Rights legislation, but included Goss's reluctance to remove Prest and the fact that one of Goss's advisers had publicly disparaged Langton and other Aboriginal professionals as 'Buppies' or 'Black Urban Professionals' who 'lived' and 'dressed' like whites, 'charged more' than white consultants and, by implication, were therefore not legitimate spokespeople for the general Aboriginal community.

The first version of the report was sympathetic to Langton, but placed her main criticisms in the last sentence of a 21-paragraph item. Far more space was given to the 'gin jockey' interchange; the headline featured the phrase and the body of the text repeated the whole story, including the phrase, twice. Yet at no stage did the report explore or question the meaning of this ambiguous accusation. After a comment from the Human Rights Commission that the phrase was indeed an insult to everyone, again without explaining why, the article concentrated on quoting extensively from the Goss adviser's attack on Langton and other Aboriginal professionals.

The amount of space allowed to each element of this story deflected readers' attention from the Goss government's record and whether it had condoned and practised discrimination, to the accusations over the 'authenticity' of Langton and other Aboriginal critics. In the second report, on the following Monday, the offensive phrase had been removed from the headline, and was referred to as a 'racial slur', although the interchange was again reported in the body of the text without explaining why this phrase was insulting. In this second, shorter report, the account of Ms Langton's criticisms of the Goss Government were limited to the refusal to sack Prest and the 'Buppie' attack on her. Yet the attack on her credibility as an Aboriginal spokesperson is again reproduced in full. Readers would have gained from this version very little idea of the principle or substance of Langton's criticisms. Instead, the story merely raised the question of whether she even has the right to speak from an Aboriginal position.

The definition of who is 'inside' and who is 'outside' the nation is clearly a significant media preoccupation in Australia—particularly over matters of ethnicity and race. The narrative about the nation draws heavily on metaphor, where the white blonde mother symbolises the 'heartland'. The processes through which differentiation from this heartland is manufactured, tested, challenged, undermined and reinforced forms the focus of Part III of this book. The 'making' of the nation deals with the external boundaries or borders, the heartland, who can legitimately speak for the nation, and whose voices are sanctified with the right to articulate the sustaining myths. The media play a key role in all these processes.

In Chapter 21 we explore how differences between cultural groups are constituted by the media, and which differences are valued or debased, for within the multidimensional hierarchy of social status, class, gender, race and ethnicity, age, disability, and sexuality, the media is hard at work letting some things in and keeping others out.

PART III

DIMENSIONS OF
DIFFERENCE

21

MAKING A DIFFERENCE

We have seen the process through which the internal membership of the nation is defined, in which the acceptable diversity is codified and the hierarchies enunciated. We turn now to the process of differentiation, the media work done on constructing differences and, in that process, rendering them as relationships. In media products differences are ranked either explicitly according to a dimension of power or authority, or resources (other characters, commentators, economies, ways of life) or implicitly via frameworks of social meanings. In this latter sense framing includes the conventions governing the production of media events which themselves include assumptions about audience response, though audience interpretations may vary widely.

We suggest that ranked and structured differences can be elaborated according to the following: sexuality, rationality–irrationality, violence, disease, disorder, and calamity, and according to institutional criteria such as language, family life, political stability, economic organisation, religious affiliation, and notions of justice. Various rankings were also indicated by accent, speed of delivery, camera (lighting, angle), headlining, dubbing, and commentary. In all cases these strategies and conventions took the Anglo centre as the point of reference, and others were implicitly ranked in terms of distance from the Anglo-Australian norm. Three qualifications are necessary for interpreting this material:

1 Despite the use of fixed and ranked contrasts as an aesthetic or professional device to summarise social relations (e.g. male/female; black/white; working class/middle class), signifiers such as colour, culture, class and sex often operated interchangeably—they were not fixed to a specific group of people (women, men, black, white, worker). Difference from the central image always signified something less, so that groups of people filling one side of a contrast slipped according to the contrast theme. For example, *female* often seemed to operate as a mark of inferiority. We see this when black men and working-class men are feminised in contrast to middle-class men, as an alternative to equating black/working class with violence. In these cases women, blacks (especially black men) and

working-class men were ranked on the female side of a male/female distinction. But in other cases specific women did not fit the 'female' convention, and black men were moved under the sign 'male' to be 'on side' with white men. Similarly 'black' often stands in for 'class', for example in 'black riots', where 'whites' are also visibly part of the riot, but where 'white' signifies non-working-class or *non-class*.

2   While the elaboration of difference was densely coded to differentiate Australia from the rest of the world, it also operated to indicate and rank relations/differences within Australia. This is obvious in the case of non-Anglo Australians and Aboriginal Australians, but it was also applied to females and to class differences. In these latter cases 'the typical Aussie' included women and workers (Aussie battlers, the Aussie working man), but rarely specific Aboriginals; and both groups were placed outside the norm when they were distinguished from classless Anglo-Australian males. Some examples occur in sitcoms with working-class characters such as *Hey Dad*; in ads pitched to an upmarket audience; in news coverage of wage claims, strikes and western suburbs; in the relation of women to 'important local events'; in the relegation of women to the home; and so forth.

3   The third qualification concerns how age (youth, maturity) and marital status are brought in to play, as variations on these themes. In many cases age accompanied the lower-status term (female, black, working class etc.) to denote immaturity. This was most marked in the persistent coupling of women and children in product ads where women speak baby-talk and where women and children depend on an authoritative male. However, non-Anglo Australians (male and female) are also often depicted as children: for example in the manipulation of language (interviews in English; Anglo clarification of English utterances by non-English speakers etc.); in images and expressions of high emotion and excitement; in 'these simple people' themes in documentaries and current affairs items; and in the contrast between non-Anglos and Anglos in situations involving help and advice. In all these cases, the adult, authoritative voice and position was accorded to an Anglo-Australian male, or else an Anglo, or an Anglo Australian.

But there is a twist here, that turns on media attempts to diversify 'typical Australia' according to perceived population demand (especially internal and external markets—diversification has a monetary export value, as we shall see). Television in the period from 1990 to 1993, portrayed a significantly increased number of images diversifying Australia. In these cases, however, diversification—images of non-Anglo Australians as Australians—is depicted by women and children, but rarely by 'typically Aussie males'. Several children's ads and programs have ethnically diverse casts, whereas the few images of ethnically diverse 'Aussie men' are marked as ethnic—for example, an Italian Australian in an Italian food ad; crims and nightclub owners in soapies (*E Street*) and sitcoms (*Acropolis Now*)—and are placed in a subordinate position to Anglo Australians, male and female.

Marital status adds another twist to this. Endogamy seems to be the rule, especially in differentiating 'typical Australia'. While cross-ethnic flirtations and hints of affairs have featured in some genres (ads; soaps; magazine stories and features), most of these occur among unmarried people. Non-Anglos, especially Afro-Caribbeans and Afro-Americans (but seldom Asians) are portrayed as erotic but not marriageable. Marriage is ethnically homogeneous, especially marriage that entails children (passage of 'blood'). The one exception, *E Street*, was that of a childless couple. Horror stories of cross-ethnic marriages abound, especially those about 'Filipina brides'. Perhaps the most bizarre example of resistance to cross-ethnic marriage occurred during the April 1990 viewing period. Grace Bros, a department store, ran ads for Mothers Day. There were children from many ethnic backgrounds in the TV ads, but in print ads they all had unmistakably Anglo fathers (hence they appear to have been 'adopted'—this avoids any problem with 'blood' pollution). The relationship between the passage of 'blood' and the reproduction of a differentiated nation finds its most pervasive setting in television programming and advertisements during children's viewing times.

22

MAKING CHILDREN: SUGAR AND SPICE AND TV ADVERTISING

Children's television was monitored from September 1991 to July 1992. We did not monitor the small proportion of material that is categorised as 'high quality' by the Australian Broadcasting Tribunal but concentrated on what most kids watch most of the time—what the ABT has called 'the wallpaper' programming. Much of this consists of imported animations, and it is clear that older patterns of representing non-Anglo racial and cultural groups have changed. The use of 'foreignness' or blackness to mark out the 'baddies' has diminished although it has not entirely gone; the alternative strategy, of presenting only a racially homogenous Anglo-American world of people or anthropomorphic creatures, also seems to be less common. The new trend is to include racial and cultural diversity among the 'goodies' and even, occasionally, the 'baddies'. Advertisements also reflect this trend to include both actors and animated characters who are not of northern European descent. These inclusions, however, while attractive and interesting, are made within a very narrow range of patterns. This section explores the power relations suggested by the new trend in advertisements shown in children's viewing time in Sydney during 1991 and 1992.

The impact of American models for advertisement production, even before regulations relaxed in 1992 to allow more overseas produced material, is noticeable in the relative frequency with which non-white children appear in advertisements in children's viewing time, and particularly in ads for girls' toys. This raises important questions concerning gender analysis as it is entangled with particular ideals of beauty for little girls.

The ads shown throughout children's viewing time include station identification and trailers, music ads including segments of video clips, and ads for charity organisations, food, toys and some fashion and cosmetic products. Each type of ad has its own style, which means that a wide range of messages may be transmitted in a typical break of between six to eleven advertisements, from the asexual sweetness of ads for little girls' toys to the erotic excitement of Salt'n'Peppa singing 'Let's Talk About Sex, Baby!'.

Food ads predominate. Most are made in Australia and blondness is the main attribute of the largely white Australian casts, especially of mothers providing food and little girls receiving it, although the hair colour of fathers and little boys varies more. Few Australian-made ads show non-Caucasian actors, and they are invariably children. A Red Rooster Chicken ad shows a group of dark-haired adults grouped round a laughing Asian child as the voice-over sings: 'Australia. . .your chicken is ready'. The Smarties ad ('How do you make your Smarties last?') features a very attractive Asian girl, who is shown in close-up just as often and who moves just as actively as the other, white and fair, children do. An Uncle Toby's muesli bar ad, with Lisa Curry-Kenny, has included for the first time a dark-complexioned and probably non-white child in the group receiving the confectionery. The McDonald's ads often include an Asian child in a group of children eating at McDonald's.

The non-white children in all except the Red Rooster ad, however, are always a minority and are neither the centre of the ad narrative (e.g. the birthday child is always white and blond) nor of the camera's focus. The only other notable example is the Kraft Singles ad series in which a group of very young toddlers play, while an a capella group with African–American accents sings a version of a child's rhyme about bones ('The knee bone's connected to the thigh bone. . ..'), with a chorus 'Feed Dem Bones'. Along with this disembodied presence of African–American culture, one version features two Asian children in a group of about six children, while another features two dark-complexioned children, one of whom is clearly of African descent. Kraft is an American-based transnational, but the ad was made in Australia by J. Walter Thompson, an advertising company which has the rights to market Kraft worldwide. It was considering the world market when this ad was made, with New Zealand as its first overseas target. It is interesting, although hardly surprising, that it included African–Americans and east Asians (probably Japanese) as these are the groups most often included in American advertising. Why does this Australian-made advertisement strive for an attractive image of racial diversity yet so noticeably exclude Aboriginal, Maori or other more specifically Pacific people?

There have also been reductions in diversity. The dark-complexioned (Aboriginal?) child has disappeared from the Quik ad for milk flavouring, and the end of the Bicentennial period's obsession with food ads featuring groups of people referred to as 'Australia' in the accompanying jingles, has also meant the disappearance of some other token Aboriginal presences. The most frequent representation in food, toy and game ads still made in Australia is of what one marketing professional referred to as 'the typical suburban family, the English type' (Jan Ellis, *Milton Bradley*, interview 27 May 1992).

The high proportion of children's toys marketed from America means that many of the ads for those products are also made in the USA. Prior to the deregulation of foreign content in advertising, overseas influences were still very strong; Australian producers often simply recast Australian actors and repeated the American or English original. The 1991 Barbie Video Star ad, discussed below, is a good example. Although it uses Australian actors, it follows exactly the same formulae as the 1992 Barbie ads that retain the American actors. The relatively frequent presence of non-caucasian actors in children's toy ads is probably due to the dominance of American and English models or ads, which reflect the changes in those overseas marketing strategies.

The increasing presence of non-caucasians, and particularly African–Americans, is most noticeable in ads for girls' toys, apparently because boys' toys are often battery-operated, mechanical or non-human in form, and can be shown without human actors at all, except for the occasional white hand to show the toy's scale. Where the toys are humanoid, such as the GI Joe dolls, African–American characters are represented, and the dolls show the same patterns of organisation and focus as discussed below in relation to girls' dolls, but the boys shown in the ads are still only white. Girls' toys are more often 'nurturing' toys, dolls or soft animals, which require the girl viewer to imagine herself holding them, so they demand human representations. The gender focus in the representation of racial difference therefore adds other dimensions to this discussion.

Many of the ads for girls' toys now show non-caucasian, and particularly African–American actors and dolls, in beautiful images of attractive, healthy children of mixed races playing together, all within the usual fantasy context of middle-class affluence. These are undoubtedly positive images generally speaking, and emphasise the tardiness of Australian advertisement producers to include non-caucasians in their products in this way. They do, however, relate better to (some) American populations than to Australian populations. Why have Australian producers not included Aboriginal, Asian and Pacific children in the same prominent and positive style?

There are more serious questions about the way interactions between children of different races are portrayed in these advertisements. Persistent patterns in the way each group is represented imply certain power relations and inequality of access to resources. The patterns amount to a preference for blondness over darker complexions, which operates within the representations of white children as well as between racial groups and indicates what ideals of beauty are involved in our culture's gender constructions. An interesting example of this occurs in doll advertisements that focus on sexuality, beauty and race. Three elements can be identified here:

1 There is an overwhelming dominance of blondness in these ads for little girls' toys, to a far greater extent than in ads for either boys' toys or food. This extends to a preference for blonde white girls over darker-haired girls which is extremely pronounced in the ads for Mattel products, in particular the Magic Nursery Baby and the Barbie Hawaiian Fun and Video Star dolls advertised in November 1991. In the first, the child who is the centre of the ad's script about acquiring the doll, and who is

always shown alone or in the centre of the three girl actors, is the child with the longest, curliest and blondest hair. The other fair-haired girl is given attention with giggles and smiles by the child in the centre; the third child, who is white but has black hair, receives none of the blonde girl's confidences or glances.

The Hawaiian Fun Barbie exhibits the same dominance of the blonde actor in an ad showing only two girls looking at a blonde doll. The darker-haired white girl is kept behind the fair girl, who gets to hold the doll, leaving the dark-haired child to exclaim excitedly in the background. The Video Star Barbie also has two girls acting in it, one with long wavy fair hair and the other with black hair and an olive complexion. The blonde girl is kept in the centre of the frame, and slightly in front of the other girl in each shot. When the camera moves, the dark-haired girl moves out of the right edge of the frame, while a burst of light from an earring shines on the fair girl's face. When a child's hand is shown removing the doll's light-up clip to put in her hair, it belongs to the blonde child who is then shown wearing this badge of proprietorial status.

2 Where non-caucasian dolls are shown, the visual arrangement of the dolls usually favours the blonder dolls; this is particularly noticeable with the 'original' blonde Barbie. The Video Star Barbie ad has three dolls in it, and in each presentation, the blonde doll takes the centre of the frame or the other two dark dolls' attention. The only child to handle a doll is the blonde actor touching the blonde Barbie doll, so each is seen as more active and in a proprietorial relationship.

3 Where non-caucasian actors and dolls are shown, there are obvious patterns and few exceptions. These patterns appear in ads for dolls not only in the Mattel advertisements (Barbie Sun Sensation June 1992), but in those for products made by Hasbro, and distributed in Australia by Kenner Parker (Tropical Treat Cup Cake, May 1992) and Milton Bradley (Puppy Surprise, March 1992).

The advertisement bracket in children's viewing time presents a complex and often contradictory body of images of non-caucasians: erotic and sexually related to each other in music, particularly if African–American or African–English; sexually (but wholesomely) related to whites in some food/cosmetic ads, particularly if African–Carribean; female and middle class if an African–American child interested in toys, but only if the child is the friend of the white girls who really own the toys because they are the only ones allowed to handle them; desperately ill and dependent on charity if African in Africa; but able to share some good kids' junk food if the child is middle-class Japanese or, just occasionally, Aboriginal.

Nor is a simple, unified 'message' transmitted by either the ad or the program it slots into. There are some conflicting trends as well as different issues raised in each. In children's animations, for example, where increasing racial and cultural exclusiveness is also apparent, there is no sexuality, no romantic interest between 'races' or 'ethnicities' at all; whereas in fashion/cosmetic ads and video clips there is deliberate and often light-hearted erotic suggestion in black/white contacts.

Although non-caucasian groups now appear regularly in ads shown in children's viewing time, there is a severe limit on which groups to show! In Australian-produced ads, there are almost no Aborigines visible at all, except in sport promos. This parallels the American-produced ads' exclusion of American Indians or Hispanic actors. Although Australian material shows children and adults with black or brown hair there is almost no-one who looks like a southern European or Arabic Australian unless they are being parodied in some food ads. The Asians in local and American-produced ads are usually east Asian, with few south or south-east Asians at all except in some airline and travel ads, where they are depicted as beautiful and exotic but always as flight attendants or tourist attractions.

The increasing occurrence of beautiful and engaging images of racial diversity in children's advertising is an improvement on the homogeneity of past representations. This development has occurred largely because of the increased amount of American advertising material being screened in Australia; the material reflects changing marketing strategies in the USA which in turn have arisen from African–Americans' intense political lobbying as well as the rise of a black middle class with greater purchasing power. This positive result is offset, however, by the severely restricted roles given to non-caucasian figures in all these advertisements. We are importing a representation of unequal power relations as well as a beautiful (if selective) image of racial diversity.

The range of images is severely limited to a small handful of simple stereotypes that have long been embedded in European ideology: African rhythm and sexuality, Carribean/African sensuality and carefree leisure; blacks as passive, ill and dependent; blacks acceptable in relations with whites only when subordinate and marginalised.

23

ALL TOGETHER NOW: THE NEW RACIAL AND CULTURAL INCLUSIVITY IN CHILDREN'S ANIMATIONS

Children's TV is the most worried over, most controlled, and most frequently exhorted to be 'responsible' in its self-regulation. The desire to regulate arises from the powerful although contradictory conceptions many of us hold of children, as either innocents in need of protection, or as untamed creatures in need of discipline to protect their own and others' futures. Much of the debate has been about how violence is depicted in children's TV and its effect on child viewers, but many commentators are also concerned with common biases concerning gender and racism.

Yet very few studies investigate racial or cultural difference and power relations in children's TV. When we began to observe programming for primary children shown in Sydney in 1991 and 1992, it became clear that race and ethnicity are widely referred to in animations where the central characters are human, animal or fantasy characters. We also found a significant number of recent attempts to include non-white and non-English groups in children's animated programs. We explore here the terms on which these inclusions have been made, and suggest that while they challenge established representations, many of these more recent animations depict a very narrow range of power relations, and power remains with the white, Anglo characters or their anthropomorphic animal equivalents.

With the disbanding of the Children's Programming Committee of the former ABT, most programming for children's viewing time is still completely unregulated on commercial stations and the ABC. The programming occupying most of that time is what the former ABT called 'wallpaper' material: a diverse collection of material with only a few claims to be 'high quality', much of it animated, some very old, and most of it imported. Each program is often inserted in a longer programming segment, which is introduced and compered by local hosts and given some local content. On commercial stations such material usually runs for 1 or 2 hours in both the morning and afternoon, punctuated by brackets of advertisements. These programs are therefore seldom broadcast 'whole', but are contextualised, 'nationalised' and intersected.

This has been discussed by Michaels and others as the 'transmitted text', a text which may differ significantly from the original 'whole' text of the individual program. How this is understood by the viewer is a different matter again, and greatly depends on the viewer's knowledge and expectations (i.e. culture). This can be called the 'perceived text' and may differ from one viewer to another. When people discuss their ideas about the programs they have viewed, they may reach another, consensual interpretation, which Michaels (1990) has called the 'social text'.

Our discussion of how racial and cultural differences are portrayed in children's material will concentrate on this 'wallpaper' material, to gauge the range of its representations and to examine the 'transmitted text'.

Most examples come from Channels 2, 7 and 10, from weekday morning and afternoon shows and weekend morning programs from October 1991 to May 1992. SBS has been excluded as its often fascinating programs are not accessible to many of the primary school age-group whose reading skills are too limited to cope with subtitling. Channel 9, reportedly a major player in the challenge to the ABT Children's Programming Committee, offers very little television for the primary school audience.

Animations are created from the experiences as well as the imaginations of their adult authors, and draw directly on cultural models for character and plot material. As well, animations are based on comic stereotypes, that is, on two-dimensional, easily recognisable caricatures on which simple, rapid comic or action scenarios are built. These two sources—author experience and established caricature—make it likely that many old and well-known stereotypes will appear in cartoons. Indeed, there has been a history of cruel comic representations of African–Americans in cartoons for early film shows.

On the other hand, in animation, anything is possible: heroes can be green or black or purple, depicted in realistic styles or as bizarre imaginary creatures, so while animations may simply reproduce the same range of characters and relationships as in acted programs, they can break away altogether from accepted models and present new, challenging heroes, villains, and relationships.

MEANING, TEXTS AND FANTASY

While this is a review of the content of transmitted texts, rather than an audience survey, any exploration of the meanings of animation and fantasy created for children must keep in mind how children might interpret what they read or see. Any transmitted text can have multiple and contradictory readings for different viewers, and some interpretations may run contrary to the intentions of the producers. The ambivalent relationship which fantasy and particularly animation have with 'reality' further complicates any attempt to discuss 'content' in children's programming.

Children's programs shown in Sydney in the 1990s offer glimpses of the history of children's television. The earliest 1960s episodes of Hanna Barbera's

Flintstones are followed the next week by episodes from a later series, in which some of the more blatant male-focus of the early series is reduced by an emphasis on Fred's adolescent daughter, Pebbles. There are rare occasions when the earliest Mickey Mouse mixes it with his own later manifestations, and Walt's old themes can be seen in the new, expanded range of Disney cartoons such as *Ducktales* and *Tailspin*. The 1960s satires on superheroes and the Cold War, *Rocky and Bullwinkle* and *Roger Ramjet*, still line up today in the 4–6 p.m. children's timeslot but now they jostle for space with the 1990s eco-cartoons, from the earnest superhero *Captain Planet* (who appears along with Gaia), to his tongue-in-cheek rivals, the *Toxic Crusaders*.

While many old animations are shown, fewer of the old acted children's adventure series are still around, particularly those staples of early TV, the 'cowboys and Indians' genre. *Hopalong Cassidy*, *Wells Fargo* and *The Lone Ranger* were just a few of the diverse shows in which 'badness' was frequently marked out by ethnicity, where 'villains' were always 'Indian' or 'Mexican'. The large quantity of these early programs, however, ensured some variations on the theme of the ethnic baddie: there were 'good' as well as 'bad' Indians, or the villains were white men running guns or liquor to the Indians or exploiting them in some way (which sometimes defined the Indians as weak, vulnerable or stupid). Nevertheless, viewers were often invited to sympathise with the Indians, so even the most stereotyped stories did not always identify 'goodness' with caucasian characters. Sometimes, too, the presence and power of the 'attacking' Indians offered viewers an attractive alternative to the 'good' white authority figures.

Many of these variations dwindled with the onset of the civil rights movements of the 1950s and 1960s. These and other political and sociological concerns about racism and ethnic discrimination appeared to affect the contents of children's material. For example, references to races other than caucasians were avoided—this was obvious in the early Hanna Barbera cartoons which were still being rerun as a major component of children's television in Sydney in 1991 and 1992. These included the *Flintstones* (totally devoid of the satire and biting class humour of its acted model, the *Honeymooners*), and the *Jetsons*, recently updated as a feature-length animated film. These series each avoided the major race questions of the 1960s in America by representing the working class (of the *Flintstones'* stone age quarry) and the whole of the future (in the *Jetsons*) as totally white. No variations of skin colour, voice accent or culture are allowed in these monolithically Anglo-American societies. While this strategy is present in some recent animations, and of course still evident in the reruns, it is no longer common in animations.

Some cartoon-makers have not felt any need to review the practice of defining characters by ethnicity. The Disney cartoons are an example. The earliest Disney characters were animals, such as Donald Duck or Mickey Mouse, who are shown doing very middle-class American things, such as moose hunting or big game fishing. Mickey Mouse neither refers to his own black colour nor celebrates it, unlike Daffy Duck, the *Looney Toons* character, whose cry of 'Not this little black duck!' was ironically taken up by at least some young Aboriginal viewers in the 1950s. Disney frequently cast human characters as 'baddies' or as socially or politically subordinate to the main characters and commonly used race or ethnicity to identify them. Donald Duck and Mickey Mouse were pursued by bad Indians, Russians or Mexicans, and in some very early examples, by cannibalistic Africans.

These practices have continued to the present. There are two forms: the human peripheral character and the main animal character who has been given racial or ethnic attributes. A viewer of *Saturday Disney* or any of the other Disney cartoons featured in much of the Channel 7 programming for children in Sydney during 1991 and 1992 will find that these attributes are still stereotyping traits and relations with the main 'white American' animal figures. A typical example of the peripheral human character occurs in the recent *Duck Tales* series, which continues the old acquisitive characters of Uncle Scrooge and the three Duck nephews. In an episode shown on Channel 7 on 7 March 1992, the ducks journeyed to South America looking for archaeological treasure; the subplot involved outwitting an Hispanic tour bus driver who was depicted visually and verbally as stupid and exploitative.

The newer Disney series, such as *Tailspin* and *Chip'n'Dale: The Rescue Rangers*, have no human characters at all, only anthropomorphic animals. In these, ethnic markers unmistakably delineate both 'good' and 'bad' characters. In *Tailspin* (e.g. Channel 7's episode shown on 11 April 1992) the main heroes have Anglo-American voices and middle-class clothes. Their friends include a monkey with an Afro-Caribbean accent, who wears a tropical shirt and lives on an apparently Caribbean island. Some of the villains have Anglo-American voices but many are 'foreign', such as a warthog who has an unmistakably Russian accent, wears a uniform and has an authoritarian style in which he lies to little animals. His homeland is snowbound and ringed with barbed wire; the main building looks rather like the Kremlin. It is not at all hard to work out what ethnicities are ascribed to the characters in this example, although it is not clear whether the intention was anti-Russian or anti-communist in the warthog instance, nor is it clear how a child would interpret the characterisations. What is clear is that the creators of the cartoon continue to draw on a very limited range of caricatures for character and plot material. In the *Chip'n'Dale* episode on the same date Chinese characters were caricatured either as naive, or evil and cunning, or both!

A notable Australian example of this persistent use of negative ethnic stereotypes in cartoons to indicate 'baddies' or socially subordinate characters is the *Dot* series, animated films shown on television regularly, and available on video. The original, award-winning film, *Dot and the Kangaroo*, portrayed Aboriginal men in a traditional stereotype, as physically fine and healthy but extremely menacing and dangerous. They are shown engaged in a ceremony depicting a kangaroo hunt, after which they and their dingos pursue Dot and her female kangaroo protector, only to be scared away by a trick that plays on the Aboriginals' fears of the bunyip. The portrayal of the 'baddies' in *Dot and the Whale* is just as disturbing: as Dot tries to save a beached whale, the villains try to have the whale cut up to be sold. These villains are 'mediterranean' and 'oriental' caricatures whose voices are accented to ensure recognition. These men, like many post-war migrants, are fish-shop owners. They are depicted as mercenary, stupid and cruel, in an extremely vicious, negative stereotype of southern European and Asian migrants.

A popular strategy to avoid delineating the ethnicity or race of 'baddies' and heroes has been to turn them into space monsters, robots or fantasy figures to whom a racial or ethnic label was irrelevant. Initially, the goodies remained white, as in *The Transformers* and the *Vultron* animations, as if their audiences (assumed white) needed this identity marker. So for a long period 'cleaning up' potentially derogatory stereotype 'baddies' left a homogeneous cast of identifiably human 'goodies', all white and usually male.

The presentation of racial and ethnic caricatures as 'baddies' was revived by the hugely successful *Teenage Mutant Ninja Turtles*. This American cartoon was an early example of the industry's acknowledgement of the dangers of chemical and radioactive contamination, and might be compared with 'eco-cartoons' such as the French *Smoggies*, and the American *Toxic Crusaders* and *Captain Planet and the Planeteers*.

Some might argue that the *Turtles* are an example of 'non- racist' practice because the heroes are non-human and green. Yet the ethnicity (and indeed race) of all the characters is only thinly disguised: the scripts, the Turtles' voices and accents, and the material culture surrounding them inside their sewer, identifies them unequivocally as adolescent, west coast, white Americans. (Their addiction to pizzas simply suggests the limits of the multiculturalism-equals-different-food position.) The Turtles' mentor in the cartoon version of the original comic is Splinter, the Japanese Ninja who has been mutated into a talking rat. This 'good' Japanese is essentially the 'wise oriental' stereotype; the other 'good' characters are all drawn as caucasian.

On the other hand, all the 'badness' in this series emanates from the Japanese villain Shredder and the evil Foot Clan, whose members look like faceless machines but are known to be human Japanese Ninjas. A monster from outer space (a disembodied brain looking for a human form) provides the Shredder with super hi-tech equipment but all the malice stems from the human Japanese villains. Even the historical glimpse of the Foot Clan when Splinter was a devoted member (the Clan presumably is the source of his education and 'wisdom'), is parodied and its honoured leader shown as ignorant, foul-mouthed and easily misled by the wicked Shredder. Two working-class Americans (one caucasian, one Afro-American) become dupes of the Japanese Shredder; for their stupidity they are mutated to fighting versions of wild animals, and other villains take either monster or mechanical forms. The persistent theme of the series, however, is that Japanese culture has generated this relentless evil threatening to overtake America, and from which only the Turtles can save the nation. Is this a descendant of the cowboys and Indians plot? If so, how often might alternative interpetations be made? Do any children side with the Foot Clan?

The depiction of ethnicity and race is a complex matter of constructing characters by visual, sound and plot components, with references (at times satirical) to stereotypes and caricatures. Obscuring one or two elements, such as skin colour and physiognomy, may still leave the overall racial or ethnic reference of the character intact, so long as their voice, surroundings and the plot continue to stereotype them.

Most recently, and of more interest as it will undoubtedly continue as a trend in children's animation, goodies have been given racial or ethnic diversity and in some cases baddies have as well. These attempts to include diversity are important because the creators of racially or ethnically defined characters must also create relationships for these characters, thereby revealing their own assumptions about power. How children then intepret these narratives is another question. It is interesting, however, to review the content of some recent animations in these terms, particularly as some have very self-consciously incorporated racial and ethnic issues. One example is the Hanna Barbera cartoons—here we look at *The Smurfs*.

The Smurfs form a significant proportion of the programming for children on Channel 7's *Agro's Breakfast Show*. Ethnicity in the earliest series of this 1970s cartoon was relatively uniform: the main characters were little blue elves or gnomes, who lived in pre-industrial Europe and whose main enemies were non-humanoid animals and an apparently caucasian and human-sized wizard. In the later series, however, the Smurfs travel through time and space, which ensures many opportunities to portray 'human' difference and power relations.

There is a strong presence of Africans among the humans visited in this way by the elves, and the representations of traditional African agrarian lifestyles are consistently positive. There are occasional African 'baddies', such as tricksters who are reformed by the Smurfs, but these are far outnumbered by delightful African children of both sexes and all ages, and by wise and interesting African adults, storytellers and artists. These Africans all have names like Aeyisha, names used frequently by African–Americans today in celebration of their African heritage. Yet in all this time-travel there are no visits to any contemporary African or African American communities, so the affirmative and respectful images of Africans remain remote in time and space for American audiences.

Other people are not so lucky! In March 1992 in an episode of *The*

Smurfs the elves travelled to a Pacific island, where the depiction of traditional life was riddled with some of the oldest and most vicious caricatures of Polynesian societies. The dominant person in the village is shown as an enormously fat woman, who enslaves her own people and the Smurfs in the service of a carved stone idol of a cruel god who demands human/Smurf sacrifices. *The Smurfs'* respectful treatment of oral tradition in African life has reverted here to the old western caricatures and contempt for 'heathens' and 'superstitions' in its treatment of Polynesian subjects. It seems that *The Smurfs* reflects the positive impact of America's new marketing focus on Afro-Americans, at least in regard to treatments of traditional Africa, but persists with negative caricatures of other non-caucasian races and non-western cultures.

Arising from an idea by Ted Turner, *Captain Planet and the Planeteers* is a high-powered attempt to apply all the things that make successful cartoons (e.g. crusading hero and lots of hi-tech action) to an ideologically sound approach to increasing environmental awareness. The cast includes the voices of many famous and politically active performers like Sting and Whoopie Goldberg. In general, it is successful: engaging, exciting, it gives child audiences at least as much optimism often as fear and depression about enormous issues like overpopulation. There are some doubts about its finer political points; for example, the fact that its solutions arise from magical powers rather than the Planeteers' own resources might discourage children from taking political action; and it equates nuclear warfare's destructiveness with that of 'vandals' who 'deface property'. Nevertheless, the animation tries very hard to represent non-Anglo races and cultures, as well as women in general, in roles which are at least as active and intelligent as those for western males.

The main plot has the earth approaching environmental crisis, and Gaia (Whoopie Goldberg) selecting 'five special young people' to save the planet: three teenage boys from the USA, Africa and the Amazon, and two young women, from the USSR and Asia. Gaia equips them each with power over one element of nature, such as fire or wind. When these 'Planeteers' combine their powers they can call up Captain Planet, 'earth's greatest hero', who looks like a green but very spunky Superman! The 'good' characters are carefully balanced by race and gender, and possess far more diverse ethnic/cultural characteristics than are usually present in animations. For example, their voices are accented appropriately at least to the continent of their origin instead of with the ubiquitous north American Anglo cartoon accents.

The 'baddies' are more uniformly Anglo-American (including Sting), including a white American woman and some mutant characters with Anglo-American accents. In an interesting and probably unintentional association, a humanoid–rodent 'baddie' is depicted in a hooded shawl which strongly resembles an Arabic man's headwear. This small piece of carelessness highlights the general absence of any Arabic (or Muslim) presence among the

Planeteers, suggesting perhaps the limits of the producers' ideological correctness.

All the characters get a scrupulously fair cut of the action: in every episode each character uses his or her individual power before they join forces to call up Captain Planet. The character development is not so evenly shared by gender. Each male character not only gets a go at the heroics but also has a crisis of confidence, but the female characters are less fully rounded, although Linka, the USSR character, has lots of power and vigorous conflict with Wheeler.

The stories generally deal with urban and western problems, although these are not limited to the USA. They include nuclear power (the scientists are white); overpopulation (rats in a western urban setting); and littering (Kwame confronts white western urban citizens). There is some exploration of third world situations too, as in the episode about a cure for a new plague; the only cure is found in a South American rainforest plant, threatened of course by the burning of the Amazonian forest. In this episode the local Spanish-descent 'mestizo' cattle farmers destroy the forest for quick profit, in conflict with the indigenous forest people (like Mati). This is an interesting depiction of conflict between non-caucasian groups, but even this episode falls back on the old pattern—the local non-white elite were misled by the real villains, the profiteers who are all either white or non-human or mutants.

Despite its modern complexities *Captain Planet* contains subtle racial and ethnic caricaturing and establishes a hierarchy of power and dramatic interest for its characters, as follows:

1   The dominant 'good' mythic/hero figures, Captain Planet and Gaia, are overwhelmingly American, even if Gaia is played by an African-American. It might be considered important to target American children as their country is a major energy user and polluter, but the Americanness of the heroes also presumably reinforces any viewer's concept of international American dominance. Furthermore, since the physiognomy of both is caucasian, even if one is green and the other brown, so the major hero is most closely identified with white Americans, and Gaia, though she has an African–American accent, is an exotic character who has no distinct cultural trait other than her voice. Despite attempts to avoid the established representations of power relations, the series continues to associate the greatest power with white Americans; it allows an African–American woman a disembodied presence at the top, but does not include an African–American man, nor any readily identifiable person from a *contemporary* African–American community.

2   Ethnic and/or racial stereotyping persists in the Planeteers' 'powers' and character development, which provides several sub-plots. The American Planeteer, Wheeler, has the power of fire; its qualities of unrestrained

dynamism have long been appropriated by 'Aryan' and northern European societies. The other caucasian character, Linka, from the old Soviet Union, is given the power of wind and the attributes of cool logic and rationality, the obverse side of old northern European self-representations. Although Linka is given a strong role (especially as she is often in direct conflict with the American Wheeler), the other female Planeteer, the 'Asian' Gi, with the power of water, is the least developed personality, which suggests that the producers find it hard to come to grips with the complexity of Asia and America's ambiguous relationship with it.

The main personal tension in the series arises between the impulsive, insensitive Wheeler and the others. Linka frequently expresses irritation but most of the moral weight is given to the responses of Mati (the indigenous Amazonian who has the power of heart), Kwame (the African with the power of earth) and Gi (from an unidentified part of Asia, with the power of water). Wheeler's crassness is often met with shouts of 'sit down Yankee!'. Yet all this maintains the dramatic focus on Wheeler/USA, who has to be constantly re-educated and perhaps this keeps viewers' attention on the white, western Americans.

ROMANCING THE TRADITIONAL

Two Planeteers are depicted as pre-industrial: Mati, the indigenous Amazonian with the power of heart (emotional sensitivity) and Kwame, the traditional African farmer with the power of earth (which means being able to conjure up huge mounds of earth and rock as obstacles to baddies). These two non-western male characters are the most romanticised/mysticised. Kwame tends to make 'wise', philosophical sayings while Mati has all the emotional sensitivity, moral goodness and unifying power. The presence of Africans and African–Americans is powerful, in Kwame and in Gaia's voice, but no African–Americans are represented visually or culturally. It seems easier to celebrate a 'traditional' culture now distant in time and place than to acknowledge a powerful contemporary sub-culture which is seen by some white Americans as threateningly close.

Several conclusions can be drawn from this analysis:

- A few animations persist with negative caricatures of non-western human characters, and/or use derogatory racial or ethnic caricatures to delineate anthropomorphic animal characters.
- Cartoons still give non-human or unnaturally coloured hero figures racially and ethnically specific characterisations, as *Teenage Mutant Ninja Turtles* and *Toxic Crusaders* do. The depiction of ethnicity and race is a complex matter of constructing characters with visual, audio and plot

components, and integrating established (if at times satirical) stereo-types/caricatures. Obscuring one or two elements, such as skin colour and physiognomy, does not disguise a racial or ethnic identity or type if voice, surroundings and plot place a character in a particular stereotype.

- In many cartoons, whether or not race or ethnicity is specified, there is a hierarchy of colour, with lightness/whiteness associated with the most 'goodness' and power, amongst both 'goodies' and 'baddies'.

- There are now several animations that present non-Anglo, non-western human characters in permanent and prominent roles; some of these are only subordinate to the main hero and villain, locked into permanent dependence on the more powerful caucasian characters. Others alter the appearance of the main characters, but give them white American accents, scripts and material culture. Only a very few allow real alternatives to the narrow limits of older characterisations, and even the better ones, like *Captain Planet*, maintain the white American character, voice style and cultural attributes in high profile. Some of the most prominent non-caucasians in this series are of African descent, but even here the current cultural and social characteristics of African–Americans are omit-ted. There is romanticised traditional Africa, but where is south central LA?

- In the growing ethnic and racial diversity evident in contemporary cartoons, there is a markedly more positive representation of African–American characters than there has been in the past. This is the most prominent non-caucasian group shown and most representations are sympathetic or try to be, although they are still drawn from a fairly narrow range, and power invariably resides with the caucasian characters.

- Non-African descent groups are far less positively represented in contem-porary animations. Polynesians, Jews and particularly Asians (the Japanese in *Ninja Turtles*) are still given negative representations. However, since the Japanese in *Ninja Turtles* hold great power, the power relations of this cartoon are left open to the interpretations of its young viewers.

We have now examined how differentiation works for specific audiences, in this case children. Yet the work of constructing the Other and presenting him/her is heavily influenced by stereotypes for audiences other than children, and in circumstances that claim to represent reality. We now examine a format and an audience remote from breakfast television cartoons and children: the only national news daily, *The Australian*.

24

MAKING *THE AUSTRALIAN*

The editorial stance of *The Australian* newspaper has prompted us to explore our contention that the mainstream press can maintain a negative influence on the issue of racism so that non-Anglo groups and their interests are subordinated. Smitherman-Donaldson and Van Dijk explain that 'the discursive reproduction of racism is the enactment or legitimation of white majority power at the micro levels of everyday verbal interaction and communication'. (1988:17)

The Australian is the flagship of News Ltd, the Rupert Murdoch group of media companies in Australia. Its generally conservative political position, its strong identification with free market economic policies and its primary market among the technocratic and business elites (e.g. through its regular sections on computers and higher education) suggest that it reflects the values and attitudes of that social stratum. In terms of social values *The Australian* reflects the interests and orientation of the New Right more precisely than its major (regional) competitors, the Melbourne *Age* and the *Sydney Morning Herald*, do.

The Australian has concerned itself with government policies on multiculturalism and racism for many years, and its position has remained almost unchanged over recent years. It has made its opinion pages available to critics of multiculturalism such as former Melbourne University psychology academic Dr Frank Knopfelmacher, its own foreign affairs commentator Greg Sheridan, and its regular economic and social affairs commentator P. P. McGuiness. It offers the views of Phillip Adams as a proponent of multiculturalism in the name of balance.

The Australian's editorial position on the Human Rights and Equal Opportunity Commission's Inquiry into Racist Violence, commenced in 1989 and completed in 1991, indicates a firm commitment to a position that denied structural racism existed in Australia. In an editorial on the first hearings of the Inquiry (28 August 1989) it advises the Inquiry Commissioner Irene Moss not to find that racist violence was 'the tip of an iceberg of racism [for if it did so, it] may be dismissed as just another manifestation of the grievance industry'. It continued: 'Australia has been virtually free of institutionalised racism. . .Australians are not perfect; neither are we to any significant degree, racist'. According to this editorial, the conclusion to be drawn from these last two decades is that 'questions of race need to be handled with sensitivity to the feelings of the dominant race [sic], no less than those of racial minorities'.

The Australian expresses a most important perspective here: 'racial minorities' need not imply a power relationship nor any particular legitimacy or illegitimacy—the term could simply refer to relative numbers. 'Dominant race' with all its overtones is not, however, simply a numerical term—it refers to power and legitimacy; domination implies higher status, greater rights, wider claims. What indeed is this dominant race to which *The Australian* refers? Is this race aware of its common racial feelings?

The statements that minimise the issue of racism, though offered in an unselfconscious and matter-of-fact manner, expose an agenda in which the hierarchy is unquestioned and unquestionable, and in which minorities should keep quiet and toe the line. Since the concept of race hardly qualifies as a scientific descriptor of social behaviour, whose values are laying claim to speak for the whole 'race'?

We are reminded here of the writing of Herbert Spencer, a mid-19th century social Darwinist, one of the forebears of scientific racism, who coined the phrase 'survival of the fittest' and whose theories of social evolution were based on a perception of social development from the homogeneous to heterogeneous. Homogeneous societies were savage and barbaric, and those that survived did so by evolving into more complex and 'market' oriented systems of interdependencies (Bock 1978:65; Peel 1985: 814–15).

The release of the report of the National Inquiry into Racist Violence prompted *The Australian* editorialists to continue their discourse on race. Under the heading 'Hysteria Will Not Rid Us of Racism' (22 April 1991) the editorial attacked the report as hysterical reportage and exaggeration. Responding to the editorial, this time under a heading 'Facing up to racist cancer', two letter-writers condemned the editorial and asserted the reality and extent of racist violence. One writer claimed sustained harassment by 'xenophobic males' and the other wrote: 'no doubt. . .the majority of sub-missions were both accurate and honest attempts to assist the Government to assess and redress the problem of racist violence in this country' (1 May 1991).

We would conclude from this that a strong belief exists in the heartland of the media, as expressed in *The Australian*, that the social and economic system is fair and reasonable, that sustained action is neither prudent nor necessary to address any inequalities others claim to exist, and that minorities have no role to play in setting the social agenda.

The media do consistently develop ideas, images and themes about particular ethnic minorities and racial groups. Their departures from the assumptions of Anglo-Australian norms are demonstrated in a range of genres. We now review the process of creating the Italians for Australian media audiences in dramatic television representation.

25

MAKING ITALIANS IN AUSTRALIAN TELEVISION DRAMA

As the largest non-Anglo-Saxon immigrant group in Australia, Italians have had an indelible influence on local language, social customs and food, but their dramatic representation in Australian theatre, cinema and television has never reflected this influence. One of the few drama series on commercial television that deals with Italian immigrants in a historical perspective, *Fields of Fire* (1988–90), shows how Italians are mainly portrayed as volatile and often corrupt background figures in a story about a young British immigrant. *Fields of Fire*'s dramatic parameters were established by its Anglo-Australian producers' concern with providing entertainment for a predominantly Anglo-Australian audience.

Apart from SBS, Italo-Australian writers, directors and film-makers have had little opportunity to produce their own stories, despite the considerable talents of film-makers like Franco di Chiera, Monica Pellizzari and Luigi D'Aquisto (whose 1988 film about Italian migrants in Melbourne, *Hungry Heart*, did not receive even a cinema release). Rosa Colosimo, a Melbourne-based film and television producer who has promoted Italo-Australian films and television series for two decades, describes how Italians are portrayed on Australian television:

> Unfortunately the Italian characters who appear on the small screen are the usual stereotypes, the usual clichés, the natural progeny of racism. The husband is a fruiterer called Luigi or Giuseppe, and is stupid, possessive and suspicious. The wife is fat, dressed in black, with no makeup, and is called Maria or Concetta. The sons have little intelligence but their parents want them to become doctors or lawyers, while the daughters are absolute geniuses who their parents do not understand in their insistence that the woman's place is in the home, preferably in the kitchen. There is no need to go on, you can imagine the rest all too well. (Colosimo 1987:153)

Colosimo's scenario can be recognised in comedy programs such as the ABC's *Home Sweet Home* (1981), which focuses on the internal conflicts of an Italo-Australian family, and Anglo-Australian dramas where Italians, often portrayed by Anglo-Australian actors, appear in 'bit parts'.

It also applies to the historical survey of images of Italians in American film and television contained in Allen L. Woll and Randall M. Miller's book *Ethnic and Racial Issues in American Film and Television*, where the two principal traditional stereotypes of Italian-Americans are identified as Mafiosi-type criminals and working-class comic buffoons. Woll and Miller also claim that Italian women have usually been portrayed either as passive and kitchen-bound, or passionate, overtly eroticised figures. They conclude:

> The Italian has generally appeared as a creature of passion, an emotional being given to excess in love or hatred, whose religion, culture, and condition seemingly explained his exaggerated behaviour. (Woll and Miller 1987: 275)

While Italo-Australian characterisations in television comedy and drama have tended to be 'softer' than American prototypes like the Corleone family in *The Godfather* (I and II), *Rocky* and *Rambo*, they have frequently exhibited similar traits to those Woll and Miller describe. The first important portrayal of an Italian in Australia occurred in *They're a Weird Mob*, which British director Michael Powell directed in 1963 with Italian actor Walter Chiari playing the role of Nino Culotta, the nom-de-plume of author John O'Grady's unashamedly assimilationist novel. Nino was a relatively mild comic figure, an Italian journalist who observed the foibles of Australians, but this mildness concealed a propagandist who concluded that the Australian way of life was the best in the world, and that non-Anglo-Saxon immigrants to this country should forget about their ethnic heritage and become Australians.

The first dramatic portrayal of Italian immigrants to Australia 'from the inside' was Michael Pattinson's film *Moving Out* (1983), which dealt with the generation gap in an Italo-Australian family, a standard scenario for dramatisations of non-Anglo immigrants in Australia. Gino Condello (Vince Colosimo), a 15-year-old Italo-Australian who considers himself a streetwise native of North Fitzroy in Melbourne, is faced with a newly arrived Italian family, and his own family's decision to move to the outer western suburbs of Melbourne. Gino's developing relationship with the recently arrived Maria forces him to come to terms with his own ethnicity and the fact that he is a 'wog' despite his efforts to Anglicise himself, and the film ends with his acceptance of his dual culture. Helen Garner and Jennifer Giles' book developed from Jan Sardi's screenplay of *Moving Out* became a set text in some Australian schools, but it was not screened on television until many years after its cinema release. Rosa Colosimo has expressed reservations about *Moving Out* as an accurate reflection of contemporary Italo-Australians:

> The film was critically acclaimed, but we made it 15 years too late and it has some grave defects. The ending in which Gino returns to his origins is too facile,

and the Australian characters are all unsympathetic or racist, which is not entirely accurate. We are quick to condemn the prejudices of others, but we don't even notice our own. (Colosimo 1987:154)

Waterfront, a 6-hour television drama series about the Melbourne water-side workers' strike in the late 1920s, was screened on Channel 10 in 1984 and was the next important attempt to dramatise Italians in Australia. The protagonists of *Waterfront* are mostly Anglo-Australian: the main character, the unionist Maxey, was played by Jack Thompson, and Warren Mitchell, Noni Hazlhurst, Ray Barrett and Chris Hayward all had major roles, along with Greta Scacchi as Maxey's Italian 'love interest', Anna. But it included a major subplot about Italian migrants who were used as strikebreakers, and began with the migration to Australia of Professor Chieri, an anti-fascist militant from Turin, and his family—upper middle-class Italians who have difficulties adapting to the 'classlessness' of Australian society. *Waterfront* was written by Mac Gudgeon, directed by Chris Thompson and produced by Bob Weis, who hired Rosa Colosimo as an adviser for the sections dealing with the Italian characters in order 'not to repeat the errors of others'. As a result, as Colosimo recounts:

> At last, in 1984, Italians were portrayed not just dressed in black, but as intellectuals, political activists, fair-haired and thin, Italians who played the piano and had fun. The Australian hero fell in love with the Italian heroine. It was a very complex and convincing work . . . Italian dialogue was heard for what I believe was the first time in the history of Australian commercial television. (1987:154)

Channel 10 wanted to eliminate all the Italian dialogue from *Waterfront*, but Bob Weis refused to allow this and leaked Channel 10's decision to the press, with the result that only a few cuts were made, and English subtitles were used for the Italian scenes for what was probably the first (and last) time on Australian commercial television. Like *Moving Out*, the screenplay for *Waterfront* was subsequently published as a novel, compiled by Sue McKinnon. Like its predecessor it presented a sympathetic, but Anglocentric view of the Italian characters 'from the outside'. One particularly contentious scene in *Waterfront* portrays a confrontation between striking Australian waterside workers and Italian and Greek 'scab' labourers, which McKinnon, describing the sequence of events in the television film, is at pains to present sympathetically. This dramatisation, despite its good intentions, nonetheless depicts the Italian workers as ignorant, disorientated, and even of fascist persuasion, while its attempt to show Anglo-Australian good intentions giving way to mild racist abuse is clumsy. Although it sincerely attempts to portray the experiences of some educated Italian migrants in Australia, *Waterfront* ultimately confirms Rosa Colosimo's claim:

> I believe that we Italo-Australians should relate our own experiences and lives, and not leave the job of representing us to others, whether they're Italian or Australian. This doesn't mean that these others are not excellent directors, screenwriters or actors, but they can never really understand us, or know what it means to be Italo-Australian. It is our responsibility to tell our own story, and the cinema is probably the best medium for this, as long as we can avoid the pitfalls of stereotypes. (Colosimo 1987:154)

It was not until 1989 that any advance on *Waterfront*'s portrayal of Italians in Australia was made with *The Magistrate*. A 6-hour mini-series about an Italian magistrate searching for his son in Australia, co-produced by the ABC, Rete-Italia and TVS Television, it was written and produced by Chris Warner, and directed by Kathy Mueller. Warner's previous work for television included the SBS series *In Between* (1988) about young people from Turkish, Vietnamese, Anglo-Australian and other backgrounds; these were mostly lugubrious, pessimistic portrayals of young non-English-speaking people in Australia. Warner originally attempted to set up *The Magistrate* with SBS, but when the budget of this multinational production began to escalate, SBS was forced to pull out and the ABC took over. A major factor in the success of *The Magistrate* project was the engagement of Italian actor Franco Nero, who has appeared in more than 100 Italian and international films since 1963, to play the series' protagonist, Paolo Pizzi. As Nero explained in an interview:

> I accepted the offer because I liked the script. It was not an easy decision to reach due to the fortunate fact that I am much in demand . . . But I am a strange actor, maybe the only Italian actor who is constantly working abroad. I can speak different languages and have worked with people of many different nationalities. Most stories of the Mafia have focused on the crime connection between Italy and the USA. This is something new because of the Australian link. (*Cinema Papers*, May 1989:12)

Nero is rarely off-screen throughout *The Magistrate*, and he imbues the eponymous protagonist with a moving dignity; he is mostly quiet, rational and subdued, contravening the impulsive, passionate and effusive Italian stereotype. Although Pizzi does not avoid showing emotion—he cries in a particularly poignant scene with his father, an immigrant to Australia (played skilfully by Melbourne actor Osvaldo Maione), his control of emotion in his battle against the Calabrian 'Ndrangheta, who have killed his wife with a bomb, is particularly powerful. The *Sydney Morning Herald* television drama critic, Robin Oliver, considered *The Magistrate* 'close to the best British work in the serial thriller area' (*SMH* Guide, 13 Nov. 1989), an indication of the series' somewhat Anglocentric restraint.

In dealing with themes related to Anglo-Saxon notions of the Mafia, *The Magistrate* works from a premise fraught with the danger of reinforcing film and television stereotypes of Italians as criminals, but it largely succeeds in subverting these stereotypes (and the criminal element in the story involves the Calabrian 'Ndrangheta, not the Sicilian-based Mafia).

The characters of *The Magistrate* express a wide range of attitudes and behaviour affecting Anglo-Australians and Italians. The ocker detective Davies is well-meaning and sympathetic towards Pizzi, respectful of his Italian idiosyncrasies, and willing to learn from his experience, both in Italy and Australia. The local police in the fictional Victorian town of Woongabbie, which has a reputation for marijuana-growing by its Calabrese community, brutally harass Pizzi's brother Leonardo (Joe Petruzzi), which provokes a public demonstration by the Calabrese fruitgrowers. Anglo-Australian prejudices towards Italians are counterbalanced by Italian tendencies to regard Australia as a British colony lacking the history and cultural traditions of Italy. 'So much for British justice', comments Pizzi after police order him to leave Australia. 'This is Australia' is the reply, with a hint of republican sentiments.

In *The ABC of Drama* Elizabeth Jacka expresses a different viewpoint:

> This is one of the most aesthetically satisfying of the mini-series shown (by the ABC) in 1988–89. Not every part of it is a masterpiece (the first hour is terribly slow and deliberate but then it finds its rhythm beautifully) but it is among the most structurally ambitious and robust in content terms. It is the story of a Calabrian magistrate involved in investigating Mafia control (sic) of the drug trade. . .Once it hits its stride, *The Magistrate* is a very exciting thriller—but it is also a complex family saga and an exposé of the drug trade, with a glance at journalistic ethics along the way. . . It is also a welcome change from the predominantly Anglo fare of ABC drama and was something of a landmark in being the first co-production with an Italian partner. (Jacka 1991:88)

Jacka also points out that *The Magistrate* was only the eleventh drama program on multicultural themes that the ABC had produced since 1975 (1991:68). The series had a rather lukewarm reception when it was screened on the Berlusconi-owned private TV channel Rete-Italia in Italy in 1990, partly because it appeared subdued and low-key in comparison with the popular Italian Mafia mini-series, *La Piovra* (The Octopus), which has had at least three sequels to date. In *La Piovra*, Michele Placido plays a policeman whose family is killed by the Mafia, and who sets out on a bloody vendetta. The high-powered violence, action and emotion in *La Piovra* (which SBS has so far screened twice in Australia) is more sensational than the relatively contemplative concerns of *The Magistrate*, which is more relevant to Australia on account of its incisive observations about Italo-Australian relations.

In 1990 the ABC's record for positive portrayals of Italians took a downward slide with *Police Crop*, a fictionalised one-off drama about events surrounding the murder of Canberra Assistant Police Commissioner Colin Winchester. Originally entitled *The Black Hand*, echoing at least two early American sensational Mafia films whose titles derive from the racist expression 'the black hand of the dago', *Police Crop* was billed as a follow-up to *Police State*, a successful and often comic drama about Joh Bjelke-Petersen and the Fitzgerald Inquiry. Both programs rated very highly (18 and 22 in Sydney) and Jacka regards them both as interesting examples of the docudrama genre:

> . . .they are the first time the ABC has made docudramas which, as well as being very appropriate vehicles for such [controversial] material, are a good strategy for making programs quickly and cheaply so that they are able to be seen by audiences while the issues are still current and are thus able to have an effect. (1991:68)

Police Crop, written by Ian David and directed by Ken Cameron, buys straight into Italian-Australian Mafia mythology, deriving its revised title from a police-sanctioned dummy marijuana crop instigated by Joe Verducci, a man with Calabrian syndicate connections (or connections with the 'Ndrangheta, not the Mafia, as the film implies). The program starred the Italian actor Luciano Catenacci, who played Pizzi's treacherous former tutor, Silvestri, in *The Magistrate*, and Catenacci, along with Italo-Australian actors Rob Ruggiero, Vince D'Amico and Joseph Spano, struggled to imbue his role with some dignity. 'No prizes for who they're playing!' commented an anonymous item listing the Italian actors in *Police Crop* in the Sydney *Sun-Herald* (18 Feb. 1990). The fact that the program was made 'quickly and cheaply' is evident in its producers' last-minute realisation that the Italian characters would have to converse with one another in Italian, and that sections of David's script would have to be translated. Frank Cavanagh, the Italian dialogue consultant for *The Magistrate* who Anglicised his real name on the credits of *Police Crop* to distance himself from the project, was engaged to translate and to coach Catenacci in English. He did such a good job that the supposedly 'evil' Italian characters spoke so fluently they put the Anglo-Australian cops' relentlessly scatological banter to shame. Marion McDonald, reviewing the program in the *Sydney Morning Herald*, commented:

> It was a curious—and unintended, surely?—effect of this sensational docu-drama that the alleged Mafiosi came out of it virtually looking like Honest Joes, or Giuseppes. I put it down to the subtitles. 'We can't let these crooks take our

work and money.' That is the sort of thing they are supposed to have said. 'We'll have to put in another crop to pay for the lawyers.' The police by contrast employed an earthy argot, often alluding to each other's ears and arseholes. This may well be a true picture, however. Even in your reviewer's relatively sheltered life, the good guys have not necessarily been the smooth talkers.' (*SMH* 24 March 1990)

The tortuous, twisting plot of *Police Crop* made it difficult to follow, although its general picture of widespread police corruption and cover-ups was clear enough.

In perpetuating myths of marijuana-growing Mafiosi, *Police Crop* repeated common stereotypes, while its portrayal of Italians as shadowy background figures in an Anglo-Australian cop drama reversed the gains made by *The Magistrate* with its Italian protagonist.

Signs of widespread concern among Italo-Australian communities about the Anglo-Australian tendency to associate Italian immigrants with marijuana growing and the Mafia are indicated by *Victoria Market* (1982), a play by Nino Randazzo, the editor of the Melbourne-based Italian newspaper, *Il Globo*. Subtitled 'The Genesis of a Myth', *Victoria Market* deals with the serial murders of Italian stallholders in Victoria Market in the mid-1960s, and was performed in Italian at the 1982 Melbourne Italian Festival. Randazzo has described the play as. . .

. . .a message, a protest against those elements, both Italian and Australian, of constitutional power who have created the myth of 'the Mafia in Australia'. Lawyers, journalists, police officials, politicians, academics and professional racists have hidden and are still hiding their complicity and vested interests, prejudices, and sometimes their crimes, corruption and lust for power and privilege under the convenient cloak of the 'Mafia in Australia', a myth which originated at the beginning of the 60s and which continues to crucify the Italians of Australia. (Randazzo 1982)

Victoria Market is a plea for justice and an end to prejudice. It also suggests that the Australian tendency to use the term 'Mafia' indiscriminately (as in 'New South Wales Labor Party Mafia', 'gay Mafia', 'feminist Mafia', 'multicultural Mafia', etc.) support the argument for precision when it is applied to its country of origin. The play has never been performed in English, although it provided the basis for a highly distorted screenplay by two Anglo-Australian writers, entitled *In Duty Bound,* which has fortunately never reached production.

The Italian narrative in Australian drama suggests that the issue of how Australia is represented in the media reverts time and again to control over the scripting and production process. The media can appropriate all too easily a minority (some of which may be criminal but most of which is not) to promote some other commercial goal. We turn now to the construction of the Other through comedy. Laughing at or with the Other becomes crucial for understanding the tensions revealed by our interrogation of the media.

26

WOGS STILL OUT OF WORK: AUSTRALIAN TELEVISION COMEDY AS COLONIAL DISCOURSE

In his studies of how the media represent ethnic minorities the Dutch sociologist Teun van Dijk has suggested that the reader or viewer of mass media texts stores 'hidden information' about the world and other national-ities in the form of 'models' and 'scripts'. The former are personal impressions based on individual experience, while the latter are 'culturally shared, and hence more social. . .which feature the stereotypical information members of a culture or group share about everyday events and episodes'. (Van Dijk 1988: 228). These notions, insofar as they relate to ethnic stereotypes, can be extended to fictional modes of representation, particularly comedy, which traditionally has involved a high degree of caricature and stereotyping of ethnic groups, and relies on an audience's recognition of certain common 'models' and 'scripts' relating to both their own and other nationalities.

The use of stereotypes is not always detrimental to those on whom they are placed: for example, in the comedy show *Wogs Out of Work* the affec-tionate caricaturing of ethnic minorities, or 'out groups', also challenges the dominant Anglo-Australian 'scripts' and 'models'. However, despite being one of the longest-running live theatre shows in recent Australian history, *Wogs* appears to be the exception that proves the rule, by playing up stereotypes in order to undermine them. Most representations of non-Anglo-Saxon migrant groups in Australian comedy, both on stage and television, confirm common, negative Anglo-Australian stereotypes, whether generated by Anglo or non-Anglo comics. Such a perception must be understood within a wider framework—the processes of colonisation in Australia, colonisation by whites of blacks, and the colonisation by Anglo Australia of all other immigrants. A key component in this process of colonisation is mimicry (Bhahba 1990), which Robert Young (1990) explains as follows:

> The mimic man, insofar as he is not entirely like the coloniser, white but not quite, constitutes only a partial representation of him: far from being reassured, the coloniser sees a grotesquely displaced image of himself. Thus the famil-iar. . .becomes uncannily transformed, the imitation subverts the identity of that which is being represented, and the relation of power, if not altogether reversed, certainly begins to vacillate. . .The surveilling eye is suddenly confronted with a

returning gaze of otherness and finds its mastery, its sameness, is undone. . .Compared to ambivalence. . .mimicry implies an even greater loss of control for the coloniser, of inevitable processes of counter-domination produced by a miming of the very operation of domination, with the result that the identity of colonizer and colonized becomes curiously elided. (1990:147–8)

Mimicry becomes a much more subversive dynamic in the hands of non-Anglo comedians who portray Anglo-Australian authority figures, like Simon Palomares' portrayal of the tolerant, trendy MP espousing multiculturalism as a trendy, yuppie notion of togetherness in *Wogs Out of Work,* or Nick Giannopoulos' cleaner describing the Anglo yuppies in his neighbourhood in the same show, or his portrayal of the 'wog' kid in a blond wig, trying desperately to emulate a surfie. In these cases the mimicry becomes a political strategy that mocks and undermines the colonial apparatus.

FROM *WOGS OUT OF WORK* TO *ACROPOLIS NOW*

In the rare cases in Australian comedy when the unequal balance is redressed, and migrants are given the opportunity to speak for themselves, the tendency has been to mimic common Anglo-Saxon representations of migrants for maximum laughs, due to the pressure of the Anglo tradition of comedy and Anglo market forces. This is evident in the work of the Italo-Australian comedians Vince Sorrenti and Joe Dolce, both of whom work mainly in live theatre. Sorrenti specialises in dirty jokes and comic references to his mother in Sydney's western suburb of Punchbowl. He wrote a series of articles for the *Sydney Morning Herald* in 1991, reflecting on his recent trip to Italy, and caricaturing male Italians' most widely stereotyped behaviour: driving fast cars, spending large amounts of money and exhibiting chauvinism in their dealings with women. Dolce's most well-known production was the 1980 pop song hit 'Shaddap Your Face', which caricatured popular conceptions of Italian mispronunciations of English. In both cases, self-deprecation and replaying common Anglo stereotypes of migrants is the predominant comic strategy. The same is largely true of *Acropolis Now*, the first Australian TV comedy series with non-Anglo-Saxon migrants as protagonists, portrayed by non-Anglo-Saxon actors.

The Greek protagonists of *Acropolis Now* are migrants rejecting both the cultural pressures of their parents and the dominant trends of Anglo-Australian 'skip' culture, yet they are so caricatured and stereotyped that they are almost indistinguishable from Con the Fruiterer. British actor Warren Mitchell—well known to Anglo-Saxon viewers as the right-wing racist Alf Garnett in *Till Death Do Us Part* plays Kostas, the father of Jim (Nick Giannopoulos) in the opening episode. The first series of *Acropolis Now* appeared on Channel 7 in August 1989, and the second in August 1990, where it was shown immediately before *'Allo 'Allo* and *Fast Forward*, which seemed to reinforce its racial stereotypes and caricatures. At a conference on scriptwriting and multiculturalism held at the Australian Film, Television and Radio School in September 1990, Simon Palomares, the Spanish-born writer of *Acropolis Now* and its stage predecessor, *Wogs Out of Work*, stressed that the main priority of *Acropolis Now* had quickly become to 'keep it on the air', and maintain a kind of comedy which kept the audience ratings as high as possible:

> Whatever the criticisms of the show are, [they] pale in comparison with its main success. . .that it's on air. If *Acropolis Now* is not there, there's nothing to replace it. . .You've got to have a platform. If you lose that platform because you're too loud, or. . .too radical, or. . .waving too many flags for too many different causes. . .you've got nothing to say. And our main concern now is to keep *Acropolis Now* on air. If we have to do it through comedy. . .or stereotypes. . .or racism, sexism. . .we'll do it. Because it's keeping ethnics on television.

But at what cost? Palomares' justifications, which involve an Uncle Tom-like subservience to the dictates of commercial television, were answered by the Greek-Australian performance poet PIEO:

> I don't care about your ratings. I don't care if you're making a million dollars or ten cents. You're offending me. . .You are the buffoons that we as whites and as blacks and as migrants can all laugh together [at]. (AFTRS Conference, broadcast on SBS *Vox Populi*, 2 December 1990)

This notion of quasi-sacrificial migrant 'buffoons' points to a degree of caricature in the show which debases the dignity of its Greek migrant characters and offends intellectuals like PIEO and the writer George Papaellinas. Palomares justified the show's caricatures in terms of what he saw as an internal balance, maintained by the extremely sexist behaviour, loud clothes and generally gross behaviour of Memo, the slightly less exaggerated antics of Jim and the female character Effie, to the relatively 'straight' and rational demeanour of Rick (the character Palomares plays), the ocker caricature of the Anglo-Australian cook Skip, and the 'straight' Anglo-Saxon female character Liz.

But there are more complex dynamics at play. The show's producer, Peter Herbert, has described Liz as. . .

> . . .the Anglo-Saxon voice of reason in the wog chaos [who] represents the signposts of normality among the culture clash of the Greeks and Spaniard. Liz unravels the mayhem. (*Sun-Herald Sunday Magazine*, 12 August 1990)

In this role Liz becomes a middle-class anchor figure for Anglo-Saxon audiences, at once sanctioning (but occasionally reprimanding) and interpreting the chauvinist behaviour of the working-class Greek males and representing a norm of behaviour against which their extreme antics can be judged. Her status as the voice of the colonial power apparatus is affirmed by Nick Giannopoulos: 'She is virtually our translator. Our ethnic eccentricities go through her and her understanding is like the audience understanding' (*SMH Guide*, 13 August 1990). Liz and Palomares' 'straight man' Rick, who is educated and relatively sophisticated, combine to represent a norm of acceptable behaviour against which the transgressions of Memo, DJ and Effie, the 'wog girl', can be measured.

Palomares has acknowledged that his models for the program are American sit-coms such as *Happy Days* (whose Italian American protagonist Fonzie, he points out, is also a 'wog') and *The Cosby Show*—both safe, middle-class programs with an assimilationist focus. *Acropolis Now*, he pointed out, 'ran out of things to say about ethnicity after the first seven episodes':

Power and comedy: Liz and Effie (Tracey Callender and Mary Coustas) from Acropolis Now.

We've got 22 minutes a week to do a show. We would be trying to put in a minute of something that really says something about the culture we come from, that makes a difference. The rest of the time we have to spend making a gag every ten seconds, otherwise we won't stay on air. (AFTRS Conference, SBS *Vox Populi* 2 December 1990)

There is no doubt that *Acropolis Now* has an enormous appeal for its target audience—teenagers of Greek extraction. In December 1990 Tony Mitchell interviewed some of the 600 Sydney migrant teenagers who came nightly to see *Acropolis Now On Stage* at the Enmore Theatre in Newtown, most of them travelling from inner western suburbs. The vast majority of them saw nothing offensive or even unrealistic in Memo, who was the favourite character of most, and they rejected the suggestion that the show might confirm Anglo-Saxon prejudices about Greek Australians. Many of them admitted that characters like Memo were 'exaggerated', but thought this was necessary to make the show funnier. Some had seen *Wogs Out of Work*, and saw little difference between that show and *Acropolis Now*, apart from a transfer to television which modified its language and gave it a sitcom format. Few of these teenagers hesitated to refer to themselves as 'wogs' although they acknowledged that 'depending on how it was used' it could still be a term of abuse. It was clear that as far as its target audience was concerned, there was nothing in the show that contributed to racist attitudes (Mitchell 1992).

The portrayal of the series and its characters in the Anglo-Australian press, on the other hand, reveals an ambivalent assumption of token migrant viewpoints by Anglo-Australian journalists, which includes an appropriation of the term 'wog' in its newly liberated mode as a term of defiance and self-assertion for non-Anglo youth. Frank Gauntlet, for example, the British-born theatre critic of *The Daily Mirror*, wrote a feature article on *Wogs Out of Work* headlined 'The Cosy Nostra: Woggy Web just keeps on working', which sanctions its title by quoting George Kapiniaris:

Wogs was a killing word 20 years ago, now it's become something else and I think this show has done a lot to take the edge off that. The word wog used to be derogatory but now it's basically a way of saying that's what we are. (*Daily Mirror*, 30 November 1989)

Gauntlet goes on to discuss the 'sinister connotations of the Wog invasion', referring to the amount of employment *Wogs Out of Work* and *Acropolis Now* have provided for NESB actors—14 actors and 14 musicians had performed in different versions of the stage show. The term 'sinister' evokes a yellow-peril (NESB) takeover of the acting profession that is only faintly tongue-in-cheek, while Gauntlet's description of these actors as a 'comic cosy nostra' suggests an incestuous in-group akin to the 'gay mafia' which is often accused of dominating Sydney theatre.

Another British journalist, Robin Oliver, described the 1990 series of *Acropolis Now* in the *SMH* Weekly TV Guide under the banner 'Wogs, Wags and Gags', followed by the disclaimer 'the trio of comics who made "wog" a title worthy of pride are about to begin a new season on television' (*SMH Guide* 13 August 1990). A by-product of this shift in meaning of the term 'wog' was its continued use with impunity by some Anglo-Australians.

In an essay entitled 'Some Theoretical Notions and Preliminary Research Concerning Derogatory Ethnic Labels' (DELs), the American sociologists Greenberg, Kirkland and Pyszczynski conclude that. . .

> . . .DELs are verbal expressions of prejudice with psychological impact that can encourage negative behaviour toward out-groupers. Clearly there is an urgent need to know much more about their causes and effects, because the ethnic prejudices to which they seem to contribute continue to encourage conflicts throughout this heavily armed multiethnic world. (1988:90)

This tentative conclusion is based on a study of the use of specific terms such as 'nigger', which has undergone a similar shift of emphasis in American black communities through its use by rap groups like Niggers With Attitude. Greenberg and his colleagues include the more generic term 'wop' ('without papers'—an illegal immigrant) but the term 'wog', being a predominantly British DEL, is not mentioned. Thought to originate from 'golliwog', it has been used in Australia as a term of racist abuse for any non-Anglo-Saxon outgroup, but by 1987 it had been adopted by those outgroupers themselves as a defiant term of identity. Although this shift by no means eliminated the use of the term 'wog' by Anglo-Saxons as a term of racial abuse, a good deal of responsibility for its change of emphasis could be claimed by *Wogs Out of Work*. After filling the 700-seat Athenaeum Theatre in Melbourne with mostly Greek and Italian migrant youth from the western suburbs of Melbourne for nine months in 1987, *Wogs Out of Work* played at the Enmore Theatre in Sydney for 16 months, and toured all over Australia. Its sympathetic portrayal of the dilemmas of young Australians from non-Anglo-Saxon backgrounds proved a rallying point, and as Hilary Glow pointed out in her review of the show in *New Theatre Australia*, displayed. . .

> . . .ideological concerns. . .not the least of which is its re-appropriation of the term 'wog'. . .In much the same way as the term 'black' was re-appropriated into the discourse of the Black Movement, here, too, there is an attempt to invert the denigratory connotations of 'wog'. To some extent, the show still uses recognisable representational practices ('wogs' as excitable, or stupid, or obsessed with food etc.) but it is concerned to move beyond the reproduction of

stereotypes and to challenge the attitudes and assumptions that underlie them. It is no small part of this show's success that 'wogs' become the subject of celebration rather than denigration. (1987:24–5)

Largely due to the show's sympathetic portrayal of a wide spectrum of young second-generation Mediterranean migrants, migrant women workers, and social outcasts, together with its satire against Anglo-Australian yuppies who affect a token concern about 'new Australians', it brought new audiences into the theatre. The term 'wog' became for many young Australians of non-Anglo-Saxon origin a positive expression of their deviation from the norm, which was represented by the slang term 'Skip', which *Wogs Out of Work* also introduced. As George Papaellinas has said of the show:

It was. . .some of the most sophisticated humour I've ever had the privilege to watch, simply because it took the whole 360 degrees and spoke affectionately about where these people lived and. . .came from, and that's a class and gender issue as well, not just something called ethnicity. [It] spoke out of a lot of pain at. . .the people who had caused the pain, but also involved them in it. But *Acropolis Now*? No. (AFTRS Conference, SBS *Vox Populi* 2 December 1990)

Acropolis Now appears to have undone its predecessor's involvement in gender and class issues, and Anglo-Australian guilt, and its shift of emphasis in the word 'wog'. In his review of *Acropolis Now* in the *Sydney Morning Herald*, Simon Kent praised the show for its 'abundance of self-deprecation that can only help to endear the program further to viewers who may have once shied away, taking heed of the warning to beware of Greeks bearing gifts' (*Sydney Morning Herald*, 23 August 1989). Kent's assumption that self-deprecation is a desirable comic mechanism to woo Anglo-Australian audiences reflects how the focus of *Wogs Out of Work* has changed in *Acropolis Now*: the 'court jester', buffoon-like mode permits Anglo-Saxon viewers to take a condescending view of Greek behaviour that confirms outmoded stereotypes. A 1990 *TV Week* article provides evidence that the show's Greek protagonists support this shift in emphasis from defiant affirmation to self-deprecation. Called 'Every Skip's Guide to Wogtalk', it uses the term 'wog' no fewer than 13 times, draining it of all but its most deprecatory connotations. The article consists of a mock glossary, compiled by Nick Giannopoulos and George Kapiniaris, of terms used by 'wogs'. These include 'Wog breath: A person who should brush his/her teeth with toothpaste, not garlic', and the term 'wog' is defined as 'People of Southern European origin or Middle Eastern persuasion (Maltese, Egyptianese, Arabese, Turkeys, Lesbianese)' (*TV Week* 8 September 1990). The negative connotations of the word 'wog', as it is used in racist Anglo-Saxon discourse, seem to have returned in full force, a tendency confirmed in the show by gags like Memo's 'I'm not stupid, I'm Greek', and puns on 'Cretan' and 'cretin'.

It could be concluded from this evidence that the ultimate effect of *Acropolis Now* has been to reverse all the gains in race relations and NESB migrant self-esteem achieved by *Wogs Out of Work*. From the perspective of an educated, middle class 'concerned Anglo', an absence of positive portrayals of Aboriginal or non-Anglo-Saxon groups in Australian stage and television comedy continues, and pejorative portrayals or exclusion remain the norm. But this does not account for the evidence that working-class NESB migrant young people find nothing offensive about *Acropolis Now*. For them it provides an important focal point for outgroup identity, and fuel to fight against discrimination by 'Skips'. Evidence of a widespread tendency among teenage girls of Greek descent to dress up and imitate Effie (*Sydney Morning Herald* 11 February 1990) suggests a form of mimicry which is a defiant enactment of an exaggerated ethnicity, one that challenges the strictures and constraints imposed by their migrant parents and their stigmatisation by Anglo-Australians.

Craig Brown has claimed that 'Comedy sitcoms such as *Acropolis Now* are acting as successful bridging programs, getting the networks, the public and sponsors used to the idea of ethnic culture on television' (1992: 56), but this 'bridging' process is extremely slow and has yet to yield any visible results. *Acropolis Now* may have led indirectly to gains in NESB migrant representation on television, but there is still no other NESB-dominated comedy program like the BBC's *Tandoori Nights* on Australian air waves. The fourth series of *Acropolis Now*, which began on Channel 7 in February 1992, replaced the relatively rational and balancing presence of Simon Palomares as Rick with a new Sicilian character, Alfredo (Nick Carrafa), a more burlesque type of 'straight man' whose supposed intellectual capacities are presented in caricatured form. The *Fast Forward* comedienne Nikki Wendt's frantic, slapstick style as the new waitress Suzanna similarly exaggerates the relatively rational role of Liz. This throws all the emphasis of the comedy on the uniformly over-the-top Greek-Australian trio of Jim, Memo and Effie, an NESB version of the Three Stooges who are proceeding to cancel out many of the advances in comic portrayals of non-Anglo migrants achieved by *Wogs Out of Work*. Italo-Australian cartoonist Rocco Fazzari, whose caricatures of Effie have featured frequently in the *Sydney Morning Herald,* commented on an episode of the 1992 series of *Acropolis Now*:

> . . .it's worse than the scratch across my Nana Mouskouri album. . .One hopes that Effie and crew will try and rise to greater heights. They might be wogs in work at the moment, but they might as well be selling bedroom settings at Nick Scali's with this effort. (*SMH Guide* 24 February 1992)

In general terms, Australian television comedy in the early 1990s shows few indications that a further stage can be reached in migrant representation in the mass media, where Aboriginal and migrant performers have space to play roles, both straight and comic, which do not require them to caricature or stigmatise their ethnicity.

The differentiation of the Australian population remains a complex process of negotiation and open resolution. While the diversity is more clearly represented now than ever before, the differentiation still seems to be following that concern expressed by *The Australian*, that the superiority of the dominant culture must remain unchallenged.

PART IV

MEDIA PRACTICES AND AUDIENCE PERCEPTIONS

27

STRUCTURES OF CONTROL

The output of the media provides a fertile field in which to explore the processes by which race and ethnicity are given everyday meaning. While it has become apparent that the media are active in constructing narratives of race and ethnic difference, it is also clear that different audiences construct their own meanings. We have also seen that despite government and community concern about the practices that reproduce racially and ethnically differentiated media products, they continue to do so in ways that systematically disadvantage, stigmatise or marginalise minorities. How, then, do the structures of media control operate, how are the practices of media production sustained, and what do audiences think of the results?

We begin with the formal institutions of regulation, government and industry bodies. The complexity of the constitution of the Australian States and the Commonwealth and their labyrinthine connections always make it difficult to determine the dimensions and import of state policy. If we take this ensemble of governments, often in conflict with each other, sometimes acting in agreement, as the 'state' in Australia, we can tease out some general tendencies in policy, or at least identify the focus of debate and sketch the links between these areas.

At the Commonwealth level alone there are at least ten bureaucracies with some stake in the cultural policy areas which bear on racism and the media. The major government departments are as follows:

- The Department of Immigration and Ethnic Affairs (DIEA), concerned with the selection, admission and settlement of immigrants, and its semi-autonomous creature, the Bureau of Immigration and Population Research (BIPR).
- The Department of Arts and Administrative Services (DAS), with its specific responsibilities in cultural policy, including the certification of 'Australianness'.
- The Department of Attorney-General, concerned with the legal management of racism and human rights and censorship (AG).
- The Department of Prime Minister and Cabinet, with its concern for

social justice, and its 'offices' for the Status of Women (OSW), and Multicultural Affairs (OMA).

- The Department of Transport and Communication (DOTAC) which controls the electronic communication sector, and has as its creature the Australian Broadcasting Authority.
- The Department of Foreign Affairs and Trade (DFAT), which manages the relations between Australia and other countries whenever these are affected by Australian representation of the 'foreign', as with the film *Turtle Beach* and the TV series *Embassy* in relation to Malaysia.
- The Aboriginal and Torres Strait Islander Commission (ATSIC) which has responsibility across the board for the indigenous population.

There are also various statutory bodies which carry specific responsibilities—the Australia Council for the Arts (responsible through DAS), the Australian Broadcasting Commission (ABC), and the Special Broadcasting Service (SBS), responsible through DOTAC. This list excludes state and territory bodies that have sometimes overlapping, sometimes complementary and sometimes conflictual relations with the Commonwealth on these matters—for example, Departments of Aboriginal (and Torres Strait Islander) Affairs and Ethnic or Multicultural Affairs commissions or bureaus.

Such a multiplicity of participants already suggests that the layers of policy and implementation, whatever they might be, are heavily influenced by the specific bureaucratic interests of individual sectors and by the range of non-government (but sometimes advisory) organisations and groups that seek 'speaking positions' and claim an authenticity of perspective.

The policy questions occur here as they do elsewhere, at three levels (see also Pettman 1992). The most accessible is the level of espoused policy, the formal ideology as it were of the Australian state. Here we find the National Agenda on Multiculturalism, promulgated in 1989 and articulating a range of strategies. The National Agenda, emerging after a tumultuous series of political arguments during the mid and late 1980s over the place of multiculturalism in Australian society and in government policy, specifically includes the place of the media in multiculturalism. That policy is corporate and bureaucratic in its goals and processes and concerned with economic efficiency, cultural identity, and social justice.

The public ideology is an important indicator of social direction, but it is less than accurate about the experience of those ostensibly affected by it. So we move to a second level, the level of 'accommodation' where policy goals are translated into strategies and goals for equality and equity. Here we find a rather different picture, in which targets are set but rarely met, in which bureaucracies such as the Office of Multicultural Affairs reject draft after draft of government department access and equity plans, where bureaucrats seek forms of words to defend entrenched practices, and where patterns of inequality are renewed rather than eroded (Meekosha et al. 1987; Ferguson 1986; Pettman 1992; Cunningham 1992a). Here we see the very real conflicting political claims for and against multiculturalism given expression in decisions about resources, programs, services and grants. All too often the fallout from these conflicts leaves ethnic minorities and indigenous people on the margins.

Finally to a third level of policy, in which things happen to people in their everyday lives. Here the bureaucratic discourses hover on the edges of human relationships, where 'economic efficiency' overcomes concerns for social justice, so that cultural difference becomes either the target of harassment or the framework for exclusion.

A useful example of this process of ideology transformed into practice appears in the attempt by Actors Equity to reflect on the casting practices of the Australian television industry (Communications Law Centre 1992). The union had for some years expressed concern at the poor opportunities for NESB and Aboriginal actors, at the typecasting of those who were employed, at the practice of 'blacking up' white actors to appear Aboriginal (or otherwise 'ethnic'), and the standard practice of always allocating non-specific ethnic parts to Anglo actors. The 1989 licence renewal hearings for television in Sydney gave the union a chance to press its case, in conjunction with the Tranby Co-operative College for Aborigines. Channel 10 admitted that there were problems with Aboriginal representation and agreed to meet Equity to develop a procedure for greater Aboriginal representation. Despite Equity approaches after the hearings before the Tribunal, no such procedures eventuated and Channel 10 continued its traditional practices. Channel 7 told the Tribunal it was negotiating an agreement with Equity; despite Equity developing a draft code for negotiation, by 1992 Channel 7 had simply failed to respond. Similarly, Channel 9 expressed some interest in such a proposal—nothing has emerged. Equity's attempt to get some broad agreement with the Federation of Australian Commercial Television Stations also met with a simple response—silence (Communications Law Centre 1992: 19ff).

Here we have the layers in practice. The government policies include the national Agenda on Multiculturalism, with its concern for social justice and cultural identity; the state (NSW) Anti-Discrimination Law, making it illegal to discriminate on the grounds of race or ethnicity when offering employment or providing a service; the ABT Codes on adequate and comprehensive services, which seemed to have required recognition of the ethnic makeup of the population in a broadcast service area as a factor in the granting of licences. The ideology of adequate representation is clearly espoused.

The Tribunal hearings offered the locus for the 'second level' negotiations—how can we as licensees find a way to agree to some of what the 'community' wants in order to get our licences and be away?

Finally, the 'third level', the sounds of silence, where the commercial channels, once relicensed, simply do nothing, refuse to answer requests, and get on with business as usual (except for the minor matter of gaining government agreement to reconstruct the Tribunal so it more closely reflects the interests of the broadcasters and thus hopefully will not trouble them again with these vexatious matters).

This is one example of a perplexing phenomenon, well recognised by policy analysts. Broad social movements gain a wave of public support to achieve gains in the political and legislative arena; politics as a symbolic exercise enshrines these gains in laws and statements. These symbolic gains then have to be put into practice in an environment highly sensitive to the 'real' commitments of the power blocs that lie beneath the public rhetoric. For instance, Castles et al. (1988) trace the unstable passage of multicultural- ism as a policy of government, from its emergence under the Fraser Liberal government in 1978, through its transformation under the early years of Labor (and its near terminal state in late 1986), the reaction of the broad ethnic movement, and its re-emergence as the National Agenda hooked to the department of Prime Minister and Cabinet in the late 1980s. Detailed field research (Meekosha et al. 1987) documented how public servants, charged with policy implementation, maintained that at its nadir the policy was waved aside in direct negotiations with ethnic communities. It was only with its constant reassertion and, more important, its resourcing, that the policy articulated as ideology was translated into action.

Cunningham, in his recent discussion of cultural policy, argues against Castles et al., who have been highly critical of multiculturalism as national ideology, that multiculturalism does serve as a basis for the development of national community cultural production; if Australian governments had not espoused something like that policy, for all its imperfections, the space to struggle for change at the 'sharp end' would disappear (Cunningham 1992a:43).

Government policies can best be understood as temporary expressions of the ideology of the state, representing the accommodation of competing interests, framed by the underlying imperatives of liberal capitalism, for social order and economic integration. Multiculturalism as a policy has not achieved significant change in the commercial media, though its impact on the state sector has been crucial—SBS quite simply is the most outstanding expression of multiculturalism as policy. With all its contradictions, with the specific and community ethnic tension, with its class and cultural predilections, the organisation shows up the three levels of policy most clearly. It exists as a creature of the policy of multiculturalism; its internecine struggles (in radio and television individually, in its staffing policies, between ethnic radio and multicultural television, with its audiences, with community leaders, with DOTAC, and with the ABC) are all evidence of the second level of policy. For its audiences its impact varies—eliciting anger, joy, excitement and frustration, but affecting the quality of people's lives by empowering some and constraining others (Jakubowicz 1987).

Government policies, as they affect race, ethnicity and the media, are a crude mix of conflicting goals, let loose in a marketplace where government intervention is viewed with suspicion from hostile quarters. Cutting across those policies, and undermining or reinforcing their impact, are bureaucracies, power blocs, commercial interests and social movements seeking to seize the chance to move forward on their own terms. In each surge, the evidence suggests that the more vulnerable and marginalised groups have the greatest difficulty keeping up with the game.

Government regulation of the media in relation to race and ethnicity, as distinct from its more general regulation of race and ethnic relations in all other areas, is confined to arms'-length involvement by the former Australian Broadcasting Tribunal. At the time of writing the Australian Broadcasting Authority, with a responsibility to look first to industry self-regulation before it could issue any mandatory guidelines, has endorsed the commercial industry codes of practice for race and ethnicity. At first the industry seemed to have been reluctant or unaware that the Authority was expecting these guidelines to work better than the old broadcasting standards did. Yet federal and state government regulation of the media over race issues is limited. It has no control over the print media, other than to prevent discrimination in employment or in the offering of goods or services, or to censor obscenity or violence. Until late in 1992 the electronic media were also constrained by standards issued by the ABT.

AUSTRALIAN BROADCASTING TRIBUNAL—UNTIL 1992

The key Tribunal standards referred to gratuitous racial vilification and to balance in news reporting. There is an interesting but forever unresolved question as to whether the adequate and comprehensive requirement of the licences issued to broadcasters can be construed to require adequate and comprehensive coverage of ethnic and Aboriginal issues, and employment on air of Aboriginal and ethnic 'talent'. Submissions to the 1989 Sydney hearings by Tranby Aboriginal College and the Communications Law Centre argued that current licensees have failed their responsibilities to Aboriginal people. The television channels responded to that submission in May 1989. In each case they rejected the claims made by Tranby, and provided a detailed list of initiatives which would respond to urban Aborigines' specific and general needs and open up Aboriginal experiences in Australia's society. Channel 7 claimed that the news and current affairs programs, *Hinch*, *Wombat* (a children's program) and several travelogues would meet these needs and indicated that two episodes of *Rafferty's Rules* (a series about a magistrate) dealt with racism and black deaths in custody (developed in conjunction with the Aboriginal Legal Service), while *A Country Practice* had two blocks planned at that stage on Aboriginal issues. Ernie Dingo's role in *Fast Forward*, a comedy program, was also mentioned. Furthermore Channel 7 argued that its Head of Children's Programs had made a particular point of using *Wombat* to convey information about Aboriginal culture, and kept in touch with the Department of Aboriginal Affairs on these matters.

Channel TEN 10 also identified its news and current affairs programs, as well as several children's programs such as *The Mulligrubs* and *Off the Dish*. Channel 9 supported Tranby's proposal for a conference with the stations in its submission and named a range of programs with either Aboriginal motifs and/or actors, such as the documentary *A Dreaming of Lords*, the movies *The Last Wave* and *We of the Never Never*, the role for an Aboriginal actress in *The Flying Doctors* series, the telemovie *Cyclone Tracy*, and an episode of *Mission Impossible* entitled 'Cattle King' (ABT 1988c). There is no doubt that the commercial networks are aware that their responses to race and ethnic differences and conflict is a matter of public concern and one for which they may be held to account. The Tribunal did not report on the licence renewals before its abolition and replacement by the Authority; it may be a long wait before the strength of the complaints and the quality of the responses by the channels are adjudicated.

It is interesting to explore two examples of Tribunal responses to claims of racial vilification, with their markedly different outcomes. The first covered the radio comments of Ron Casey which referred specifically to Asians (Chinese and Japanese in particular) in derogatory and offensive ways.

The Australian Broadcasting Tribunal found in March 1988 that Casey had breached Radio Program Standard 3 (RPS 3) and that radio station 2KY was therefore in contravention of section 99 (1A) of the Broadcasting and Television Act 1942. Casey's statements were deemed likely to incite or perpetuate hatred against or gratuitously vilify a person or group on the basis of race. In particular he made comments about Japanese on Anzac Day 1987, and about Asians and Chinese in October 1987 and February 1988.

2KY's initial reaction to the April 1987 matters was to defend Casey and argue that 'because of the free-flowing or unstructured nature of Mr Casey's breakfast program, Mr Casey was likely to use and has used terminology expressed by his listeners. . .' (ABT 1988b). The October 1987 broadcast had Casey recommending jaundice and plastic surgery for the unemployed husband of a woman caller (to make him Asian-looking so he could benefit from preference supposedly given by the Commonwealth Employment Service to Asians over Anglo-Australians). The Managing Director of 2KY John MacBean, who was also President of the NSW Labor Council, then suspended Casey after a Tribunal notification of a complaint to the station. Casey was later put back on air after apologising in a joint statement with MacBean.

The February 1988 comments intensified the uproar. New complaints were lodged, and when the Tribunal found one of these complaints upheld (5 April 1988) Casey was suspended by MacBean (6 April 1988). He was then 'the equal top rating AM announcer in Sydney' (interview 2BL Andrew Olle/John MacBean 0840 6.4.88). According to MacBean, Casey had become 'carried away with his own rhetoric on this question of immigration and . . .on Asians in particular'. By the end of July 1988 MacBean had relented, and Casey was back on air, with a long delay 'dump button'. In late September a federal court order was issued on behalf of Casey, restraining the Tribunal from proceeding with the Inquiry. Casey emerged from the whole exercise as a hero; perhaps not widely celebrated for his stance on immigration restriction, but regularly invited by the press to comment on that.

Issues affecting refugees and immigrants were also relevant to Aborigines. The feelings expressed by Aborigines across the country about how the media report their lives and present their problems suggest that there is a dichotomy between white media representations of Aborigines, and Aboriginal perspectives. One important example of this was the controversy over the Channel 9 *60 Minutes* segment entitled 'The County', broadcast nationally in July 1989. The segment was made by reporter Mike Munro, and followed months of police action against Aborigines in Sydney's inner-city Redfern area. The media had carried a series of stories linking Aborigines to crime and violence, particularly those living in the confined area around Eveleigh Street. The reports had included the South Region Crime Squad raid on the National Aborigines Day picnic in a local park (14 July 1989), a confrontation between Aboriginal youths and police in Eveleigh Street over an allegedly stolen car (25 May 1989), the police shooting of Aboriginal David Gundy, and an alleged 'Redfern riot' in August 1988. Police were reported to be concerned that Eveleigh Street had become a no-go area; the media persistently reported the area as 'lawless' (e.g. *SMH* 5 Sept. 1988).

'The County' followed the night patrol from Redfern police station into the Aboriginal areas, showing shots of intoxicated Aborigines living in squalid conditions, and interviewing whites who claimed to be former residents of the area, forced out by Black violence. Several intoxicated Aborigines were 'interviewed', as were Aboriginal community workers. The title, 'The County', came from the local police term for the Aboriginal area: 'Coon County'. It was a classic reinforcement of the media myths about Aborigines—long lingering sequences focusing on the squalor and the poverty. Moore and Muecke (1984) have pointed out the importance of grasping the position of the Aboriginal subjects in any representation of them—the Australian media repeatedly (even if unselfconsciously) present Aborigines as incapable, degenerate and primitive. Their differences are always signs of inferiority—at best 'natural' rather than 'civilised'.

The story was widely seen—at the time *60 Minutes* was battling to regain its ratings leadership, recently lost to Channel 10's *Comedy Company*—and the segment was vigorously advertised. Its broadcast drew an enormous and angry reaction from the Aboriginal community of Redfern; it felt that its problems had been maliciously exposed to ridicule and hatred. During the week after the broadcast, over 100 local people met to protest about the program, and declare the Eveleigh Street a media 'no-go' area (*SMH* 31 May 1989). This was a sadly futile exercise in a situation where police media officers fed reporters their line on the local area; other popular current affairs programs such as Channel 7's *Hinch* also sent crews into Redfern, produced similarly patronising and racist material; were approached by local Aborigines concerned to set the record straight, interviewed them and then did not put the material to air, usually because it was not considered 'newsworthy'.

Two Aboriginal organisations made complaints to the Australian Broad-casting Tribunal (Youth Action and NSW Land Council), claiming that the programs were in breach of Television Program Standard TPS2—they were likely to incite or perpetuate hatred, or gratuitously vilify a group on the basis of its race. The station was asked to comment—Channel 9 disagreed that the program was 'extremely offensive, degrading and detrimental to Aboriginal people', and denied it was 'inaccurate, inflammatory and promoted negative attitudes towards Aboriginal people'. Its Director of Broadcasting Policy, R. Sorby, claimed that the program was 'a constructive attempt to explain what was and is happening to inner city Aboriginals'.

The Tribunal then rejected the complaints, accepting Channel 9's defence, and deciding that the report. . .

> . . .of this controversial and very sensitive issue of public interest was handled in a responsible manner. It is appreciated that the report may have offended some viewers. Nevertheless, it is considered that in the eyes of the 'reasonable viewer', that is a viewer who is susceptible to some degree of incitement to racial hatred, the report was unlikely to have incited or perpetuated hatred against, or gratuitously vilified Aboriginal people.

Since the report reinforced the most popular prejudices about Aborigines and police views of the situation, one may well ask what the program could have done to convince the Tribunal that 'susceptible people' would have their hatred against Aborigines perpetuated. With that, the Tribunal referred the complainants to the Code of Ethics of the Australian Journalists' Association and suggested that the union might be the appropriate place to 'express your concern'—implying that an ethical breach may have occurred but not a breach of standards.

This whole episode exemplifies one of the central problems concerning media and racism. The white-controlled media and its government regulators have their view of what they are 'reflecting' (not, in their view, 'constructing'). The minority community has no control over how its comments will be used, nor what aspects of the community will be selected to reflect things as the media see them. For instance, one Redfern Koori, Alan Johnston (Aboriginal liaison officer with Redfern police) interviewed for the *60 Minutes* program gave evidence to the National Inquiry into Racist Violence. Johnston noted: '*60 Minutes* had me sitting behind a camera for a heck of a long time but they did not grab hold of one thing that I felt was a positive thing that needed to be said over the media that evening' (HREOC 1991). What would have happened if a middle-class immigrant group had been reported this way? The Tribunal's acknowledgement of the offence does not acknowledge that it was Aboriginal viewers in particular who were deeply offended and upset. The program adopted a standard position: pity, and abnegation of responsibility.

For Aborigines in Redfern the electronic media are one of the major weapons of their oppression, and one they seem helpless to resist. It represents them over and again as either threats or victims—as did the *60 Minutes* piece. Only rarely is an Aboriginal or pro-Aboriginal voice heard in a context in which the speaker is powerful and in control: usually this occurs in specialist programs. For example, the ABC's radio religious program *Chronos* covered a local Redfern priest who supported Aboriginal allegations of police harassment in the wake of February 6 1990 police raids; it also explored the possibility of property developers wanting Aborigines expelled from the area so it can be redeveloped (2BL Sydney 16 Feb. 1990).

The Tribunal's refusal to act on Aboriginal complaints about 'The County' was scarcely more acceptable to the complainants than its reaction to the Casey case. Obviously the concepts outlined in the program standards were unclear and difficult to act upon, but the Tribunal had the power to investigate the standards and how they might be modified. The Tribunal could also have been requested by community groups to hold such an investigation, and it did inquire into the Right of Reply after a request from People for Animals in 1989. In this case the animal protection group had insufficient time to consolidate and present their views on duck hunting; it asked the Tribunal to hold an inquiry into whether there should be a standard to guarantee aggrieved groups a right of reply.

The saga of regulation of racist commentaries on air, particularly on radio, eventually led in early 1992 to the ABT announcing an inquiry into the racial vilification policy of its radio and television standards. The inquiry had been recommended to both the Office of Multicultural Affairs and the Human Rights Commission National Inquiry into Racist Violence (Jakubowicz 1990; Goodall et al. 1991) and had been pursued by the Communications Law Centre on behalf of Actors Equity, a union particularly concerned about casting policies and the opportunities for ethnic and Aboriginal actors. The ABT agreed to act, producing a background paper on the issues in February 1992 (ABT 1992).

During 1991 the Tribunal had ruled on two major complaints about radio talkback announcers Ron Casey and John Laws. Casey was found to have breached the guidelines in 1990 and placed under tight conditions by the Tribunal after a period off air. Late in 1990 the radio station itself filed a complaint with the Tribunal to test whether Casey's latest statements in June 1990—that 'boat people be stamped on the forehead with an "Australian reject" sign and sent home' (*The Australian* 3 May 1991)—were in breach of its standards. This time there was very little response by ethnic communities, who had mounted a strong campaign in the previous case only to see Casey reprimanded but allowed to remain on air. The Tribunal found that Casey had 'used offensive and insulting terms', but had not breached the standards. The move by 2KY to test the boundaries for their prize performer seemed to have paid off. He was now effectively free to say what he wished, with the steam and energy of his critics apparently exhausted.

The Laws case was more complicated. The Tribunal, having been fought by Laws through the federal court at every stage, ruled finally that concerning Aborigines, Laws had breached the standards (vilifying them on the basis of their race), including an interchange in 1987 on 2GB with an Aboriginal caller whom he described on air as 'so typical of so many of your race. You're belligerent, you're a bully, you're a loud-mouth, you're ill-informed and you're plain bloody stupid' (*Sydney Morning Herald*, 13 July 1991). However, by the time the decision was announced, Laws had left 2GB and moved to 2UE so that nothing could be done—the company that had employed him had sold the station, and his new station was not being liable for his previous actions (*The Australian*, 14 October 1991).

The regulations were cumbersome, expensive and difficult to enforce and demanded much community time and energy. Evidence of affront and suffering was required for the Tribunal to find a breach of the standard. With the replacement of the ABT by the Authority late in 1992, the regulatory framework changed. From now on the industry was to set its own standards and deal with complaints by itself. The public spotlight would disappear into a cumbersome, internal process.

The structures of control seemed unable to combat anything but the most extreme examples of racism and racial vilification, and the experience of media employees did little to correct this impression. We now compare the ABC and SBS based on the views of media workers who are Aborigines or of ethnic background, or who were responsible for inducing change in these organisations.

28

MEDIA PRACTITIONERS

We have sought views of minority media practitioners as most analyses of such situations tend to reflect the perceptions of the media mainstream and those who wield power in the system.

Many people from Aboriginal and non-English-speaking backgrounds feel that TV and the media in general would reflect Australian society more accurately if employment practices throughout all sectors of the media were more representative of people from minority communities. As the media is owned and managed almost exclusively by Anglo men, issues concerning the employment of staff from minority backgrounds remain controversial, and for these people access to jobs in the media on any level is very limited.

On commercial television there are a very few non-Anglo faces. The ethnicity of behind-the-screen staff is unmonitored, and commercial broadcasters have no obligation to adopt representative or equitable employment practices. The absence of data on the backgrounds of commercial television employees has made it impossible to include the employment practices of commercial broadcasters in this discussion. As the commercial stations reach a far larger audience than the public service broadcasters, ABC and SBS, it is most important that management adopt more accountable and representative employment practices and strategies.

ABC and SBS are bound by section 22B of the Public Service Act to adopt equal employment practices to ensure that. . .

(a) appropriate action is taken to eliminate unjustified discrimination against women and persons in designated groups in relation to employment matters in the Department; and

(b) measures are taken to enable women and persons in designated groups to—
    (i) compete for promotion and transfer in the Department and in the service generally; and
    (ii) pursue careers in the Department and in the service generally, as effectively as other persons.

The 'designated groups' are 'Aborigines and Torres Strait Islanders, people of non-English-speaking background and their children, and people with physical or mental disabilities'.

Section 22 of the Public Service Act also requires the employment of an EEO officer to develop an EEO program and deal with cases of alleged discrimination. Part of the EEO officer's job is to monitor station employment practices in terms of gender and ethnicity. It is therefore possible to assess employment practices at ABC and SBS, and to see how staffing affects programming, program content, and the representation of people from minority backgrounds.

SBS

The Special Broadcasting Service is known to many as the 'ethnic station'. It was established (under the Broadcasting Act 1942) on 1 January 1978 to provide multilingual broadcasting services. (SBS Corporate Plan 1990–93:29). In 1979 SBS began producing experimental ethnic television programs for transmission on the ABC. In 1980, the Federal Government 'accepted the principle that a permanent multicultural service rather than an ethnic television one should be established' (SBS Corporate Plan 1990–93:30). SBS Television began broadcasting in Sydney and Melbourne on 24 October 1980. SBS's perception of its role is stated in its current mission statement:

> The SBS's mission is to contribute to a more cohesive, equitable and harmonious Australian society by providing an innovative and quality multilingual radio and television service which depicts the diverse reality of Australia's multicultural society and meets the needs of Australians of all origins and backgrounds.

Because of its multicultural brief SBS has by far the most diverse staff of any TV station. It is therefore the most interesting macro-environment within which to analyse staff attitudes to employment practices relating to ethnicity and gender, and how these practices affect program content. It allows us to examine the experiences of media workers from non-Anglo backgrounds, the positions they are employed in, and who has the ultimate power over issues of representation. This discussion is based on a series of interviews conducted in 1991 with people working in SBS television management and in the news and current affairs department.

The SBS EEO Program 1989/90 recognises the following characteristics of SBS's 'Organisational Culture':

- the multicultural/multilingual objectives of SBS;
- the ethnic composition of the workforce;
- the 'outside recruitment' of many senior staff.

Andy Lloyd-James, the Head of SBS Television describes SBS as 'one of the big ticket items of multiculturalism, it actually represents it as a corporation'.[1] He states that 'everything which the network does is designed to drive forwards the notion of a harmonious society. To that extent, News and Current Affairs are actually the front-runners for us because they are the programs which are actually dealing daily with the daily realities of life in this country'. SBS presents a multicultural face to its audiences—news presenters Lee Lin Chin and Mary Kostakidis, for example, are unusual in that they are both women and from non-English-speaking backgrounds. Considering this 'multicultural face', and the multicultural focus of SBS, it is surprising to find that the picture behind the camera is different; that in 1990 there were eight journalists from English-speaking backgrounds, only four from first-generation non-English-speaking backgrounds, and two from second-generation non-English-speaking backgrounds.[2] In news and current affairs, as is the case in SBS television in general, most employees of non-English-speaking background are in the lower pay categories.

Andrew Potter, Head of SBS News and Current Affairs, is aware of the importance of employing people from non-Anglo backgrounds as presenters, yet acknowledges that even in terms of 'on-screen' cosmetic representation 'we could be found to be way short of the mark'. As stipulated in the EEO program, SBS senior staff are largely recruited from outside the organisation. SBS EEO officer Jim Tsoukalidis attributes this practice (which prevents the promotion of existing staff) to notions of Anglo or English cultural and institutional superiority, or 'a fair degree of cultural cringe about the ABC. . . if you can't get anybody from the BBC'. The result of this practice is that upper management at SBS is recruited either from BBC or ABC television, and is therefore almost entirely dominated by English or Anglo-Australian men. According to Tsoukaladis

. . .it's necessary to look at what you might call key positions, and the question of the effectiveness of an organisation. If you're producing an output which affects people from an EEO target group, then having members of that EEO target group involved in making decisions means that they are more likely to reflect what their needs are. Now that applies here. There are five key positions that affect television. That's the Executive Director of SBS, the Head of Television, the Head of Local Production, the Head of News and Current Affairs, and the Head of Programming. Of those five positions there is only one of a non-English-speaking background.

---

1. Andy Lloyd James interviewed by Lois Randall, 11/9/91.
2. Information provided by Jim Tsoukalidis, SBS EEO Officer, 1991. All direct quotes in this chapter are taken from interviews undertaken by Lois Randall or Kalinga Seneviratne.

All these key positions at SBS are filled by men. In the top pay bracket, none of the top ten positions are filled by women. In the second highest bracket, 8 of the 20 positions are filled by women, and of these only one is from a non-English-speaking background. In the lowest pay bracket, women fill 39 of the 78 positions. Of these, 32 are from non-English-speaking backgrounds. Women are poorly represented in SBS in general. However, most women from English-speaking backgrounds are employed at the middle of the range (ASO level 4, 5 and 6), whereas women from non-English-speaking backgrounds are concentrated in the lowest pay scale, mainly as contractors with no permanent positions, or in the ASO 1 category.

In terms of Aboriginal representation on SBS staff, SBS did not employ its first permanent Aboriginal member of staff until 1989. Since then management strategies for the employment of Aborigines have been formed via an often painful process of trial and error—the pilot Aboriginal program *First In Line* suffered a high turnover of Aboriginal staff. Rhoda Roberts, who worked on *First In Line* as a presenter/journalist, attributes this to the fact that 'there were non-Aboriginals, who had no understanding of the Koori way, dictating'. She also points out that 'it was a first' for management, who 'thought that if they stepped in every five minutes when something went wrong, it would appear like whitey telling blackie what to do—the old mission mentality. And they were really so sensitive of that, that they wanted to avoid it at all costs. So in fact they stood back and never said a word for a whole year, whereas they should have stepped in'.

Due to a long overdue recognition that Aborigines remain under-represented on SBS staff, an Aboriginal training and employment strategy has been developed with target levels for employing at least 20 Aboriginal staff over five years, and an Aboriginal officer to run the scheme. General staff and management awareness of Aboriginal issues has improved slowly (proportionately with the increase in Aboriginal staff) to the stage where SBS has established an Aboriginal Unit.

From SBS management's point of view, the *attitudes* of employees are more important than the employment of staff from 'ethnic' backgrounds, in ensuring an 'accurate reflection' of Australia's multicultural society in programming. Lloyd James, for example, recognises that 'if you're trying to reflect the reality of Australia in the 1990s your make-up should to some extent reflect it', yet he places more importance on his belief that people choose to work at SBS because they are commited to multiculturalism: 'I genuinely believe that . . . people work at SBS because they've got a commitment to the notion, because this place gave them a chance and in giving them a chance opened their eyes.' While it may be important to 'open the eyes' of many people working in the media, the overall employment practices at SBS give the impression that management is more willing to give Anglos 'a chance' to experience working in a multicultural environment than to give people from non-Anglo backgrounds 'a chance' to work in executive decision-making positions.

Journalists from non-English-speaking and Aboriginal backgrounds at SBS agree that the only way to reflect Australian society accurately in the media is by employing staff on all levels, from management to journalists, who represent the diversity of Australian society's sectors and communities; and they agree that equitable representation on the station staff should go beyond 'on-screen' presenter positions. Irene Buschtedt, producer of *Vox Populi*, affirms that 'what appears in the program reflects the sort of people that are working within the station'.

Rhoda Roberts, reporter/presenter for *Vox Populi*, highlights the importance of on-staff representation for Aboriginal people:

> I think most journalists should be able to cover an Aboriginal story. . .but there's still a lot of ignorance and myths. . .It's not as if our government is telling us the truth—they haven't for 200 years. We are looking at a generation that had no formal education in Aboriginal studies. Journalists have never learned. But if they've got someone Aboriginal there telling them, working in the industry they'll start to learn. People have come to me and said 'we want to do a story on such and such, is it O.K. to get this old man?' . . . Now they are actually coming and asking questions like that. So I think that's a step forward.

SBS's programming also reflects the make-up of its staff in that it places Australia culturally in Europe to a large extent. Irene Buschtedt has said:

> . . .it'd be nice to have a bit of extra money to give us [*Vox Populi*] the opportunity to employ more people to work on the program on a permanent basis from other ethnic backgrounds, to widen it a bit—to maybe have Asian representation on the program. . .we're well represented in the European front. . .maybe someone from the South Pacific area. Our neighbours.

Access to employment in the media is thus a very important aspect of ensuring a more accurate representation of Aborigines and Aboriginal issues, as it is for people from non-English-speaking backgrounds, mainly because it provides cross-cultural contact. A vital part of the education process for all staff is having contact with people who understand media processes and who come from the diverse communities that make up the station's audience.

SBS employment practices are based on the merit principle. While it is bound to EEO, there is no overall affirmative action or quota system in operation for employing people from different backgrounds other than the Aboriginal employment scheme. Lloyd-James rejects such systems:

> If you move away from a merit principle, then you run the risk of having less

> than effective minds at work. Working in television is a position of such appalling power, that the thing you've got to pay most attention to is the quality of the people, the quality of the minds that are making it.

SBS employment practices therefore seem to imply that non-Anglo minds and abilities are more likely to be inferior.

Andrew Potter also points out that 'in the end you employ the best person for the job, and with 10 per cent unemployment there's a fairly big market to pick from'. The questions of how 'best' is judged, and by whom, do not seem to have been seriously considered by SBS management. Commenting on this problem, EEO officer Jim Tsoukalidis notes: 'We. . .need to codify a lot of employment practices—to actually sit down and say "this is the way that we will go about filling a job, this is the way we will write a selection crieria so that it's not biased, this is how we will select the selection committee" '.

Some Aboriginal journalists and staff from non-English-speaking backgrounds reject the quota system on different grounds, feeling that it would undermine their professional confidence if they thought they were employed to fill a quota, not for their skills. They also expressed concern that a quota system would lead to tokenism and the employment of people with inappropriate skills. Tsoukalidis, however, feels that—as with the case for Aborigines at SBS—affirmative action is a necessary starting-point: 'I tend to reject the concept of tokenism. You have to start somewhere, and hopefully it will lead into something else better.' Rhoda Roberts says: 'I really hope one day that it doesn't matter if you're Aboriginal or Greek, you're there because you're the reporter. That'll happen, hopefully, when we've got more skilled people.'

Training, with some sort of affirmative action component, is therefore a key issue. Before people from minority backgrounds can acquire jobs in the media, they need the skills to compete for jobs on an equal basis. Again reflecting on the *First In Line* experience, Tsoukalidis points out:

> . . .in that program we didn't have any training assistance. The budget only covered salaries. What I would like to do now is look at the budget of a program like that and include a training component which could possibly come out of a different fund, so there would be a mixture of on-the-job and more formal training at the Australian Film TV and Radio School. That's the strategy now to work out a training component *before* people start.

Such training initiatives are important because they allow people from non-English-speaking and Aboriginal backgrounds to get a foot in the door at SBS. However, it is also important to realise that many people from non-English-speaking backgrounds who do have media skills and experience have been unsuccessful in seeking employment at SBS.

SBS recruited its first three news trainees in 1991: one for TV, one for radio and one as a joint radio and TV trainee, a position kept specifically for an Aboriginal or Torres Strait Islander. The other two trainee positions were specifically for people from non-English-speaking backgrounds. These positions had been initiated and developed with funding from the Office of Multicultural Affairs and the Department of Employment, Education and Training. Roberts is enthusiastic over cadet traineeships:

> They don't just do Aboriginal stories, which is really important. The more Aboriginal reporters we see, reporting on all kinds of things, then the public views us as part of this society, which we are. At the moment people think it's a myth out there that we exist, because people look at television as if it's a mirror of our society. . .Now the more Aboriginal faces they see on television then that myth starts to get broken down.

Access and equity should not mean that people from minority backgrounds are confined to programs about their particular communities or other minority communities. For SBS news and current affairs employees, however, there is some concern about the apparent confinement of ethnic and Aboriginal staff to ethnic and Aboriginal issues. The more mainstream current affairs programs—*Dateline*, for example—are staffed by mainly Anglo journalists, while *Vox Populi* is staffed by journalists from non-English-speaking backgrounds. *Vox Populi* journalist Emilia Bresciani explains:

> They should have people like myself in *Dateline* if we're going to make some kind of impact, but we at *Vox Populi* do have a wider audience, and it's not just the home of the wog. . .but I suppose it will take some time for *Dateline* and for people at SBS to realise that in variety lies success. I suppose society is very much scared of change.

Despite SBS's exclusively multicultural brief the overall picture remains controlled by Anglo managers who apparently continue to apply Anglocentric criteria in their selection and placement of staff, and an Anglo or European perspective to programming. While there have been some positive new initiatives, particularly in improving the on-air representation of Aboriginal people, most staff from non-Anglo backgrounds and 'other' perspectives still seem to be confined to specifically 'ethnic', 'Aboriginal' or 'community' programs by a process that keeps the 'hard news' and current affairs programs and the station as a whole controlled by Anglo-Australians.

As Irene Buschtedt, SBS's producer of *Vox Populi* points out:

> . . .systemic discrimination is one of the hardest forms of discrimination (a) to pick up, and (b) to combat. It does manifest itself by having very few people

from non-English-speaking backgrounds in higher echelons or even highly graded journalists, A1s, chiefs of staff, producers, or whether they're on the foreign desk with the expertise that they have. If you look at the management structure of any commercial or non-commercial TV station it is primarily Anglo-Saxon, and that takes a long time to overcome.

When asked about the notion of taking on NESB trainees at managerial level, as well as trainee journalists Buschtedt responded:

Practical, yes! I just don't know whether Australia is mature enough yet as a nation to take that on. It took a long time for women to be recognised and be seen as capable of doing work at the same level, and of a better quality than men. I think it'll probably take at least that long—and that's several decades—for people of non-English-speaking background to be accepted. And you get the double whammy if you are an immigrant and a woman. It's probably easier if you are an immigrant man to move up the scale faster. That's reality. . .It would be nice to think that one day the Executive Director of SBS could be someone from a non-English-speaking background.

While SBS obviously employs people from a diversity of backgrounds, elements of the discriminatory employment practices are still common throughout the media. Many observers feel that to fulfil the aims outlined in its mission statement, SBS management needs to make a genuine financial commitment to establishing programs and initiatives that will open up management to people from non-English-speaking and Aboriginal backgrounds, and to improve the overall representation of cultural diversity on and behind the screen.

ABC

The ABC's charter was amended in 1983, and now requires the Corporation to broadcast innovative and comprehensive programs that 'contribute to a sense of national identity and inform and entertain and reflect the cultural diversity of the Australian community'. Yet the predominant voice of the ABC, as personified by the presenters or anchors of its news and current affairs programs, is still Anglo and male. To create a more accurate reflection of cultural diversity, the ABC has adopted several strategies for increasing its representation of people from non-Anglo backgrounds on screen and on staff, since 1988. These include:

- the introduction of an Aboriginal Employment Development Policy (AEDP), with a Co-ordinator of Aboriginal Employment and Training, and an Aboriginal Programs Unit;

- the employment of a Special Recruitment Officer, and a Multicultural Programs Unit;
- affirmative action targets and traineeships.

While these initiatives have led to some changes, special recruitment has been severely limited by the ABC's current budget restrictions, which have resulted in redundancies and staff cuts, and by entrenched attitudinal 'employment barriers' for people of non-Anglo backgrounds and women.

According to Lis Rust, Special Recruitment Officer:

> I think that television has all these ways of defending the status quo. The way in which people's screen presence is determined needs to be changed. There should be a more flexible approach to how people sound and how people look, because to me it still seems that we have this very monocultural notion of the way people are supposed to come across on air. . .It's a very male approach still, in that men are seen as being authoritative presenters. So there's still all those barriers that need to be broken down. They are in a sense attitudinal barriers but they manifest themselves as structural barriers because they make it very difficult (a) for people to get in, and (b) for them to move on once they're here.

In its 1989 EEO program ABC TV set affirmative action employment targets for women, NESB and Aboriginal people, based on a percentage breakdown of the Australian population as a whole. Therefore the targets set are 50 per cent for women, 25 per cent for NESB people, and 2 per cent for Aboriginal people. The EEO unit has deliberately adopted these targets rather than quota systems because the latter are considered discriminatory, and because of a wariness about bringing employees into a hostile environment. The potential for resentment from other staff towards specially recruited employees has been exacerbated by the current employment climate of staff cuts. As Lis Rust points out, in the current climate of job cuts resentment is inevitable: 'There have already been rumblings around the place from other staff, like "how come Aboriginal people are getting special treatment when I've been made redundant and I've been here for 10 years and I don't think it's fair" '.

The sensitivity of station staff towards 'special' recruitment programs highlights the importance of merit-based employment as a means of countering resentment towards affirmative action programs. According to Rust: 'We can't abandon the merit principle—that's been one of the cornerstones of selling this whole thing about Aboriginal employment. When Aboriginal people apply for those positions they go through exactly the same selection process. And it's the best person for the job.' Despite the fact that employment must, by law, be on a merit basis, perceptions of special treatment reveal a general ignorance by ABC staff of the meaning and practicalities of affirmative action employment programs.

Despite this adherence to merit-based selection principles, perceptions of 'special treatment' put enormous pressure on Aboriginal staff to prove themselves. Rust comments: 'The track record of Aboriginal employees themselves—particularly in journalism where one of them has won two coveted awards, and the work in the Aboriginal Programs Unit—has gone a long way to breaking down some of those stereotypes. There's no doubt that Aboriginal people do have the skills and the ability.'

Christine Sammers, formerly a producer with the now defunct Multicultural Programs Unit, is concerned that suspicions of tokenism can undermine the confidence of specially recruited employees, and she holds management responsible to ensure that this doesn't occur:

> The NESB trainees are suffering a bit because they think other people will think they didn't get there on their own merits. They start to question their own abilities and their self-confidence is undermined. I've even had the odd sly comment against me, but then I remind them of my previous experience. It's important that management does the groundwork for NESB employees to go into that work environment so the rest of the staff understand what the issues are, and the trainees are not just put in cold.

The current recession, which has imposed on the ABC significant budget cuts, has meant that while it is still Board policy to reaffirm a commitment to cultural diversity and employ people from minority backgrounds, overall staffing has been reduced. Rust has had to postpone her active recruitment plan and only outside funding has made it possible for the ABC to employ people from non-English-speaking backgrounds. Over the last three years the Office of Multicultural Affairs has funded nine NESB trainee journalists in ABC news and current affairs, and one multicultural researcher in *The Investigators*, one of ABC TV's highest rating programs. This research traineeship, however, has been filled by an Anglo-Australian, even though applications were submitted from NESB people with relevant experience. While the selection committee considered that according to merit-based employment principles the successful applicant had the most appropriate skills, this selection decision emphasises how hard it is for NESB people to gain even specifically designated multicultural positions.

Similarly, the Aboriginal Employment Development Program is based on funding from outside the ABC. The Department of Employment Education and Training (DEET) has provided the program with 75% of its salary and costs for the last three years, and has just committed funding for training Aboriginal staff for the next five years. Since 1989 this program has led to the recruitment of 36 Aboriginal/Torres Strait Island staff members, which as the EEO report points out 'is more than halfway towards achieving its target of employing 57' (Special Broadcasting Service 1990). Most of these employees have been placed in a range of positions directly involved in program-making, in the Aboriginal Programs Unit, in news and current affairs, or in other areas where they can have a say, and influence program policy and the organisation as a whole.

Frances Peters, producer with the APU, maintains that 'most Aboriginal people who work at the ABC are trainees'. It is important that the ABC offers these trainees permanent positions upon the satisfactory completion of their training. Although these are positive steps towards achieving greater diversity of staff, it is revealing that both these special recruitment and training programs have survived the current employment climate only because they are funded from outside sources. Fred Kelly, Co-ordinator of Aboriginal Training and Employment, acknowledges that without the DEET funding, the progress made in the last three years in terms of Aboriginal employment 'would have taken at least ten years'.

The Aboriginal Programs Unit has proved extremely successful in producing high-quality programs on Aboriginal issues for general audiences. Frances Peters explains how the unit operates: 'We have a philosophy that no program is made by non-Aboriginal people. All the directors, producers and researchers are Aboriginal people who work in APU. . .I think the main priority is having Aboriginal people being the ones to have the political and creative control, editorial control over our programs.' The *Blackout* series is really a first for Australian television because it broadcasts Aboriginal programs in prime time. Vaughan Hinton, (non-Aboriginal) executive producer of the unit, explains that 'a prime-time program such as *Blackout* gets 1.5–2 million viewers and they are viewers across the whole demographic segment of viewers'.

While a specifically Aboriginal unit might seem to limit Aboriginal staff and issues to one program strand instead of including them in mainstream programming, Peters stresses that the unit is an important first step. In the long term, however, she believes that 'instead of just seeing the Aboriginal program unit. . .the most practical thing to do is to have Aboriginal people [as] producers and directors and writers or journalists, infiltrating. . . the already existing areas so the [Aboriginal] perspective is made mainstream, so it's not just, "hey this is just an Aboriginal program!"'. The perspective should be shared in all the areas.' Fred Kelly applauds the AEDP for the achievement of three Aboriginal directors of *Blackout* and four working in mainstream programming. Christine Sammers in 1991 spoke of the Multicultural Programs Unit:

It's a stage thing—although our unit is marginalised in terms of resources, staff and access to production funds. . .we are also effecting change. Even though multiculturalism is still seen as a marginal issue because it is not crucial to the agendas of program departments, our unit *is* promoting cultural diversity through mainstream programs.

Rust, like Sammers, was frustrated by the financial restraints they both operate under.

I'd like to see a much more serious commitment made by ABC management in terms of trying to address this whole notion of cultural diversity, in terms of the resources I have available. This needs to be regarded as a priority, not to be shoved aside when we have redundancies or staff cuts or budget cuts. . .or because it's all too hard, and it's just disposable. This is a multicultural society, and you can't go on pretending that it isn't. . .you have to have enough resources and the right sort of support to. . .be effective. I think that every single vacancy we have between now and whenever should be targeted to people of NESB and/or women. Because we haven't met our targets, we've got a long way to go, and if we are serious then that's what we have to do!

The EEO report has identified 'employment barriers' for Aborigines, NESB and women. These barriers are mostly matters of attitude, and arise from a general lack of understanding of the important contribution that staff from minority backgrounds can make to programs. The News and Current Affairs Department, for example, has very few people from non-English-speaking backgrounds holding editorial positions or able to contribute directly to program content or perspective. Sammers attributes this to a general assumption that multicultural programming means lowering program standards. She believes that for many ABC staff, multiculturalism is 'synonymous [with] lack of excellence, because by definition if it was excellent it would already be there on the agenda and on the screen'.

Frances Peters asks why people have assumed that allowing Aboriginal people to present programs without spokespeople or white narrators would limit the quality of programs. She maintains that the *Blackout* programs are good documentaries by anybody's standard, and achieve international sales: 'David Hill was over the moon about our last series. There were excellent reviews and that's because we know that we are actually catering to a national audience.'

Sammers also feels that change has been very slow because most people in the ABC have never been asked to think about their performance in terms of cultural diversity; they block it out because they don't understand it or feel that it's important.

So getting it on the agenda is a big thing. They think they don't know where to find NESBs, they think that people won't be able to speak English and they'll have to worry about translators and interpreters and subtitles, and that is extra levels of complication. So it's whether they think that it's important enough to warrant the time and worry. The 'how to' is like a self-censorship thing, saying it's too hard. And. . . they don't know! I've had executives at the ABC tell me that they've never been in a house of someone from [a] NESB. . .so to them it is a big hurdle to overcome. . .They see me, second generation, as totally assimilated and just like them. Someone who identifies ethnically, to them, still speaks with a very heavy accent and lives in Marrickville.

As part of an initiative to counter similar stereotypes and ignorance about Aboriginal people Fred Kelly, Aboriginal Employment and Training Co-ordinator, has established cultural awareness seminars. These have been run in Sydney and Melbourne and include a panel of Aboriginal people speaking about their life experience and dealing with being taken away from their parents, brought up on missions, or living in a racist environment such as Wilcannia. The seminars start with a quiz about Aboriginal culture. Lis Rust comments:

From my own experience the seminars are very effective. They are done in a way that makes you, as a non-Aboriginal person, realise that you know absolutely nothing about Aboriginal culture at all. It makes you take stock, and for a lot of ABC people it's the first time they have actually thought about some of these issues. . .it makes you realise how much you've got to learn. . .and how difficult it must be for Aboriginal people trying to contend with that ignorance about their culture, their belief and their customs. . .Everyone who's been on them say it's made a fundamental difference [to] how they're going to operate in the future because it's given them all this information that they didn't have before, never been taught at school, never had any notion about looking at things from an Aboriginal perspective.

ABC management, like that of SBS, is dominated by Anglo men. According to the EEO report 'human resource data indicates that the organisation's managers are predominantly male and that occupational segregation by gender is slow to change' (Special Broadcasting Service 1990). Rust has experienced more resentment to the informal *Network 99* women's meetings than to any of her other recruitment and training programs: 'The culture of television so far as most women here at Gore Hill are concerned is still a very macho, male-oriented, cowboy style of management. It excludes women. . .the way your management skill is assessed here is whether you're one of the boys. It's just appalling.'

Sammers also feels that management has difficulty allowing for a diversity of perspectives because of its limited access to and understanding of multicultural issues:

I don't think it's a conscious thing where they say 'no I don't want your ideas. . .' They say 'I've built my career, and I'm in this position because I know what makes TV work, and I think this makes TV work because of my experience.' So it just reproduces itself. To try to tell people in management that a good idea is relative and relational and culturally defined is very difficult.

For the ABC to provide a more accurate reflection of cultural diversity, its management must be open to cultural perspectives other than its own. It is also important that the ABC recognises and understands the multicultural nature of its audience. Sammers claims:

There has been an element of self-censorship because they feel that they know who the audience is. . .we're. . .telling them that you don't know who the audience is. There are demographic changes. Neilson's is starting to collect ethnicity data. It's only been in the last year we've started asking the questions, SBS started asking questions. But I rang SBS and they don't have any precise ethnicity data. None of us know who's watching what station.

It seems that training programs aimed at management positions for women, Aboriginal people and NESB people are required so that minority cultural perspectives can infiltrate ABC programming.

Rust rejects the notion that people from NESB do not gain jobs in other areas of the ABC because they lack the skills:

[In] the last couple of years [I have] put together registers of freelance producers and directors, and journalists and reporters of NESB, and their educational qualifications and. . . skill levels are at least as good as [those of] people from English-speaking backgrounds who are already here at the ABC, and [they] certainly have attributes in that they speak several languages. The OMA train-eeships for people of NESB are therefore more important in that they are functioning to ensure that people from NESB get the jobs not so much through the training component [but from] providing an outside funding impetus. . .to ensure that people get in and [management realises] that there is a problem that needs to be addressed.

Even more vital is a program to educate management about the import-ance of its recognition of and commitment to cultural diversity and associated issues. Chris Sammers feels that more representative employment is only half the answer:

There is a corporate culture. For example, women have been working at ABC TV for a long time and it has taken even longer to get any further representation of women on screen. In terms of the future, people have to lead from the front. . .We need the Managing Director to be really pushing it. And down the line, the Director of Television has to be pushing it. . .We also need that constant pressure from outside groups to back up what we are doing. The ethnic communities really have to see it as a priority. Also the funding from organisations like OMA, who have concentrated on the media, is important. I think that we're still looking at the flow-on benefits of OMA funding, and it had a real effect on what we were doing.

OUTCOMES

Both ABC and SBS television have a formal commitment to reflecting the diverse nature of Australian society in their programming. Management, in both stations, acknowledges that employment practices and staff attitudes are key factors in the achievement of such goals. There is, however, a distinct gap between these ideals and the actual priorities of ABC and SBS management, as evident in their employment practices. Staff from Aboriginal and non-English-speaking backgrounds emphasise the fact that while some positive steps have been taken towards increasing staff from non-Anglo backgrounds at SBS and ABC television, most of these positions are on-screen journalistic and non-management. While this increase in on-screen representation is commendable since it visibly reflects the pluralistic nature of Australian society, there is also a real need for better representation of people from non-Anglo backgrounds in areas where they can have a direct influence in determining program content. Upper management of both ABC and SBS television remains firmly in the control of Anglo-Australian men, and there are still very few people of non-English-speaking background who have any real decision-making power in management positions.

This situation of male-Anglo media ownership and control in Australia, and the current employment environment of general staff cutbacks and low recruitment rates makes it imperative that all media management in both the commercial and public sectors recognise and understand the multicultural nature of their audiences and make a genuine commitment to accommodating people and cultures that are different from their own, on staff and in general station programming.

In terms of employment practices it is fairly widely agreed that employing people on a basis other than merit can lead to resentment from other staff. It is important for employers to consider seriously just how they judge 'merit'; to evaluate their selection criteria. Would they, for example, give a journalist position to someone from a minority background, with languages other than English, an understanding of cultural diversity, a knowledge of the social and political make-up of other regions, and an excellent record in their field in another country? Or would they favour someone with five years experience of producing stories for an Australian commercial TV news program, and who has no comprehensive understanding of important multicultural or social issues? The latter choice seems likely, since specifically funded Office of Multicultural Affairs traineeships at ABC television have been given to Anglo-Australians. The structural barriers, which are manifestations of an organisation's dominant attitudes, seem almost impenetrable.

EEO is designed to redress imbalance and counter discrimination in a situation of equal skills, and as such it is very important, but it has not succeeded in readdressing inequality of access to employment in the media, particularly in key decision-making and editorial positions. Many people who have excellent skills still don't get jobs in the media. It is argued that this is because of a scarcity of positions available, and a high level of unemployment among those who already have extensive experience. These excuses seem to stem from an underlying resistance from the status quo to allow women and people from minority backgrounds to compete on an equal basis for jobs. While media managers claim that they actively support equality of access to employment, they are in fact excluding or screening out minority groups and thereby maintaining the Anglo cultural domination of the media industries and output.

It is apparent that the major barriers to employment and representation of minorities lie in the structural self-interest and attitudes of management and programming executives, *not* expressed in station rhetoric and 'mission statements', but by their employment practices and funding priorities. Management must adjust its practices, to bring the media into line with a changing Australian society.

29

NEWS VALUES AND MINORITY JOURNALISTS

News and current affairs present us with elaborately packaged information about our society and our place in the world. This information is delivered to us by presenters and reporters who are mostly Anglo-Australian and male. We are given to believe that they are presenting the issue and the subject of the story with integrity in a balanced, objective manner. They speak to us with the voice of authority. But from what position are they speaking? Whom do they represent? What social values influence their choice and interpretation of stories? Why is it assumed that the dominant cultural perspective is objective?

News is not simply a reflection of reality. It is created through industrial processes, involving aesthetic and professional decisions based on newsworkers' social and individual judgments about their audiences and the line they want to take. Newsmaking is a process of identification and selection of stories, in which some events are noticed, others are not. The events that are noticed tend to be presented in a manner which reinforces the existing social and moral order. News is constructed and negotiated by the people who gather it and present it—it is not simply a rigid or predetermined ideology.

News values are a highly complex set of codes by which newsworthiness is judged. Internalised by news workers, these values ensure that the interests and values of the dominant culture are constantly repackaged and reproduced in news stories, and 'other' perspectives are screened out or rejected as non-newsworthy, or marginal. This agenda is set by the people who control the newsrooms and who make editorial and programming decisions. As we have seen in the previous section, these positions are almost invariably filled by Anglo-Australian men who maintain, often unconsciously, the dominant ideologies of Anglo-Australianness.

Emilia Bresciani, SBS journalist, puts it this way:

There wasn't so much a conscious restriction of presenting my point of view. There is a general restriction from the Western world towards anything else that does not reflect their way of thinking. They're so arrogant. . .Australia is perhaps a bit more guilty in that having such a multicultural population it's still playing the role of the British-type lord here when it comes to the media format, or any communication package that is ever broadcast. . .I mean the whole style of news presenting—they're very concise, very superficial, there's a very non-questioning attitude from reporters in general.

The very manner in which news is constructed, to provide a shorthand version of current events, requires newsworkers—from camera operators to editors, journalists and producers—to *choose* what images, graphics, wording and spokespeople to use. The average news story seldom runs for more than a few minutes, and news crews work to daily deadlines, which means that newsworkers make these decisions on the run. There is no time for a great deal of thoughtful selection. Standard news formulas are often used to save time, and the same audio-visual equations are constantly reworked.

Stories that do not fit into this news formula—because they may describe processes rather than events, or deal with more general community issues—are often described as 'soft', or not 'newsworthy'. Time constraints, employment structures, attitudes and funding priorities leave very limited room for the discussion of social issues or more general stories, unless they are 'cute' and can thereby be packaged into that final news item: the 'human interest story'.

Rhoda Roberts, Aboriginal reporter/presenter at SBS, asks:

> What is really newsworthy? Isn't 20 kids in Redfern on the methadone program and going to rehabilitation a good newsworthy story? Or is 20 kids overdosing in Redfern a newsworthy story? Well, we all know which one a lot of the commercial channels would pick up and that's because we've created that mould of saying 'this is newsworthy'. We've told people if it's sensational then it's news, but if it's not, it's soft. But is it?. . .you've got to start changing the image a bit, I think.

The isolated manner in which events are reported in news and current affairs can be misleading. Audiences interpret the reported incident without sufficient background information to understand the full context in which it occurred. In stories dealing with Aborigines or immigrants the incidents that are judged 'newsworthy' almost invariably involve violence. Insufficient background information can aggravate social misconceptions. Christine Sammers, in 1991 producer of ABC TV's Multicultural Unit, gives an example:

> We could provide better coverage of the ongoing issues surrounding immigration, instead of this cyclic thing of nothing, nothing, nothing, and then suddenly a news story on the 'immigration debate' emerges. We ran a six-week analysis of our news. In one example it showed how ABC radio, through their Ethnic Affairs round, had newsworthy information available on what was happening in the lead-up to cuts in immigration numbers. But ABC TV only ran one story on the day the cuts were announced. To the audience the perception was, 'Okay,

immigration has been cut. Does that mean there are too many Asians?' They never received the details leading up to the cuts.

While most newsworkers strive towards 'objectivity', it is largely unrecognised that objectivity itself is a subjective, culturally defined concept. A report of an event involving a minority community or members of a community can only be interpreted as biased against that community if the context of the event is omitted. Objectivity or balance can be achieved only if a report includes the perspective of the community or people involved. In stories dealing with Anglos this is taken for granted, yet in the ABC news coverage of the anniversary of the Wave Hill walk-off by the Gurindji people on 29 August 1991, which was hailed as the 'anniversary of the land rights movement', the only 'spokespeople' interviewed were Gough Whitlam and Paul Kelly. Does this mean that Aboriginal people cannot speak for themselves? Similarly, in an SBS news story which went to air on 26 August 1991, reporting that Yothu Yindi's song *Treaty* was the first single by an Aboriginal band to break into the charts, Mandawuy Yunipingu and the other members of the band were shown at a press conference, but the main spokesperson was Minister for Aboriginal Affairs, Robert Tickner. The story skimmed over the issue of *Treaty* and showed images of Aborigines protesting, but again no Aboriginal voices were heard.

Questions of bias rarely arise if a news report conforms with the dominant perspective. Yet the Royal Commission into Aboriginal Deaths in Custody found that Aboriginal communities are consistently unhappy with the uninformed, stereotyped coverage they receive in news and current affairs. Bias is usually recognised only if it opposes or threatens the values and social dominance of Anglo society.

Rhoda Roberts, for example, feels that at times she has to go out of her way to give the 'other' side of a story so that her work will not seem biased from a non-Anglo perspective: 'It's very hard. Naturally, they think you're going to be [biased]; that's why I say when you do stories, in actual fact you have to go overboard a little bit, by making sure the other side is represented'.

Newsmakers work on the premise that the 'national audience' shares the same values as they do; that they are programming for 'national' interests, even though this 'national audience' is nothing like as homogeneous as the upper echelons of media control in this country. Issues relating to minority 'ethnic' cultures are considered ethno-specific. Even SBS stories tend to be relegated to the so-called 'ethnic' programs such as *Vox Populi*. Irene Buschtedt, executive producer of *Vox Populi*, questions this notion of ethno-specificity: 'The issues of education, health, and violence should worry all Australians. . .I can't really think of any issue that would be ethno-specific, and not worry all Australians'.

As producer in the Multicultural Unit at ABC TV, Christine Sammers was also concerned that stories are rejected because they seem ethno-specific:

> We want our image and life experience represented across the board in all programs and content areas, and a few people are beginning to understand that this means those from minority groups appearing in mainstream stories about the economy and smog etc, not just in immigration and unemployment stories.
>
> But if the story has only non-Anglos in it they think that the story is ethno-specific, for some imagined 'ethnic community' and not for the population at large. For example, there was a play on at the Belvoir Street Theatre in Sydney [which is a mainstream venue] called *Love and Magic in Mama's Kitchen*. The cast included Peta Toppano [a mainstream 'star'] and five other actresses from Italian backgrounds. All gave fantastically strong performances—and I thought 'where are these women on our TV screens?' So I watched to see if the story would come up—it was Carnivale so it even had that tag. But it didn't appear. It was seen as too ethno-specific and of minority interest. To me it was as valid a representation of our cultural life as *Hair*, or John Williamson.

The experiences of 'ethnic' and Aboriginal journalists working in news and current affairs highlight the fact that 'mainstream' Australian society, or the 'majority perspective', can only be enriched by different cultural approaches and issues. Yet they are constantly frustrated or restricted by the 'moulding' or controlling influences of a news and current affairs agenda that is set by representatives of the dominant Anglo culture. Emilia Bresciani, SBS journalist, reports:

> It has been very frustrating for me the past five years to. . .convince others that the voice of the Third World is a very important voice. . .I have been restricted culturally, by the mould that exists in this society of which many people are unconscious slaves—and so one of the things that I want to do particularly when I say I'm a developmental journalist is to promote a different approach to news and current affairs, that departs from everybody's own cultural understanding. But it can only happen when those people consider themselves strong enough and self-confident enough to bring out their own cultural understanding of the world around them. . .It doesn't take just one person. It must take a lot of people to convince [the] mainstream approach to everything that another point of view, another way to look at life is also enriching, and therefore productive and attractive.

Rhoda Roberts, SBS reporter/presenter:

> I think they're just frightened because [only in] the last few years. . .there have been Aboriginal journalists, an Aboriginal presence on TV. So another five years

might see a change. . .we might start seeing docos made on what are considered now to be radical viewpoints. But see, it's so new. People are still coming to terms with it. The first thing they say to me is 'oh, my God, I've never met an Aborigine before, don't know how to talk to them'. But that's their view and they're actually working in the industry and they're supposed to be making the news. Then what are the people sitting at home in the lounge room thinking?

A major area of concern for Aboriginal journalists and producers working in ABC and SBS television news and current affairs is the issue of representation: how Aboriginal people and issues are presented. They feel that it is their responsibility and motivation for working in the media 'to get better coverage for our people', as Roberts puts it.

'Better coverage' has been interpreted as 'positive stereotypes' or role models by many non-Aboriginal news and current affairs executives. Their motive—including what they consider to be positive images of Aboriginality—is commendable, but this is a simplistic approach. Aboriginal people must attain positions where they can decide how Aboriginal people and issues should be covered. While role models are necessary to counter the stereotypes prevalent in news and current affairs coverage of Aboriginal people, Aboriginal journalists feel that it is also necessary to cover the many other serious issues that their people are dealing with, and that this can be done without stereotyping.

This does not mean that only Aboriginal journalists can cover Aboriginal issues. As Roberts points out, it can sometimes be difficult for an Aboriginal journalist to cover certain stories:

> It can be very hard on a journalist who's from a particular community to go and report a story. . .On the one hand you don't want to air your dirty washing so to speak, and the community can frown upon you and think you've sold out. . .There are very sensitive areas. . .drinking and child abuse and all those things that do go on in the community; as an Aboriginal journalist, it is so hard to cover because you are going to upset a part of the community, but it's something that needs to be reported, so that people know. So there are times when you can show the positive, but at times you know you don't live in a wonderful world. There are things that do go wrong and it can really rip you apart, because if you tell this part of the story as well, you know that you might never, never get back into that community, and you don't want your own community to hate you. So sometimes you have to really say 'look, someone else cover this story. . .'

It is important that coverage is informed and balanced; and that an Aboriginal perspective is given so that the misconceptions and myths about such issues can be avoided. This perspective can emerge only by consultation with Aboriginal people working in the media, and by allowing the Aboriginal subjects of a story to speak for themselves. Unfortunately, however, Aboriginal people have been consistently misrepresented, as Roberts says, 'by so many ignorant people, they just don't want the cameras any more. . . because anything they've ever seen on the TV has been negative. . .so there are other times when you can cover that story because you just know that there are people who would talk to you, who wouldn't talk to a non-Aboriginal. I know some of those old women down Eveleigh Street wouldn't even look at those cameras, but because they know it's me they'll come over and talk to me'.

Frances Peters, of ABC TV's Aboriginal Production Unit, is also concerned about journalists' tendency to go to so-called Aboriginal or non-Aboriginal 'spokespeople' for comment, rather than allowing the subjects of the story to speak for themselves. She stresses that for *Blackout*, the APU program, 'we never went to spokespeople. You see news and current affairs crews. . .grabbing people who are spokespeople, because they are not game enough to trust the story in the hands of community people. When I say community people, I mean the non-media sort of representatives of Aboriginal people.'

While ABC and SBS television have both made a commitment to employ more Aboriginal people in news and current affairs, there remains a resistance to the Aboriginal perspective in news about Aboriginal issues. Most stories about community issues are considered too 'soft' for news and current affairs, yet Aboriginal stories are restricted largely to 'soft' issues, such as art galleries or sportspeople. Roberts comments:

> When we first started *First in Line* I found it very very soft. Sure, when you start something new, you've got to ease into it, you've got to get your audience, OK. But it seemed to be all nice and pretty little art galleries. It does show that out there, there are hundreds and thousands of Aborigines who are positive role models, and they are doing really well. That's great and we should show that. But at the same time we should also say, 'look, this is how this man, Michael Mansell for instance, this is how he's portrayed in the Australian press, do you want to hear what Aborigines think of him?'. . .and do something like that, but the attitude is 'ooh, that's a bit radical.' But. . .being Aboriginal, I think, is a bit radical. You do have to question what's being radical. To be radical is to change something. Well, I don't think there's one person in Australia who wouldn't want to change some things, you know.

Stereotyping Aborigines has decreased since more Aboriginal people have begun working in news and current affairs, and this is progress of a kind, though it is qualified by a reluctance to allow the Aboriginal version of events to be presented, and to allow Aboriginal journalists to cover issues that they consider important. In a country whose very constitutional and legal structures are based on the myth of Terra Nullius, it is perhaps not surprising that an Aboriginal perspective is considered 'too radical' in a media hierarchy controlled by the perpetrators of such myths. On the subject of sovereignty, for example, Rhoda Roberts says: 'it's never touched on because people think it means that you'd have to get Gary Foley and Michael Mansell and Oh, my God, that'd be too radical!'. The representation of minorities in news and current affairs is also an area of concern for people from non-English-speaking backgrounds. As part of a strategy to increase the representation of cultural diversity and fulfil its charter obligations, ABC-TV News and Current Affairs has organised a series of forums for senior executives, producers, reporters, and production crews to discuss the implications of cultural diversity in all aspects of the production process. Christine Sammers reports:

> It's a big step—very senior people are saying to their staff 'this issue is on the agenda, let's look at the practicalities'. Most people had a general understanding of multiculturalism but there was a gap between that and their practice. We discussed specific issues to do with content and representation, like the graphics used, accuracy of archival footage, what sorts of shots—are they reinforcing stereotypes? Like when the story is about welfare do you automatically go to footage of Aborigines, and what is the effect of this?
>
> And these are complex issues because TV news is a form of shorthand. If you want to say 'immigration', and you want to make a visual image you might show an 'Asian' face because people accept this as common parlance, but if you use an English face, they'll say 'I don't understand. What's the issue?' So how to make this shorthand non-stereotypical is a real challenge.

These cultural diversity forums were held in all ABC-TV newsrooms across Australia, and the news was subsequently monitored to gauge any change. Sammers asked people 'to think about what "experts" and "talent" they use and who they "vox pop", and question whether this group really represents Australia. One of the clips we used at the seminar was about immigration, and although it was quite sympathetically done, when it came to "vox-popping" Australians about what they thought about immigration, they were all Anglo.' This shows how newsworkers make unconscious assumptions about who is 'Australian', and how news and current affairs maintain the cultural and political supremacy of the Anglo majority perspective.

Another effect of this supremacy is to make Aboriginal news and current affairs staff feel they are treated as a minority—people coming from a 'different' culture with a 'different' way of doing things. The sense of isolation and the difficulties young Aboriginal trainees experience in adapting to the secretive, competitive world of the media industries highlights the institutionalised behaviour of an industry in which the most competitive or ruthless are often considered the most successful and rewarded with promotion, particularly in news and current affairs. Rhoda Roberts describes the experience:

> We've got a couple [of trainees] here who are working for the public service and they are going through the administration. Now, these girls in another five, ten years they could be anywhere in this building, that's great. But also it's a very hard step for them, because they're coming from an Aboriginal area where competition isn't the name of the game. You don't do nasty things like fight the person you work with to get the better job. You share. That is another myth, people think that that doesn't exist in us. Any Aborigine who lives anywhere in Australia, has that sharing, caring, that's what we're brought up with. And that's very difficult to come into an area like this and with the competition you can feel so alone.
>
> Being older, perhaps we can understand and deal with the gubbah mentality. We have learned to cope in such atmospheres. Most of our education was through a highly competitive non-Aboriginal system, learning their values. But to someone younger, they may start picking up those values and think that's the way to be a good journalist. We've got to say, 'look bub, this is our way, you can write a story just as good as them'.

In the final part of this chapter we look at what some multicultural audiences think about the representation of multicultural Australia in the media and in performance. We begin with comments from audience members who attended the performance of the stage show *Acropolis Now* in Sydney in late 1990. *Acropolis Now,* a television sitcom, was based on a hugely successful theatrical production of *Wogs Out of Work,* in the mid 1980s, and was rewritten for the stage.

30

AN AUDIENCE PERCEPTION: *ACROPOLIS NOW ON STAGE*

Two boys, parents from India, Egypt:

Acropolis Now is the same basic thing as *Wogs Out of Work*. It's very true—they're able to capture what really happens in society, especially around this area—we're from Burwood, Concord, Strathfield. We live in a migrant society, it's what you see in schools. The western suburbs is a working-class area, and everything they say is very down to earth, they're not above everyone else, everyone can relate to what they're saying and what they do. That's why you see all different kinds of classes here. The schools we go to, there's more Greek and Italian and Lebanese than any other country, so we can relate to it very easily. . .It's very funny. They just talk the same, and the way they act, it's just so down to earth. They can relate to everyone, of all ages, everyone can see it, and they just know. Some of the things they come out with are so true, that we can all laugh along with it. We have the same experiences, we see it every day.

Two Greek girls from Marrickville:

We like the way they talk and how they make fun of the Greeks and how they really are.

Mixed group, mainly Greek, from Auburn and Lidcombe:

We've come to see the wogs, mate. *Wogs Out of Work* was very funny, especially the sketch where they did Aussies. *Acropolis Now* is funny and it's realistic, because it knocks the Greeks, and it makes fun of us wogs. It makes fun of Anglos too, but if we can take it they can take it. They're spokesmen. The wogs come out on top because it's about the wogs. If you make fun of someone, they're always going to come out on top. Effie's a real classic. I've met a lot of girls exactly like her. Memo is a typical Greek. Rick's the smart one, he's the only one with brains, the only one who acts normal.

A group of Croatian boys:

> It makes fun of the wogs. I don't reckon that's a good thing, but I don't like Greeks very much. If a comedy made fun of Croatians, and it was funny and it was true, I wouldn't mind it, but if it wasn't true, I'd take it to heart. *Acropolis Now* isn't really true—it's a bit exaggerated. But it's exaggerated in a proper way, not in a foul way, you know?

A group of Greek girls from Concord:

> We've come to see the show because we're Greek. No, it doesn't put down Greeks. There's a lot of humour in there, and it just gives the Australians an idea of what the Greeks are all about—the humorous side of life. Let's face it, you've got to be happy, you only live once. It's for all ages, and it's for all people, whether they're Greek or Australian or Italian . . . It's different from *Wogs Out of Work* because Liz is Australian, and Rick's Spanish—there are other people in it, and they get on better. With *Wogs Out of Work*, the Aussies and the wogs didn't get on that well, but in *Acropolis Now* they work together and stuff, so it's much better, it's happier. We're coming to see the show just to live a bit of Greece, I suppose. We can't go overseas, so why not try and live it here in Australia?

Mixed group, mainly Greek:

> Characters like Memo are true. We know, because we live it. Not everybody's like that, it depends how Greek in your way you are, how traditional you are. You find in *Acropolis Now* that it depicts family life for a Greek girl as very strict, you find Effie—she's not allowed to go out to discos on her own, she's got to be married before she can go out. No boyfriends are allowed, and when she wants to go out to a disco, she's got to be chaperoned. That's definitely true of my experience. I think Liz puts up a lot with the Greeks, but she's happy. She gets along with them, and that's the main thing. Greek people are very friendly, they're outgoing. They're a good laugh. Rick's a more conservative Greek—what you'd call the good boy round the corner of the Greek street. I think they're all attractive in their own way, but Rick's the most attractive.

An American living in Sydney:

> It's a little more open than in America. The humour is a little bit more risque—it's a lot more fun. You guys are a lot more open about race relations, you'll say a lot more about each other—just good-naturedness—whereas they're afraid to in the States. They're just so timid about saying anything, stepping on anyone's toes. Here it's a lot more good-natured, and fun. There is a lot of ethnic

comedy in the States, but you don't see much of it on TV, and when it is on TV it's very sugar-coated. Here it's more out in the open, and people will say things about one another but they don't take it real seriously in my mind. It's just a lot more fun. I love Memo—he's got the best delivery. He's an excellent comedian.

The American's Anglo-Australian companion:

I spent some time in Greece, and it's just what they go on like—it's wonderful. It caricatures Greek people, but it makes them fascinating and interesting and fun. Jeff's my favourite character—he's quite sexy.

Lebanese boy from Ashfield:

It applies to everybody—Greeks and Lebanese—the way they act. Some people may not understand. Some Australians will come to the show and they might not even know—wogs might be laughing, and Australians are going 'What's so funny?' It doesn't put wogs down, it just gives them an idea about us.

Mixed group of Greeks from Marrickville and Sydney's inner west:

We're here to see our heroes! It shows the culture of Australia and all the ethnics in Australia. Memo's the real Greek one. You have to say he does show a bit of a negative picture of Greeks, but you have to laugh at yourself and your own background. All characters that are funny have to be exaggerated, it's the caricature we're laughing at, isn't it? Rick's Spanish, isn't he? Well, why does he come across so Anglo-Saxon? He's a wog too, isn't he? I really like him, though. I'm not trying to say that Anglo-Saxon means intelligent and wog means not intelligent, I believe there has to be a line down the middle. He's fairly neutral—I'm sorry he left the show. I went to school with a few Effies in Strathfield—the hairspray, the make up—it's very true. I'm sorry to say this, but it's very true. . .She's a bit over-exaggerated, but she's pretty funny. Liz is the normal Australian type, she's a good character as well. . .I saw *Wogs Out of Work* several times. *Acropolis Now* is spaced differently, but it reminds you of the same sort of thing. . .The characters are basically the same, basically you've got a story whereas before you had sketches. . .I believe it depends on how you say the word 'wog'. If you say 'wog' in a really negative way, of course you're going to offend, but it's become really accepted now. It's just a term, a classification really, isn't it? You can say Greek, you can say 'wog'. I don't find it offensive, unless you say it in a really negative way. It's the facial expression that goes with it, I think.

31

AN AUDIENCE PERCEPTION: ETHNIC AUDIENCES AND THE MASS MEDIA

The debate over what the media actually does—and in particular what perspectives on society are conveyed by news, features and cultural programs on television, radio and in the press—involves not only academic analysts but also policy-makers and the general public. The debate moves from fact to values, from what *is* the case, to what *should be* the case. For instance, many who claim that the media should but does not report on society accurately advocate a closer link between events and their reportage by the media. For example, they argue that if 20 per cent of the population are of non-English-speaking background, then that same percentage should apply to the stories in the media about them, to their participation in television soaps and advertisements, and to broadcasting in languages other than English.

Their opponents argue that if there is little representation of 'ethnic' Australians, if issues affecting them are not featured, or if they do not appear in soaps and ads, this is a true reflection of their position in society, whether we like it or not. It is argued that 'ethnics' do not usually make interesting news stories because news is about conflict between powerful people and 'ethnics' are not very powerful; and, audiences, it is claimed, prefer characters who most resemble archetypal role models with blue eyes, blond hair, and affluence. These audiences may also include 'ethnic' Australians, who may themselves prefer idealised Anglo-Australian visions of the good life to a reflection of their own lives, which may be hard and unglamorous.

A study for the Office of Multicultural Affairs of ethnic audiences reveals significant concern about their experience of the mass media. While this study mostly reflected concern about television, it encompassed other areas (Coupe and Jakubowicz 1993). Over 60 group discussions in various languages with communities around Australia, taking in over 700 people, revealed an Australian media not capable of reflecting the desires of many of the respondents. They were asked for opinions about the following:

- Family life presented by the media and how it related to their families.
- Stereotypes of ethnic groups in advertising (or their exclusion).
- Casting in soaps and advertising.
- The immigration debate and its treatment in the media.

- News and how their community and region of origin were reported.
- The place of migrants in Australian society.
- The presentation of women and Aborigines.
- SBS and ABC (TV and radio) as a conduit for their concerns and interests.
- Their use of and satisfaction with ethnic media.
- Specific questions affecting particular groups—for example, the reporting of events in Eastern Europe, the Middle East, and so on.
- The representation of Arabs, Asians, the boat people, and so on.
- Change in media.
- Material not available to them.

We refer here to some of the main findings, though interested readers can read the report in full from the Office of Multicultural Affairs. The ethnic audiences surveyed were frequent consumers of the media, particularly the electronic media, from which they gained significant information about Australian life, even where this became rather idiosyncratic. We can see in the following table that the range of television viewing, for instance, was quite broad, with significant recourse to news of domestic and home country events.

Young people tended to watch a much higher proportion of 'soaps', and said that they saw current affairs and documentaries only when they watched TV with their parents. In general, though, the audiences were unhappy about the expression of Australian values. Often they simply did not realise that there were any Australian values present, claiming that what they saw were American or British values, or Australians mimicking them. Several felt that Australian society presented in the media seemed to lack any values—by this they usually meant moral codes in which family, parents, intergenerational and cross-gender relations were not accorded the respect that they believed was appropriate.

It was also clear that they were concerned about representation of ethnic minorities—most said that there was none on television or in the media overall. In particular, the exclusion of non-Anglo images and stories contributed to a widespread sense of 'not being Australian', although 'being Australian' was seldom considered a very attractive proposition.

Commenting on the findings the report noted the following:

The most common response, by 47 of the groups, was that Australians were 'only white', 'Anglo-Saxon', 'blonde and blue-eyed' and 'fair-skinned'. Other responses of this type were 'tall, thin and tanned', 'Paul Hogan' and 'Lisa Curry and Grant Kenny'. This blonde, Anglo norm was seen as particularly pervasive in the representation of women, when males and females were described separately, although on the whole the 'typical' Australian was likely to be masculine. These overtly physical descriptions were backed by other responses that under-

Table 1: Type of TV watched according to group (total groups responding = 47)

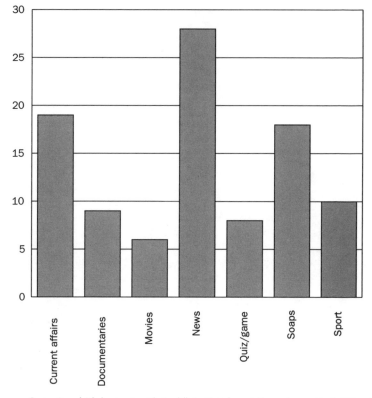

Source: Coupe, B. and Jakubowicz, A. with Randall, L. *Next door neighbours: A report for the Office of Multicultural Affairs on Ethnic Group Discussions of the Australian media,* Office of Multicultural Affairs, Canberra, 1992, p. 10; 1993, p. 10

lined how important to the groups it was to be able to see people in the media that looked like themselves and who were more representative of the ethnic diversity in Australia.

This perception of a predominantly Anglo Australia also stood for the media's exclusive representation of Anglo values, morals, culture, family structures and religion. When groups were asked how the media should show Australia, almost all of the responses related to a desire not only for a greater range of ethnicity of presenters and actors, but also for the presentation of a greater range of cultural and ethnic viewpoints. Furthermore it was specified that such presentations be positive or at least that the positive and negative aspects all ethnicities

Table 2: Australians shown on TV (total groups responding = 61)

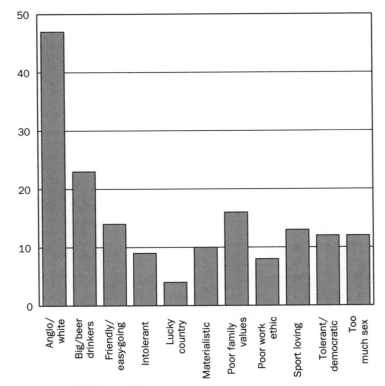

Source: Coupe and Jakubowicz 1993

and cultures be equally represented. . .the Australian media was disliked for its exclusive presentation and valorisation of Anglo-Australian people, culture and values. These were usually seen as being very different, and often inferior to those of the participants. This resulted in the majority of groups concluding that the way the media show Australian society made them feel that they were different to or excluded from Australian society. (OMA 1993: 19 ff).

The report also found that:

The Australian media were not seen to be presenting an accurate or wide-ranging reflection of Australian society. Rather they were interpreted as avenues for the communication of American or British cultural concerns, with the quality of Australian material somewhat less effective in stimulating audience involvement and response. There were real concerns at the narrowness of Australian society as it appeared in the media. The limitations of physical type, story line, and issues found in programs was a consistent theme across groups.

There was also a consistent concern that where the media reported specific issues affecting ethnic communities, this was done in either a patronising or biased way, with inaccurate or partial information typifying the presentation. The 'bad news' focus was overwhelming, leading to a view of ethnic Australians which portrayed them as conflictual, violent and uncivilised. There was widespread unhappiness with the way the media treated Asian immigrants, for example, and there was frustration with the lack of balance in reporting. It seemed to be assumed that the point of view of the audience was that of Anglo Australians to the exclusion of any other people. Ethnicity was presented continually as problematic, rarely as a positive quality of a multicultural society.

Media representation of Aborigines and Torres Strait Islanders caused some distress to the audiences. The overwhelmingly negative portrayal was seen as one-sided, unfair or too harsh. Audiences expressed the need for better information, more historical background, and a more sustained and sympathetic representation of Aborigines and Torres Strait Islanders communities.

Gender roles generated a range of responses—three main perspectives were offered. The media were criticised for presenting women only as domestic drudges or sex objects; the media were commended for valuing the role of women as mothers and as professional workers; the media were encouraged to break free of stereotypes and show women in a range of roles, and ethnic women as other than simply working-class cooks and cleaners. Significant comments were made about culturally specific notions of beauty and attractiveness serving to denigrate women who were not blonde and slim.

The ethnic media were widely used where available, and provided a useful service where English language skills were limited. In this regard ethnic radio services were sometimes criticised for being old fashioned, or limited in their coverage and accessibility, though important for cultural and linguistic maintenance (OMA, 1993: 77–8).

The outrage and insecurity voiced by many members of ethnic communities in their accounts of their media experiences indicates that they have deep reservations about the fairness, accuracy and value of the media. They want it to be better at doing its job—accurately reflecting the diversity of society. Audiences can discern the exclusions and dubious commentaries—whether they are Cambodian refugees urged to buy unaffordable disposable diapers because that is what television tells them is appropriate behaviour in Australia, or Aborigines in Redfern thoroughly exasperated by yet another program focusing on the police view, the alcoholism and the misery.

Audiences are active participants in the creation of meaning, and argue back at the media in their continual dialogue (often unvoiced) with them. The impact of this process on ethnic minorities and Aborigines and Torres

Strait Islanders has yet to bear fruit in the modification of media practice. The final part of the book reviews the implications of the material presented here, and returns to the questions with which we opened our discussion, focusing on the future and the potential for change.

PART V

THE WAY FORWARD

32

OUR PROBLEM WITH MULTICULTURALISM

The Australian political system has proclaimed a commitment to the nation as a multicultural society. The mass media provide one arena in which this commitment can be tested and its implementation evaluated. In order to undertake this evaluation we need to understand that the media are both institutions of production and organisation of information and ideology, and sites for the presentation and contested consumption of meanings. Two methodologies—from political economy and from textual analysis—are entwined to provide a cultural critique of multicultural and multiracial Australia and the media. We are dealing with a complex politics of representation, in which economic and class interests, gender relations, cultural practices and their expression through social behaviour, find daily expression in the media.

Multiculturalism remains a term wreathed with the residues of strong political and social disagreements. It is a state ideology, constructed out of the social relations of the past two decades of Australian life, and designed to sustain harmony and prevent discord and conflict. It can be used by various participants in the discourses of multiculturalism, to encompass at the same time arguments for basic human rights in Australia which transcend ethnic or racial differences, and arguments which seek to stress those differences as paramount and unbridgeable. It allows for notions of ethnic essentialism and the primacy of the ethnic group, at the same time as it can promote individual freedom from the cultural restrictions of ethnic groups. Multiculturalism can stand for a concept of society which reduces all differences to idealised separated cultures within which questions of gender or class have no purchase, or it can sharpen gender and class analyses to demonstrate the complex multidimensional aspects of contemporary identities and the competing loyalties or priorities they can encompass.

We cannot escape these ambiguities in our own work; we are therefore making an argument for a critical multiculturalism, one which comes to terms with the unique relationship between indigenous Australians and all those who came to the country after 1770. Indeed, one of the difficulties with multiculturalism as a theoretical construct remains the relationship of Aboriginal Australians to the whole idea, an issue made more dramatic after the

1992 High Court Mabo ruling with its 'rediscovery', so to speak, of Aboriginal rights to the land pre-dating European conquest (the ruling on native title and the overturning of the concept of *terra nullius*).

We recognise that the current policies used by government are heavily compromised by hierarchies of power deeply embedded in the political and social realities of contemporary Australia, where unequal relations of class and gender and ethnicity and race are reflected in and reproduced through institutions including the media. A multicultural critique of Australian society and its institutions points up the importance of continuing the critical appraisal of cultural practices, while arguing for changes and developments which reflect that critique. The insights of cultural analysts are valuable, however the implications they draw about how deeply embedded distorting and ideologically framed representations of Australian race and ethnic relations are, can become an excuse for inaction in the political sphere.

The authors of this book have worked closely with government agencies as consultants—indeed some of the research which we have used in this book has been funded by agencies such as the Office of Multicultural Affairs and the Human Rights and Equal Opportunity Commission. We are not naive about the political strategies such agencies use to advance what we would often criticise as minimalist agendas. We recognise that institutions are often enamoured of a theory of history which sees them as responding to social changes and reflecting enlightened public values, a view of them we do not always share. We recognise that many problems lie within the institutions, where there is a reluctance to change, and where agendas of critical multiculturalism can find a few champions in an environment of economic rationalism and reduction of resource inside government, and market-driven profitability in commercial media. The media reproduce the power structures of society (even if they challenge performances within those structures), so that concerted change has to address those structures directly and indirectly, and not wait hopefully for the structures to change themselves.

The future of mass media engagement with Aborigines and Torres Strait Islanders and ethnic minorities in Australia depends greatly on the structural future of the communication industries and the more controversial ideologies of nationalism and multiculturalism. We have seen how much energy the media invest in defining differences and constructing social hierarchies. We have shown that while these practices are not usually organised as strategies of racial domination, they seem to reinforce existing hierarchies and do not change until forced to engage in sustained struggles by minorities and their allies. While there is no unilinear march towards a brave, new world, there are many innovations and reactions, victories and defeats, initiatives and reinforced traditions. Popular opinion, which is said to guide and be reflected by the mass media, is a many-splendoured thing, a multitude of voices, each with very different resources available to them.

We have approached the questions with which we began this book from a position which can be best described as critical multiculturalism—a position which seeks neither to advance itself as a crusading enterprise on behalf of minorities, nor one which accepts government policies of multiculturalism as necessarily appropriate goals in themselves. We recognise that the struggles over cultural differences can range from positive affirmations of group identity, creativity and social rights on the one hand, to the brutal extermination of all 'outsiders' on the other—from respect and recognition of rights to that detestable term 'ethnic cleansing'. In carrying out our analysis we do not wish to privilege 'ethnicity' or 'race' as a dimension of social difference and inequality: we have chosen it as a problem to be investigated, arguing throughout that race and ethnic relations cannot be separated from gender and class analysis.

What then have we learned to help us answer our four questions?

- How do the media represent Australia—in its cultural diversity and social difference?
- Are these representations as a process of creating meaning, the result of conscious manipulation and active decision-making by individuals or groups within the media?
- Are they the unintended but no less effective consequence of how power is organised in Australian society, a structure of power which in terms of class, gender, ethnicity, race and political priorities is merely replicated within the media as it is elsewhere?
- Is there anything unique about the nature of communication industries in a post-colonial society such as Australia?

We have been watching an important debate develop through the late 1980s and into this decade. The debate about cultural industries and the role of cultural critics such as ourselves has been made prominent by arguments for the transformation in the relationship between researchers and the government in policy areas. In 1989 Tony Bennett of Griffith University's Institute of Cultural Policy Studies issued a manifesto arguing that cultural policy studies, in which cultural critics work in collaboration with government institutions, industry and community groups to formulate progressive social policies, had superseded what he described as 'a generalised form of social criticism', which he deemed no longer 'an acceptable mode of intellectual work' (1989:9–11).

In his book *Framing Culture* (1992a) Stuart Cunningham put forward what seems at first a similarly pragmatic argument, suggesting that simply criticising 'dominant ideas' from a detached oppositional position is dangerous; exponents of cultural studies needed to engage in the formulation of institutional cultural policy, and place themselves in the process of making policy. This implies that cultural critics should argue their case in a way that can affect government and private sector policies on mass communication, the arts and culture in general; or as Noel King has put it, 'go downtown and play a little hardball with the suits' (1992: 8). Cunningham has summarised his argument as follows:

> In the bigger picture of the politics of everyday life and the power relations embodied in its representational forms—which is the ultimate object of cultural studies—there is a large split between, on the one hand, our citizenship selves, our newspaper-reading selves, those selves that occupy positions of academic or family responsibility, in which we apply social-democratic or liberal-democratic norms, and, on the other, the oppositional rhetoric of cultural studies, which for many of its practitioners has become largely a symbolic politics. I fear that, in the establishment of cultural studies as an institutionalized and internationalized enterprise, we are responding more to the internal logics of the academy than to a wider and deeper cultural politic, the agendas of which are regularly articulated in the policy process. (1992b:542)

Meaghan Morris, an Australian cultural critic with a prominent international reputation, renowned for her detachment from Australian institutional bodies, has asserted the importance of Australian cultural traditions of opposition such as feminism, gay and lesbian politics and critical multiculturalism. These radical positions have no place in Cunningham's advocacy of abandoning oppositional stances in favour of a unilateral engagement with the grey bureaucratic prose of socially dominant cultural institutions. Morris (1992b) considers that Cunningham's argument excludes notions of 'difference' and sets in motion 'a circle in which academics will teach and analyse policy in order to generate policy—limiting our discourse accordingly, and calling this discourse 'criticism' (1992b:545). She cites the case of feminist semiotic analyses of media advertising, which Cunningham rejects because they do not use 'content analyses based on accepted sampling techniques', and comments: 'Since the study of representation now occurs worldwide across a vast range of fields from philosophy to literature to medicine, this is tantamount to demanding that all such study in Australia be carried out as amateur social science'(1992a:38–9).

Morris also cites the work of Sneja Gunew, a prominent advocate of critical multiculturalism whose work as a cultural critic of non-Anglo and migrant Australian literature reaches an international audience as well as participating in local and national debates about multiculturalism. Gunew's work exemplifies the type of 'multivariate' cultural criticism that Cunningham's policy schema excludes, even though Gunew herself has been an active participant in the policy process through her membership of the Australia Council. Morris also expresses concern at Cunningham's 'manichean' division of 'citizen selves' and 'critical selves', thereby excluding 'the critical self' from notions of national citizenship (1992b: 549–50), a process analagous to that of the construction of 'images of themselves against others' which constitutes a national imaginary. This suggests that the aims and goals of cultural policy studies may be just as unrealistic as some who advocate engaging with government claims to find cultural critics.

Our critical perspective in policy analysis and cultural studies starts from a recognition that governments are concerned with representing those social interests which are best established and most powerful. Particular governments may vary in how they want to advance those interests, and may have different priorities. The decade after 1983 in Australia was dominated by a federal government with a mildly reformist social justice agenda, in which equity for minority groups and a recognition of Aboriginal rights were prominent on the policy platform. Various strategies erecting this platform were adopted though we find it most significant that the mass media were left almost untouched by any direct government strategy—unlike the case in gender issues where media attention was directly targeted by a powerful women's lobby. It was only in 1992 that the changes to broadcasting regulations occurred, and then the 'reform' moved towards industry self-regulation.

Government strategies on ethnic relations found their clearest expression in the realm of Access and Equity through the monitoring of government agency actions by the Office for Multicultural Affairs. It is again significant that OMA did not begin to pay much attention to the media until the early 1990s (when our research group among others, began to press the issues in a wider public arena). Yet despite the policies concerning access and equity for non-English-speaking background immigrants, only moderate advances had been made in the relevant government media organisations.

As we have seen, neither the ABC nor SBS has opened up its senior management positions to people from outside the ABC/ex-BBC Club (or should we say to men from outside these areas—women do not feature in the senior management of either organisation). The typical 'credit' line for television production at the ABC has almost totally Anglo 'creative' personnel, although many of the technical personnel are immigrants—for instance, Czech and Polish camera people or video technicians. In 1993 SBS again appointed an Anglo Australian (ex-ABC executive, though with a Scandanavian grandparent) to fill the top job vacated when Brian Johns went to the Australian Broadcasting Authority.

We conclude from this that organisational resistance to change, often justified in terms of minority groups' lack of 'local experience' or 'inappropriate cultural styles', has resulted in a series of media practices concerning employment, and thereby media products. While community concern presses for action which then produces changes in media programs and press content, yet these changes lose much of their potential because media managers resist them. Not a conspiracy, but certainly a ritualised set of behaviours which reinforce the ethnic and racial version of the 'glass ceiling' complained of by so many women in the media and large organisations. The glass ceiling is apparently transparent but contact proves it to be impermeable.

৩৩ MEDIA REPRESENTATION

The media representation of Australia's cultural diversity reproduces many of the elements of an earlier (and unsatisfactory) epoch in North American media. Social difference is rarely noted, with the most significant occasions likely to occur in the national broadcasters, though we noticed that on one commercial channel the most likely appearance of an Asian Australian—apart from the news reports of their apparently endless involvement in knifings, bashings and drug smuggling—occurred in the program *Australia's Most Wanted*, where they became once more the objects of social suspicion. Where cultural and racial differences are incorporated into media the tendency is to offer an impersonal, passive view, with minorities given an active voice only in the context of violence, comic relief, or stereotypes.

Greenberg and Brand (1993a) have asked how we are to understand the effects of such representation on both majority and minority audiences. Are stereotype and exclusion less worrying for, attractive to or even recognised by audiences, than those programs and stories which try to explore the complexity of a world in which issues of race and ethnicity abound? This problem was raised by two current affairs programs—Channel 9's *The County*, and the ABC's *Cop It Sweet*—which showed Aborigines, police and Redfern from the respective perspectives of the police and of a journalist more sympathetic to the Aboriginal experience. Both programs caused immense controversy, and raised Aboriginal community involvement in the debate about the representation of Aborigines in the media. The issues raised there contributed to pressure for change.

There are now more Aboriginal and Torres Strait Island voices being heard and read in the media than there were five years ago—though programming and press content still does not reflect the public expectation identified by Bostock (1993), Nugent et al. (1993) and Coupe and Jakubowicz (1993)—that is, that Australian audiences want a greater diversity of representation.

There are now Aboriginal journalists and current affairs presenters (in limited numbers) and Aboriginal characters are being written into television soaps, if not in central roles, then in significant episodes. Some of these deal with Aboriginal community issues, though most still depend on stereotypes

THE DAILY

Telegraph Mirror

EVERY CHILD TO LEARN ASIAN

TUESDAY DECEMBER 8 1992   Printed and published by Nationwide News at the office of the company, 2-4 Holt St., Surry Hills 2010

Every child to learn . . . What exactly is 'Asian'?

that offend Aborigines (as in Aboriginal youth cast in the teenage soap *Home and Away* who were presented as a social problem). During the recording periods there were few Aboriginal journalists in any media, and so Aboriginal presence was confined to that of mute victims or perpetrators of strife. This situation has changed significantly since mid-1991, due mostly to Aboriginal activism and to a response by the national broadcaster, the ABC, in opening training and reporting positions to Aboriginal journalists.

Aboriginal reporters are now more frequently heard on both ABC radio and television, the Aboriginal news magazine show *Speaking out* is heard on Radio National in prime time (6.30 p.m. on Sunday), higher levels of Aboriginal production on the TV *Blackout* program have been more widely seen because of its shift to the earlier time of 8.30 p.m. and ABC-trained Stan Grant has become the highly publicised anchor man for ATN 7's evening current affairs program, *Real Life*. These Aboriginal journalists will, however, need some control over the *production* of news stories if Aborigines as spokespeople and authorities are to appear in them.

Several mini-series have involved 'ethnic Australians' or issues concerning race and ethnic relations in Australia—*Vietnam* is probably the most dramatic of these, with its narrative of Anglo-Australians and Vietnamese interacting over a long period (see Cunningham 1989: 44). Yet the mainstays of Australian media portrayals of social difference are oddly remote from the social realities of everyday Australia—minorities make the news as threat or challenge, but scarcely appear anywhere else. It was not until early 1993 that Annette Shun-Wah was employed by the ABC to front a youth music program and other cultural programs after many years at SBS.

To summarise: there has been some progress but also many opportunities lost. The nation that is represented is not, for many Australians, the nation of which they are a part. It is not only ethnic Australians or Aborigines and Torres Strait Islanders who have expressed these views—they are widely held among Anglo-Australians.

34

A CONSCIOUS AIM?

While some groups seek to change the way the media relates to Aborigines and Torres Strait Islanders and ethnic minorities, and there is some government involvement to support them, is there any active opposition to these changes? What would count as evidence of such opposition?

Changing the perspectives and directions of the media—major organisations deeply embedded in society's cultural practices—requires a serious commitment by all the players. Multiculturalism as government policy has been with us in Australia since at least 1978; Aboriginal self-determination is a younger policy though backed in the past by opposition to discrimination declared by both sides of mainstream politics. Yet the evidence reveals very slow change, no widespread recognition of the issues from the media, and a history of indecision over direct action.

Earlier studies of bringing about change in government organisations concerned with services suggests that change has to occur in two directions—the structure of the organisation has to change to ensure the stakeholders have influence over outcomes of decisions, and the services have to change to meet the needs and expectations of stakeholders (Meekosha et al. 1987). General policy commitments and statements of principle per se are not sufficient to bring about changes that may seem to threaten or displace the old guard, either by challenging their claims to competency, or by directly replacing them. So change requires the personal commitment of senior decision-makers and managers; active resistance to change also requires such commitment, though apathy (a typical expression of racial intolerance) can and does achieve a great deal on its own.

We have indicated that the key decision-makers in most media organisations share broadly similar social characteristics—except for the women's press, they are nearly all men, mostly over 40, of Anglo-Australian or British background, imbued with a media ideology that justifies views that more or less uphold the social order. Thus the media are controlled by a minority of the population, one that attempts to speak for the majority, but does so through a limited range of discourses. This minority controls the flow of communication, circumscribing the approved stories and perspectives.

There are organised racist bodies in Australia which have been involved in violent attacks on ethnic and religious minorities, which have promoted fascist and xenophobic literature, which have daubed walls with graffiti, and sought to confront and victimise anti-racist activists. Their activities, when they have come to public attention, have been deplored and rejected by most of the media. The major media issue seems to have been whether the exposure of these activities promotes (by publicising) the behaviour of small extremist groups who can only survive through publicity. Government bodies have argued that the media should play down such events. In other cases—for instance where the issues of immigration and race are mixed with those of sexuality (as with the racist attacks in the late 1980s on the Gay Immigration task force) governments have distanced themselves from the issue.

On the other hand some media have actively pursued racist groups, arguing that exposure forces the hand of government to condemn them and stimulates public debate which might lead to government action—against racial vilification, for example. Key media examples of this include *The Bulletin*'s stories on neo-nazi groups and the ABC Radio National's programs about former Nazis and war criminals in Australia.

While the current pattern of minor progress is not a deliberate strategy to minimise access to and representation of Aborigines and Torres Strait Islanders and ethnic minorities, it clearly does result from other conscious action. Perhaps the strategy which has led to only limited progress is not as clearly expressed as *The Australian*'s editorial defending the interests of the 'dominant race'; nor as crudely self-interested as the persistent Press Council ruling that Aborigines would be offended but most other Australians would not be; nor as bureaucratically hamstrung as the old Australian Broadcasting Tribunal with its circuitous and ultimately useless attempts to control gratuitous racial vilification in the electronic media. The conscious element lies in the commitment to sets of professional values by media practitioners which unselfconsciously integrate perceptions of racial and ethnic hierarchies as expressed in speech and intonation and cultural priorities. Unless those practitioners are consciously and actively provoked to change, they will reproduce themselves and their world views endlessly.

Embedded in how the media go about their business are traditional systems and processes which media workers find it very difficult to challenge. A scriptwriting conference tosses around ideas for the next string of episodes for a soap—where will the ideas for change come from unless the group contains people who are sensitive to the issues and prepared to articulate views other than entrenched ones? A journalist facing a Chief of Staff of the old school finds she can write a story that conveys the minority position, only to discover the story reconstructed and over-simplified into the worst stereotypes, and overridden by photographs that victimise her informants, and by headlines that reinforce the most oppressive perceptions of the situation. Advertising copywriters and producers pull together a promotion for coffee which appropriates the lyricism of Kenyan Africans overlaid with music of Soweto, and end the television narrative with a white man drinking the coffee, so that they encapsulate in 60 seconds the history of western imperialism in Africa and the European celebration of the exotic, and reinforce the audience's sense of the Other simply as a fount of pleasure for the 'dominant race'.

Perhaps the answer to the question whether the pattern we experience here is the result of conscious action, is to reverse the query and ask: what conscious activity could change the pattern, and what would prevent it?

35

CRITICAL MULTICULTURALISM AND THE STRUCTURE OF POWER IN THE AUSTRALIAN MEDIA

The advent of multiculturalism as a social program in Australian society has its roots in the late 1960s, a period of turbulence and change not only in Australia but elsewhere. By the late 1960s the migrant workers' movement and the more broadly spread ethnic community struggles against assimilationism and cultural denigration were finding shape in a project that became known as 'cultural pluralism'.

The Australian policy responses to these social movements, and the deeper social stresses in which they were rooted, were affected by overseas experiences, and in particular, the models emerging in Canada.

The sense that the nation was equivalent to the people, so that national unity required social homogeneity, was gradually replaced by the concept that the nation was a coalition of interests. The pressure from the workers' movements forced another concept: that the cultural coalition could work only if socio-economic inequality was not linked to cultural differences. Another tension to be addressed was that of 'multiracialism'—it was significant that the Australian agenda extinguished this term, as though the constant voicing of 'culture' could erase the problem of the term 'race', and offer cultural accommodation as the solution.

A dominant consensus was then forged; it linked parts of the leadership of the trade union movement, the government, key parts of the bureaucracy and the leadership of many ethnic community organisations. It found its expression in the idea of a multicultural Australia. Issues of class (and gender and often race) were swept to one side, or spoken of only sotto voce; problems that affected the immigrant communities were reduced to cultural issues, often expressed in terms of their lack of and need for information. The multicultural agendas that came out of the late 1970s (the Galbally position of 1978), and the reviews of the 1980s (the Jupp review of 1988, for instance), and the Federation of Ethnic Communities Councils of Australia annual meetings, reiterated the new orthodoxy of special needs. They spoke little about how the working class in Australia was becoming ethnicised, nor about the tight link between particular ethnic and class experiences, because it was the vision of the ethnic petit bourgeoisie, its middle class and intellectuals, which sketched and then coloured the national agendas.

The new agendas of ethnicity steadily lost their concern for rights or for transforming Australian society. They sought protection to remain different; they were drawn into a milieu that still continued to marginalise them and to offer recognition for their special needs. It did not refashion the broad cultural agenda as a diverse arena. The ethnic lobbies arena turned into bureaucracies and consultative bodies, and became less effective in influencing wider social processes. Where voices advancing a more critical multiculturalism did emerge, as with the writing about immigrant women's experiences by cultural activists such as Sneja Gunew, there was caustic opposition from the core cultural elites (eg Dessaix 1991). They still held the strong perception that there were universal values of excellence as embedded in Northern European/White North American cultural practices—usually English, French and German—and that the ethnic experience from elsewhere was somehow secondary and 'folkish'.

Thus multiculturalism as a social agenda, rather than as a social reality, has occasionally affected the media. In this book we have explored many of them, demonstrating that patterns of institutional power are permeated by cultural hierarchies and processes which reproduce cultural dominance. Yet does this allow us to criticise the media practices? If the patterns of inequality continue throughout Australian society, why should the media, which often claim merely to reflect reality or creatively refashion it for entertainment, be held accountable? Surely that one institution (however diverse it may be) cannot be held responsible for the experience of Aborigines and Torres Strait Islanders, nor immigrants and ethnic Australians?

Our answer must lie in the analysis we have presented of the media—it is made up of conscious actors working in organisations, constantly making choices, and very often these choices are directly concerned with cultural representation: employing staff or contracting writers, purchasing and pro-gramming material, printing stories, selecting images and so on. While the fact that the media are part of the power structure of Australian society may help explain the pattern of media representation, it does not excuse it.

36

POST-COLONIAL AUSTRALIA: CHALLENGE FOR CHANGE

In the mid-1960s the National Film Board of Canada linked itself with the University of Newfoundland community extension program to explore the role of film (and later video) as a stimulant for social change. In a series of films which became known as *Challenge for Change*, media workers became involved with local communities. They attempted to help them tell their stories—the communities took part in the story construction and editing— and helped them to use the new media to organise their own community action and present their views. In Australia this project was influential in the establishment after 1972 of the Community Video Access centres, which led in the early 1990s to community television.

Over that same period another discourse has emerged in literary and cultural studies: post-colonialism. Post-colonialism as a political concept has a long history—Labor Prime Minister Whitlam used it in 1972. However it has a more recent provenance in textual theory. Post-colonial projects have found their strongest expression in work by intellectuals in positions in formerly colonised societies. The work of Edward Said, the American Palestinian who has written extensively on European constructions of non-European societies (as in *Orientalism*, Said 1978), Homi Bhabha (a British-based Indian) and Gayatry Spivak (an American-based Indian and feminist scholar), have advocated the untangling of contemporary non-European societies from the stories about them written from the perspective of the cultural élites of their former colonial rulers.

In Australia the discourses of post-colonialism unfold in three ways; they affect different parts of society quite differently but sit adjacent. First is the emergence of Aboriginal and Torres Strait Island perspectives, where the decolonising exercise is a process of rediscovery and affirmation of cultures submerged or distorted by the white invasion, and the assertion of a composite consciousness in contemporary society.

The Mabo decision has transfixed Australian society and the media with the realisation that the foundation myth is just that, a myth. The News Ltd newspapers have tended to demand that the government move as rapidly as possible to 'clean up' the situation by removing any threat to the European seizure of land. For the first time in Australian public history Aboriginal issues have become core issues for the future of Australian society. In conjunction with the outcome of the Black Deaths in Custody and the Racist Violence inquiries, with their recommendations on indigenous media, Mabo has shown exactly how important the media are in allowing communication in Australian society, and how difficult it is to hear Aboriginal voices for more than a moment in the melee.

The implications for Aboriginal media workers lie in the development of expressive modes that re-engage traditional expression with Australian society—an example in the visual arts is the Utopia women's art collective in Central Australia. By mid 1993 Aboriginal media workers had come together through the establishment of the National Indigenous Media Association (NIMA), which linked local media associations around the country. At an indigenous media conference in April 1993 the call was made for an aggressive policy on the Australian media and on media training. NIMA called for the establishment of an Aboriginal network along the lines of SBS. It also demanded that training for non-Aboriginal media workers include compulsory study of Aboriginal issues.

Aborigines face a continuing post-colonial (or even colonial) social environment, in the sense that the settler society is unlikely to be sent packing. Non-Aboriginal Australians meet other issues, and not all are experienced in common. This second post-colonial expression in Australia focuses on the republic, disengagement from the British Crown and the assertion of the unique 'nationhood' of Australia. This story recurs frequently throughout Australian media discussions of the nation, its boundaries (social, physical, cultural) and its future. Here we find the definitions and struggles over the nation, in which the symbols of the crown and monarchy are pivotal. While some elements of the 'multicultural Australia' have entered the republican debate (indeed the Prime Minister appointed an SBS television news reader, Mary Kostakidis, to be the 'ethnic' on his minimalist republican advisory committee) the tension is mostly about England and Australia. The concern for the meaning of 'nation' has led to changes, even in the deregulated media environment.

The movement towards media industry self-regulation has required television and radio organisations to prepare codes of practice, including those in relation to minority groups, and professional industry bodies have also tried to set out goals. The Screen Producers' Association of Australia has developed the following code:

1 Scripting
Strong consideration should be given to the creation of characters which reflect Australian multiculturalism including characters of non-European and Australian indigenous backgrounds.

2 Casting

Particular emphasis should be given to non-traditional casting, that is the casting of actors of non-European and Australian indigenous backgrounds in roles where ethnic origin is irrelevant to the character.

3 Extras casting

A proper balance of non-European and Australian indigenous extras should be used so as to reflect the current condition in Australian society.

SPAA believes that the presence of these people in our society should be properly represented in our films and television programs. While recognising the legitimate role of government authorities to monitor the portrayal of cultural diversity in the media, SPAA believes that progress in this area is best achieved by education and awareness programs and effective industry self-regulation.
(Quoted by Davern, OMA 1993: 44–5).

A third post-colonialism exists for other non-Aboriginal Australians, who face the peculiar problems of immigrant people who enter a society only to find its primary avenues of communication blocked, and themselves hobbled as they try to enter the communication field. Here we find 'non-English-speaking background' people, with an extraordinary diversity which government language tries to define and unify in a statement of what they are not. They are not concerned about the umbilical link to the UK, but with a redefinition of their place in Australian society. The Australia Council, through its 'Arts for a Multicultural Australia' policy, adopted in 1993 after an extensive review of previous practices, has begun to work out how this vision of a diverse Australian society might be realised.

As others have shown, institutions committed to multicultural principles still face large problems. For instance, the FECCA review of federal government department Access and Equity policies, made in 1991, noted of SBS: '[it has undertaken] a calculated misuse of the access and equity principle to justify the abuse of its charter' to shift television programming to 50 per cent English language (Milne and Zelinka 1991: 135).

The national challenge requires rather more sustained action than has occurred so far. At the OMA-sponsored seminar on the media and cultural diversity held in May 1993, the industry presented two broad positions. First was the argument presented primarily by the Federation of Australian Commercial Television Stations (FACTS) through Tony Branigan—that the situation was in hand, the codes reflected community standards, and change would eventuate. Second there was the frustration voiced by several younger media professionals from outside the dominant culture, anxious that change would be so gradual as to be unnoticeable. As the former Multicultural Programs Unit head at the ABC put it, 'This industry is the greatest load of buck passers I have ever met...the producers say there are no writers. The producers say the casting directors don't know how to do their job. The casting directors say there are no actors. The heads of television say it's not their responsibility and it just goes on and on and on. The buck stops in two places. The buck stops with the owners of the media and the buck stops with Federal Government instrumentalities' (Christine Sammers, OMA 1993: 98).

As a society we are involved with the continuation of what is quite clearly a cultural struggle, on many levels and in many arenas. It is a struggle in which the creative and political energy of those who wish to communicate their ideas will join with those concerned to bring about change in institutions, and challenge the established orders. As ethnicity and racial differences move closer to the centre of the world political stage, equitable access to communication becomes crucial to ensure a socially just society. To date the Australian media have performed fairly poorly against their own standards, and have failed to live up to their claims. In international terms Australia may appear a tolerant and open society, but there are doorways still blocked by cultural prejudices protecting hallowed interests. While the litany of class, gender, race and ethnicity may sound out of date to some proponents of the post-modern age, we conclude that these elements remain central to the issue of inequality. The media will continue to provide one of the key sources of power for defining the future—for a society concerned with social justice the media still need to engage more fully with racial and ethnic diversity.

The development of a more effective media will require that the media and other institutions of multicultural and multiracial Australia construct a sustained strategy to achieve change. A successful strategy will include action on:

- employment practices, including training, recruitment, promotion and executive control;
- media representation, including a focus on scripting, producing, directing, reporting and reconceptualising Australian society as diverse and conflictual;
- audiences, including research on their expectations and their capacities and desires for change.

A socially responsible media, one which is actively engaged in exploring the multicultural reality, remains a long way off. Industry self-regulation may ensure that the status quo remains unchallenged; political and social action are required to ensure the challenge is sustained.

REFERENCES

Aboriginal Deaths in Custody, Royal Commission into, 1991, *National Report*, 4 vols, Australian Government Publishing Service: Canberra

AGB Australia 1990, *Youth, media and multiculturalism*, Office of Multicultural Affairs, Canberra

Andersen, Robin 1991, 'The press, the public and the new world order', *Media Development*, October, pp. 20–6

Ang, Ien 1991, 'Global media/local meaning', *Media Information Australia* no. 62, pp. 4–8

Anthias, Floya 1990 'Race and class revisited—conceptualising race and racisms', *Race and Class*, pp. 19–42

Appadurai, A. 1990, 'Disjuncture and difference in the global cultural economy', in Featherstone, M. (ed) *Global Culture*, pp. 295–310

Atwood, R. and McAnany, E. (eds) 1986, *Communication and Latin American society: Trends in critical research. 1960–1985*, University of Wisconsin Press: Madison

Auguiste, Reece/Black Audio Film Collective 1989, 'Black Independents and Third Cinema: The British context in Willemen and Pines (ed.) *Questions of Third Cinema*, pp. 212–17

Australian Broadcasting Corporation (ABC) 1989, *Thoughts that glow and words that burn: An ABC guide to non-discriminatory language*, Australian Broadcasting Corporation, Sydney

——1992, *Becoming Australian: A report on progress toward further representation of Australia's cultural diversity on ABC television* Australian Broadcasting Corporation, Sydney

Australian Broadcasting Tribunal (ABT) 1988a, Letters of response on file with the Australian Broadcasting Tribunal, Channel 9 doc. 33, Channel 7 doc. 19, Channel 10 doc. 13, at IL/88/174ff, Australian Broadcasting Tribunal, Sydney

——1988b, *Information Paper, (IP/88/63)*, May, Australian Broadcasting Tribunal, Sydney

——1988c, *Australian Content Inquiry: Summary of Public and Industry General Submissions and Responses to the Australian Content Inquiry*, Australian Broadcasting Tribunal, Sydney

——1992, Inquiry to Review Radio and Television Program Standards relating to Discriminatory Broadcasts [RPS 3 and TPS 2(b)] *Background Paper no. 1, IP/91/86*, February

Bailey, F.G. 1977, *Morality and expediency*, Blackwell: Oxford

Balibar, E. and Wallerstein, I. 1991, *Race, nation, class: Ambiguous identities*, Verso: London

Balibar, Etienne 1991, The national form: history and ideology, in Balibar and Wallerstein, *Race, nation, class: Ambiguous Identities*, Verso: London pp. 86–106

Banton, Michael 1983, *Racial and ethnic competition*, Cambridge University Press: Cambridge

Bell, P. 1993, *Multicultural Australia in the media*, Office of Multicultural Affairs: Canberra

Bennett, Tony 1989, 'Culture: Theory and policy', *Media Information Australia*, no. 53, August

Berry, G. and Asamen, J.K. (eds) 1993, *Children and television in a changing socio-cultural world*, Sage: Newbury Park

Betts, Katharine 1988, *Ideology and immigration: Australia 1976 to 1987*, Melbourne University Press, Melbourne

Bhabha, H. (ed.) 1990, *Nation and narration*, Routledge: London

Birrell, R. and Birrell, T. 1987, *An issue of people: Population and Australian society*, 2nd edn, Longman Cheshire: Melbourne

Blainey, Geoffrey 1984, *All for Australia*, Methuen: Sydney

Blonski, A. and Freiberg, F. 1989, 'Double trouble: Women's films', in Moran and O'Regan (eds) *The Australian Screen*, pp. 191–215

Bock, K. 1978, 'Theories of progress, development, evolution', in T. Bottomore and R. Nisbet (eds) *A History of Sociological analysis*

Bonney, B. and Wilson, H. 1983, *Australia's commercial media*, Macmillan: South Melbourne

Bostock, John and Nye, L. Jarvis 1934, *Whither away?: A study of race psychology and the factors leading to Australia's national decline* Angus and Robertson: Sydney

Bostock, Lester 1993, 'From the dark side: Survey of the portrayal of Aborigines and Torres Strait Islanders on commercial television', *Supplement to Monograph 3*, Australian Broadcasting Authority: North Sydney

Bottomley, G., de Lepervanche, M. and Martin, J. (eds) 1991, *Inter-sexions: gender/class/culture/ethnicity*, Allen & Unwin: Sydney

Bottomley, Gill 1992, *From another place: Migration and the politics of culture*, Cambridge University Press: Melbourne

Bottommore, T. and Nisbet, R. (eds) 1978, *A History of Sociological Analysis*, Macmillan: New York

Bowman, David 1992, 'Do we laugh or should we cry?—Report of the Lee Committee on newspaper monopolies and foreign control of the press', *Modern Times*, Fitzroy, Vic, May, p. 11

Bowser, Benjamin and Hunt, Raymond (eds) 1981, *Impacts of racism on white Americans*, Sage: Beverley Hills

Brown, Craig 1992, 'Ethnic stereotypes in television', *Cinema Papers*, no. 87, March–April, pp. 54–6

Bryant, J. and Zillman, D. (eds) 1993, *Media effects: Advances in theory and research*, Lawrence Erlbaum: Hillsdale, NJ

Carey, J. (ed.) 1988, *Media, myths and narratives: Television and the press* Sage Annual Reviews of Communications Research, vol. 15, Sage: Newbury Park

Cashmore, E. Ellis 1987, *The logic of racism*, Allen & Unwin: London

Castles, S., Kalantzis, M., Cope, B. and Morrisey, M. 1988, *Mistaken identity: Multiculturalism and the demise of nationalism in Australia*, Pluto: Leichhardt

Clegg, S. 1989, *Frameworks of power*, Sage: London

Colosimo, R. 1987, Cinema e televisione: La presenza italiana, *Il veltro*, no. 31, Jan–Apr, trans. T. Mitchell

Communications Law Centre (CLC) 1992, *The representation of non-English speaking background people in Australian television drama*, Communications Law Centre: Kensington, NSW

——1993 *Media self-regulation and cultural diversity* (Background documents), May, Communications Law Centre: Kensington, NSW

Coupe, B. and Jakubowicz, A. with Randall, L. 1993, *Next door neighbours: A report for the Office of Multicultural Affairs on ethnic group discussions of the Australian media*: Office of Multicultural Affairs: Canberra

Cumberbatch, G. and Howitt, D. 1989, *A measure of uncertainty: The effects of the mass media*, John Libbey: London

Cunneen, Chris 1989, The newspaper reporting of crime, law and order in north-west NSW, *Journal of Social Justice Studies*, no. 2

Cunningham, S. 1989, Textual innovation in the Australian historical mini-series in Tulloch and Turner (eds) *Australian television: Pleasures, programs and politics*, pp. 39–51

——and Docker J. 1991, 'Criticism, history and policy' *Media Information Australia*, no. 59, pp. 27–30

——1992a, *Framing culture: Criticism and policy in Australia* Allen & Unwin: Sydney

——1992b, 'The cultural policy debate revisited', *Meanjin*, vol. 51, no. 3, Spring

——and Turner, G. (eds) 1993, *The media in Australia: Industries, texts, audiences*, Allen & Unwin: Sydney

Curran, James et al. (eds) 1977, *Mass communication and society*, Edward Arnold: London

—— et al. (eds) 1986, *Bending reality: The state of the media*, Pluto: London

Daniels, T. and Gerson, J. (eds) 1989, *The colour black: Black images in British television*, British Film Institute: London

Davis, G. 1988, *Breaking up the ABC*, Allen & Unwin: Sydney

Dermody, Susan and Jacka, Elizabeth 1987, *The screening of Australia: Anatomy of a film industry*, vol. 1, Currency Press: Sydney

——1988, *The Screening of Australia: Anatomy of a national cinema*, vol. 2, Currency Press: Sydney

Dessaix, Robert 1991, 'Nice Work if you can get it', *Australian Book Review*, Feb–Mar, 128, 22–28

Docker, John 1991, 'Popular culture versus the state: An argument against Australian content regulations for television', *Media Information Australia*, no. 59, pp. 7–26

Dowmunt, T. 1992, 'Satellite dreaming', *Artlink*, vol. 11, no. 1/2, pp. 39ff

Edmunds, M. 1989, *They get heaps: A study in attitudes in Roeburn, Western Australia*, Aboriginal Studies Press: Canberra

Edmunds, Mary and James, Roberta 1991, *Black and white and read all over: Discourse, media and attitudes*, Australian Institute of Aboriginal and Torres Strait Islander Studies: Canberra

Elder, B. 1988, *Blood on the wattle: Massacres and maltreatment of Australian Aborigines since 1788*, Child and Assoc.: Sydney

Featherstone, M. (ed.) 1990, *Global culture: Nationalism, globalization and modernity*, Sage: London

Federation of Australian Commercial Television Stations, 1993, *Commercial Television Industry Code of Practice*, FACTS: NSW

Ferguson, K. 1986, *The feminist case against bureaucracy*, Temple: Philadelphia

Feuer, J. 1986, 'Narrative form in American network television' in McCabe (ed.) *High Theory/Low Culture: analysing popular television and film*

Flew, T. 1991, 'Foreign ownership and Australian content: Do they matter?' *Media Information Australia*, no. 62, pp. 22–30

Gilroy, Paul 1982, *There ain't no black in the union jack*, Routledge: London

Glow, Hilary 1987, *New Theatre Australia*, no. 2, December, pp. 24–5

Goodall, H. 1990, 'Policing in Whose Interests? Local government, the TRG and Aborigines in Brewarrina, 1987–1988 in B. Morris and G. Cowlishaw (eds) *Contemporary Race Relations in Australia, Journal for Social Justice Studies*, vol. 3, pp. 19–36

Goodall, H., Jakubowicz, A., Martin, J., Mitchell, T., Randall, L. and Seneviratne, K. 1991, *Racism, Cultural Pluralism and the Media*, Office of Multicultural Affairs: Canberra

Gordon, P. and Rosenberg, D. 1989, *Daily Racism: The press and black people in Britain*, The Runnymede Trust: London

Greenberg, B. and Brand, J. 1993a, Minorities and the mass media: 1970s to 1990s, in Bryant and Zillmann (eds) *Media Effects: Advances in theory and research*, ms version

——1993b, 'Cultural Diversity on Saturday Morning Television', in Berry and Asamen (eds) *Children and Television in a Changing Socio-Cultural World*, ms version

——Kirkland, S., and Pyszczynski, T. 1988, 'Some theoretical notions and preliminary research concerning derogatory ethnic labels, in Smitherman-Donaldson and Van Dijk (eds) *Discourse and discrimination*

Gurevitch, M., Bennett, T., Curran, J. and Woollacott, J. (eds) 1982, *Culture, Society and the Media*, London: Methuen

Hall, S. 1982, 'The re¸ ¸covery of "ideology": the return of the repressed in media studies', in Gurevitch, Bennett, Curran and Woollacott (eds) *Culture, Society and the Media*

——1987, Minimal Selves, *Identity*, ICA Documents 6

——1988, *New Ethnicities Black Film, British Cinema*, ICA Documents 7, pp. 27–30

——1992, 'The Question of Cultural Identity', in Hall, Held and McGrew (eds) *Modernity and Its Futures*, pp. 273–326

——Held, D. and McGrew, T. (eds) 1992, *Modernity and Its Futures*, Polity Press: Cambridge

Hamilton, Annette 1990, 'Fear and desire: Aborigines, Asians and the national Imaginary' *Australian Cultural History*, no. 9, pp. 14–35

Henningham, J. 1988, *Looking at television news*, Longman Cheshire: Melbourne

——(ed) 1990, *Issues in Australian journalism*, Longman Cheshire: Melbourne

Herman, E. and Chomsky, N. 1988, *Manufacturing Consent: The Political Economy of the Mass Media*, Pantheon: New York

Hodge, R. and Tripp, D. 1986, *Children and television: A semiotic approach*, Polity Press: Cambridge

——and Kress, G. 1988, *Social semiotics*, Polity Press: Cambridge

——and Mishra, V. 1992, *Dark side of the dream: Australian literature and the post-colonial mind*, Allen & Unwin: North Sydney

Hooks, Bell 1992, *Black looks: race and representation*, South End Press: Boston

Human Rights and Equal Opportunity Commission (HREOC) 1991, *National Inquiry into Racist Violence*, Australian Government Publishing Service: Canberra

Jacka, E. 1991, *The ABC of drama: 1975–1990*, Australian Film Television and Radio School: Sydney

——1992, Globalisation and Australian film and television, in Moran (ed.) *Stay Tuned: An Australian Broadcasting Reader*, ch. 34

Jakubowicz, A. 1987, 'Days of our Lives: Multiculturalism mainstreaming and the "Special" Broadcasting Service', *Media Information Australia*, no. 45, pp. 18–32

——1989, 'Speaking in tongues: Multicultural media and the constitution of the socially homogeneous Australian', in Wilson (ed.) *Australian Communications and the Public Sphere*, pp. 105–27

——1990, *Racism, racist violence and the media: A report to the Human Rights and Equal Opportunity Commission National Inquiry into Racist Violence*, Human Rights and Equal Opportunity Commission: Sydney

——Morrisey, M. and Palser, J. 1984, *Ethnicity, class and social policy in Australia*, SWRC Reports and Proceedings no. 46, May, Social Welfare Research Centre: Kensington

JanMohamed, Abdul and Lloyd, David 1987, 'Introduction: Minority discourse—what is to be done? *Cultural Critique*, no. 7, Fall, pp. 5–18

Jennings, Karen 1993, 'Sites of difference: cinematic representations of Aboriginality and gender: *The Moving Image*, no. 1, Australian Film Institute: Melbourne

Jensen, K. and Jankowski, N. (eds) 1991, *A handbook of qualitative methodologies for mass communication research*, Routledge: London

King, N. 1992, 'From play to players', *Filmnews*, vol. 22, no. 8, September

Kuper, A. and Kuper, J. (eds) 1985, *The social science Encyclopedia*, Routledge and Kegan Paul: London

Kushnick, Louis 1981, 'Racism and class consciousness in modern capitalism', in Bowser and Hunt (eds) *Impacts of Racism on White Americans*

LaMay, C., FitzSimon, M. and Sahadi, J. (eds) 1991, *The media at war: The press and the Persian Gulf conflict*, June, Garnett Foundation Media Center: New York City

Liebes, T. and Katz, E. 1988, 'Dallas and genesis: Primordiality and seriality in popular culture', in Carey (ed.) *Media, Myths and Narratives: Television and the Press*

Maynard, S. 1989, 'Black (and White) images: Aborigines and film', Moran and O'Regan (eds) *The Australian Screen*, pp. 216–35

McCabe, C. (ed.) 1986, *High theory/low culture: analysing popular television and film*, Manchester University Press: Manchester

McGuigan, Jim 1992, *Cultural populism* Routledge: London

McQuail, Denis 1987, *Mass communication theory: An introduction*, 2nd edn, Sage: London

Meadows, Michael 1990, 'Portrayal of Aboriginal Australians: reporting or racism?' in Hennigham (ed.) *Issues in Australian Journalism* pp. 89–98

——1992, 'Broadcasting in Aboriginal Australia: One mob, one voice, one land', in Riggins (ed.) *Ethnic Minority Media* pp. 82–101

——and Rielander, K. 1991, 'Aboriginal and Torres Strait Islander broadcasting: A selected bibliography', *Media Information Australia*, no. 61, pp. 86–93

——with Oldham, C. 1991, 'Racism and the dominant ideology: Aborigines, television news and the Bicentenary', *Media Information Australia*, no. 60, pp. 30–40

Meekosha, H., Jakubowicz, A., Cummings, K. and Giddings, B. 1987, *Equal Disappointment Opportunity. . .?: A report to the Department of Community Services on Programs for Immigrants, Refugees and their Children*, DCS: Wollongong/Canberra

Mercer, Kobena 1989, 'General introduction', Daniels and Gerson (eds) *The Colour Black*

——1990, 'Welcome to the Jungle: Identity and diversity in postmodern politics', in Rutherford (ed.) *Identity: Community Culture Difference*, pp. 43–71

Michaels, Eric 1990, 'A model of teleported texts', *Continuum*, vol. 3, no. 2

Mickler, S. 1992, *Gambling on the First Race: A Comment on Racism and Talk-Back Radio—6PR, the TAB and the WA Government*, The Louis St John Memorial Trust Fund, Centre for Research in Culture and Communication, Murdoch University: WA

Miles, R. 1982, *Racism and migrant labour*, Routledge and Keagan Paul, London

Milne, F. and Zelinka, T. 1991, *'They may mean well, but . . .': An examination of first-round access and equity plans of eight Commonwealth Government departments*, Federation of Ethnic Communities Councils of Australia Inc. (FECCA): Sydney

Mitchell, Tony 1992, 'Wogs still out of work: Australian television comedy as colonial discourse', *Australasian Drama Studies*, no. 20, April, pp. 119–33

Modleski, T. 1984, *Loving with a vengeance*, Methuen: London

Moore, C. and Muecke, S., 1984, 'Racism and the representation of Aborigines in film', *Australian Journal of Cultural Studies*, vol. 2, no. 1, May pp. 36–53

Moran, A. 1989, 'Constructing the Nation: Institutional documentary since 1945', in Moran and O'Regan (eds) *The Australian Screen*, pp. 149–71

——(ed.) 1992, *Stay tuned: An Australian broadcasting reader*, Allen & Unwin: Sydney

——and O'Regan, T. (eds) 1989, *The Australian screen* Penguin: Ringwood

Morris, Megan 1992a, *Australian Literary Review*, no. 143, September

——1992b, 'A gadfly bites back', *Meanjin* vol. 51, no. 3, Spring

Mousoulis, Bill 1991, 'Alike/unalike: Cultural diversity in Australian independent film—an overview, *Artlink*, vol. 11, nos 1 & 2, pp. 81–2

Mowatt, John and Wall, Deborah 1992, *Filipino women in cross-cultural marriages: a training course manual for community workers dealing with the media*, Filipino women's working party, Jannali

Muirden, B. 1968, *The puzzled patriots: The story of the Australia First movement*, Melbourne

Murdoch, G. and Golding, P. 1977, 'Capitalism, communication and class relations' Curran (ed.) *Mass Communication and Society*, pp. 12–43

Nelson, C. and Grossberg, L. (eds) *1988, Marxism and the Interpretation of Culture*, Macmillan: New York

Nugent, S., Loncar, M. and Aisbett, K. 1993, *The people we see on TV: Cultural diversity on television*, Monograph 3, Australian Broadcasting Authority: North Sydney

O'Regan, T. 1993, *Australian Television Culture*, Allen & Unwin: Sydney

O'Sullivan, T., Hartley, J., Saunders, D. and Fiske, J. 1983, *Key concepts in Communication*, Routledge: London

Office of Multicultural Affairs (OMA) 1993, *Self-Regulation and Cultural Diversity: Conference Papers*, 31 May, Hosted by the Communications Law Centre, Office of Multicultural Affairs: Canberra

Peel, J. 1985, 'Herbert Spencer (1820–1903)', in Kuper and Kuper (eds) *The Social Science Encyclopedia*

Pellizzari, Monia 1991, 'A matter of representation', *Artlink*, vol. 11, nos 1 & 2. pp. 80–1

Pettman, Jan 1992, *Living in the margins: Racism, sexism and feminism in Australia*, Allen & Unwin: Sydney

Randazzo, N. 1982, 'I perche' di un dramma', *Program note, Victoria Market*, Melbourne Italian Festival

Riggins, S. (ed.) 1992 *Ethnic minority media: An international perspective*, Sage: London

Roncagliolo, R. 1986, 'Transnational communication and culture', in Atwood and McAnany (eds) *Communication and Latin American Society:Trends in critical research, 1960–1985*, Ch. 4

Rose, Steven, Lewontin, R.C., and Kamin, Leon 1985, *Not in our genes: Biology, ideology and human nature*, Penguin: Harmondsworth

Said, Edward 1978, *Orientalism*, Penguin: Harmondsworth

Schlesinger, Philip 1991, *Media state and nation: political violence and collective identities*, Sage: London

Searle, Chris 1989, *Your daily dose: Racism and The Sun*, Campaign for Press and Broadcasting Freedom: London

Shaw, S. 1992, 'The Asian screen test', *Cinema Papers*, no. 87, pp. 34–40

Shboul, Ahmad 1988, Islam and the Australian media, *Australian Religious Studies Review*, vol. 1, no. 2, pp. 18–23

Sklair, Leslie 1991, *Sociology of the Global System*, Harvester Wheatsheaf: New York and London

Smith, Anthony 1981, *The ethnic revival in the modern world*, Cambridge University Press: Cambridge

Smitherman-Donaldson, Geneva and Teun van Dijk (eds) 1988, *Discourse and discrimination*, Wayne State University Press: Detroit

Special Broadcasting Service (SBS) 1990, *Corporate Plan, 1990–1993*, SBS: Sydney
——1993, *SBS Codes of Practice 1993*, SBS: Sydney

Spivak, G. 1988, 'Can the Subaltern Speak' in Nelson and Grossberg (eds) *Marxism and the Interpretation of Culture*, pp. 271–313

Tiffen, Rod 1989, *News and Power* Allen & Unwin: Sydney

Troyna, Barry 1981, *Public awareness and the media: A study of reporting on race*, Commission for Racial Equality: London

Tulloch, J. 1989, 'Soaps and Ads: Flow and Segmentation', in Tulloch and Turner (eds) *Australian Television*, pp. 120–38

——and Moran, A. 1986, *A Country Practice: 'quality soap'*, Currency Press: Sydney

——and Turner, G. (eds) 1989, *Australian Television: Programs, pleasures and politics*, Allen & Unwin: Sydney

van Dijk, T. 1988, 'How "they" hit the headlines: ethnic minorities in the press' Smitherman-Donaldson and van Dijk (eds) *Discourse and Discrimination*

——1989, Discourse and the Reproduction of Racism, *CRES Publication Series*, Working Paper no. 6, Amsterdam

——1991a, *Racism and the press*, Routledge: London

——1991b, 'The interdisciplinary study of news as discourse', in Jensen and Jankowski (eds) *A Handbook of Qualitative Methodologies for Mass Communication Research*

Webber, Frances 1991, From ethnocentrism to Euro-racism, *Race and Class*, vol. 31, no. 3, pp. 11–17

Wetherell, M. and Potter, J. 1992, *Mapping the language of racism: Discourse and the legitimation of exploitation*, Harvester Wheatsheaf: Hemel Hempstead

White, N. and White, P. 1983, *Immigrants and the media*, Longman Cheshire: Melbourne

Willemen, Paul and Pines, Jim (eds) 1989, *Questions of third cinema*, British Film Institute: London

Willis, Anne-Marie 1993, *Illusions of identity: The art of the nation*, Transvisual Studies Series, Hale and Iremonger: Sydney

Wilson, H. (ed.) 1989, *Australian communications and the public sphere: Essays in Memory of Bill Bonney*, Allen & Unwin: Sydney

Windschuttle, K. 1988, *The media: A new analysis of the press, television, radio and advertising in Australia*, 2nd edn, Penguin: Ringwood

Winkel, F. W. 1990, 'Crime reporting in newspapers: An exploratory study of the effects of ethnic references in crime news', *Social Behaviour*, vol. 5, no. 2, June pp. 87–101

Woll, A. and Miller, R. 1987, *Ethnic and racial images in American film and television*, Garland: New york

Yarwood, A.T. and Knowling M.J. 1982, *Race relations in Australia: A history*, Methuen: Sydney

Young, R. 1990 *White Mythologies: Writing history and the west*, Routledge: London

INDEX